ABOUT THE AUTHORS

Havelock Nelson was born in Guyana, South America, and grew up in Brooklyn, New York. He has written for *Billboard, The Village Voice, New York Newsday, Rolling Stone, Musician, The City Sun, Black Beat, The Source,* and the *Boston Globe,* and is a producer of hip-hop records. Michael A. Gonzales was born and raised in New York City and has written for *Cover* magazine, *New York Talk, Black Beat,* and *Soul Underground.* He has had several plays produced off-Broadway and is at work on a novel. Both authors grew up with hip-hop music as the major soundtrack of their lives.

BRING THE NOISE

A GUIDE TO RAP MUSIC AND HIP-HOP CULTURE

HAVELOCK NELSON
AND
MICHAEL A. GONZALES

HARMONY BOOKS NEW YORK

To Mother, Father Light
—Havelock

To my MOM, Frances, my grandmother, Mary,
and the memory of Uncle Hans
—Michael

#8640

782.42164
Nelson

Copyright © 1991 by Havelock Nelson and Michael Gonzales

Published by Harmony Books, a division of Crown Publishers, Inc., 201 East 50th Street, New York, New York 10022. Member of the Crown Publishing Group.

HARMONY and colophon are trademarks of Crown Publishers, Inc.

Manufactured in the United States of America

Library of Congress Cataloging-in-Publication Data

Nelson, Havelock.
   Bring the noise : a guide to rap music and hip-hop culture /   Havelock
Nelson and Michael Gonzales.
       p.   cm.
   1. Rap (Music)—History and criticism.   2. Rap (Music)—
-Discography.   I. Gonzales, Michael.   II. Title.   III. Title: Hip
-hop record guide.
ML3531.N44   1991
782.42164—dc20
                                                              91-11240
                                                                 CIP
                                                                  MN

ISBN 0-517-58305-4

10   9   8   7   6   5   4   3   2   1

First Edition

FOREWORD

From the bohemian dives of Manhattan's Greenwich Village to MTV-blaring living rooms across the nation, hip-hop renaissance man Fab 5 Freddy has introduced new audiences to rap music since back in its earliest days. Working closely with producers, artists, managers and directors, he's probably done more than any other person to break down the barriers that kept hip hop from mainstream acceptance. In this foreward, he tells how he helped bring hip hop from the parks of Brooklyn to New York's downtown art scene in the early '80s, and then, through MTV, to a national audience.

BRING THE NOISE: *Lead us into how you started doing what you do.*

FAB 5 FREDDY: From the graffiti scene, painting subways, I moved into the gallery scene on the Lower East Side of Manhattan, where I was a contemporary of the late Jean Michel Basquiat, Keith Haring, Futura 2000, Dry Craft Zephyr . . . that whole downtown art movement. I was relatively successful there, and I eventually started exhibiting my work in museums and galleries around the world. I wasn't making a lot of money, but I was connected to the scene downtown, which was pretty much all white except for me, Jean Michel and a few other people. This was in the late '70s.

The Mudd Club days . . .

For sure. I was a big rap fan involved in painting, and I had aspirations of being involved with film. I didn't know anything technical about film, just ideas. Through my connections with the art world, I met this guy named Charlie Ahearn, who had done some Super-8 movies. I put a bug in his ear about doing something that brought graffiti together with hip-hop music and dancing because it was one culture. At that point in time, people who was down with rap wasn't really into graffiti, and vice versa.

Tell us about the hip-hop influence in Brooklyn back then.

DJs in my neighborhood would come out with their sound systems when I was coming up—people like Frankie D, Master D, Pete "DJ" Jones and Grandmaster Flowers (who inspired Flash to add Grandmaster onto his name). Them bringing music out into the parks and shit gave me something to do in the summer, something to keep me out of trouble. I used to follow these guys, and I would go asking things like, "Yo, where's the jam, where they at—what park? St. John's, Albany, where?" I got the bug and was real curious when I saw those turntable techniques go down. I used to be one of those kids at a jam who used to stand in front of the DJ *all the time.* I would party a little bit, but I was more like, Damn, what is going on with the DJ? You know, like what's that record that he's playing? Or why does it sound like that? Or how come I ain't hearing this record nowhere else in my life? I used to ask them, and they would say, "Yo, it's the Uptown sound!" I started taking train rides into Manhattan trying to find the shit. Eventually I met some graffiti guys that had some fourth or fifth generation tapes of Flash back in the early, early days. I still got some of those. Man, they're so scratchy it's like trying to tune in Flash on shortwave. But I used to listen to that shit and go "Yeah, this is the real shit!"

Did studying the DJs influence your painting?

Oh, totally. These dudes were some of the smartest people. The way the best of them put records together was nothing short of brilliant. I mean, some of them wasn't doing nothing too flamboyant on the scratching, but, I swear to God, they drove masses of people to peaks of, like, euphoria. I mean, masses of people would just be jumping off each other. It was just the height of what the shit could be at its rawest, its purest. Out-of-body experiences, with everybody there feeling it with every record that came on. Although my paintings were influenced by the way the music felt, I wanted to introduce the works as part of a complete culture because, I felt, they would have a bigger influence on people that way. I didn't want to be viewed as a folk artist or somebody who was a primitive artist, you know what I'm sayin'? It's a very rarefied, ultrawhite scene but what I basically wanted to do was set up like a cultural battering ram to show these people, well there's not just this painting, there's a music and a dance which makes it a complete culture. A style of dressing, too.

So you were influential in introducing hip hop to the downtown folks who pretty much had no idea where this stuff was coming from.

Uh huh. One-hundred-and-fifty percent of that was me. I consider myself a modest person, but there are things that I definitely did. And I did bring hip hop to the downtown bohemian subculture.

What was their initial reaction?

Incredible. It was *Interview* magazine editor Glen O'Brien who brought me into the fold and exposed me to the cream of the downtown art–literary–new wave set in the first place. I used to do camera work for a cable show he had. I was in the center of the most cutting edge people on the scene—Blondie, Talking Heads, B-52's, Sex Pistols, you name it. If the shit was happening and on the edge I was right there. I was, like, seventeen, eighteen—I used to tell people I was a little older— I mean, real intimidated by it all and I'm already Black and shit. You know, I'm saying? I used to think you had to be twenty-one to do anything and shit (laughs).

When you guys did shows, did you have hip hop playing in the galleries?
Well, that's basically how I introduced the music to the downtown scene. However, the first time I had done it was in a performance even though I actually never really considered myself a rapper. I mean, I have done some records I feel were decent, but I mostly consider myself an artist. The people downtown knew I was into the stuff, though, and the guy from the Mudd Club said, "Look, I've been hearing about this rap stuff; why don'tcha come do something at the Mudd Club?" That was, like, the whole downtown arty vibe. A motherfucker could get up there, beat on some cans—play the shit right off like, "Yo, this is my thing!"—so I performed. It was like—boom!—Yo, I could get some money doing this, because, yo, I ain't really selling no paintings! I'm in the mix, hanging with this one and that one, but I'm like the classic starving artist. Me and Jean-Michel were fucking crashing art openings so we could eat the munchies and shit. We'd snatch up some cheese and say, "Yo, let's make a hero!"
Tell us about your early experiences rapping.
I wrote some rhymes, and got this DJ from Brooklyn named Master D to accompany me. His reputation was like legend, you know? I knew how bugged-out punk rock people were gonna be there, how much they were gonna love it. But to make the shit *really* different I got this live drummer, a white kid named Lenny Ferrari who used to always tell me "Yeah, man, my father played with James Brown." He definitely could keep a beat and everything. So—boom!—we did this thing at the Mudd Club. I was crazy nervous, and Lenny busted into some chaotic punk-rock shit. It was never really off, but when the DJ would scratch in with the drummer he'd start into some even more hectic shit. I was like, "Yo, just play the beat!," but my man just kept trying to get flamboyant. But the shit came off; the people loved it: "Yo, that shit was brilliant!," "Gosh it was great! Loved it!" I

had made five hundred dollars! So much money. And they booked me again! I did the same shit.

Around 1980 I put together a night of music to go along with a graffiti art show my man Futura was curating at the Mudd with Keith Haring, Jean Michel and Ken Sharp. The idea behind the show was to change people's views of what graffiti was, because it definitely was at a point where it was coming off the subways. I also wanted to show the vastness within its parameters, all the different styles.

I also put together a night of just music, which was the first time Afrika Bambaataa played downtown, the first time he played for a white crowd. Bam had some shit he felt was punk rock. Not Sex Pistols or Clash, but "Trans-Europe Express" by Kraftwerk. That was punk rock to him, and that's where "Planet Rock" came from!

That night Bam wasn't the only uptown nigger that came down. There was like so many Black people in the Mudd Club at one time. For the first time. All the graffiti writers. Afterward they were all saying, "Yo, that was the convention!" Any nigger you wanted to meet who was your hero, he was there. Everybody was chatting and tagging up each others books. It was a big deal! *You were immortalized in Blondie's "Rapture" around this time. There must have been people in places like Kansas going, "Who the hell is Fab 5 Freddy?" Still probably didn't give a fuck about rap, but they were with Blondie. How did "Rapture" come about?*

It came out of my whole connection with Glen O'Brien and being on the whole downtown set. I had met Chris Stein and Debbie Harry on the set of Glenn's cable show. We used to get talking and I proposed the idea of doing some artwork for them. I was really curious about the whole punk thing, and they was on top of it. "Heart of Glass" was the record they had out at the time, the fucking biggest pop tune in America at the time. They was cool with me, and they decided to put me down.

And you worked on the music for Wild Style, the first movie that attempted to document hip-hop culture, with Chris Stein.

He was from Brooklyn and really into graffiti. And he saw the connection between the way most of the punk rock people didn't know how to play an instrument, and the way hip-hop people couldn't either. I was feeding off that shit.

Let's talk about some of the records you were working on.

Well, the first music thing I worked was *Wild Style.* I did all the music for the movie, and I starred in it. I was also its associate producer, and co-originator (with Charlie Ahearn) of the concept. Lenny Ferrari played the drums on that one, and don't you know motherfuckers today want the instrumentals people rapped on in *Wild Style?*

You can't find them, though.

I never put the shit out!

How come?

Like with wine, if you leave them for ten, twelve years that's when folks are ready to drink it. And with motherfuckas like Hammer and Vanilla Ice selling all those records, *Wild Style* has become that much more important. It's the first and earliest record of this genre on film. All the characters were real people on the scene. The only people acting were me and Patty Astor— the principal players. And my character, an ex-graffiti artist promoting a club in the Bronx, was based on the way I acted when I was writing graffiti as well as some of the things I saw [rap MC] Busy B doing. The title of the movie was taken from a way of forming letters invented by this kid named Legend.

When *Wild Style* came out, the biggest type of rap coming out was on Sugar Hill. It was like bands playing. People weren't capturing the essence of hip hop that was at the parties with the scratching and all that. I wasn't hearing that attitude on record. So, Charlie Ahearn and I, who understand that tone, recorded a break-beat record for use in all the different party scenes. From that break record we recorded the musical and vocal parts, cutting two pressings of the record back to back. The soundtrack was raw.

When you do hip-hop videos, you don't have the budget of, say, Guns N' Roses. Does a small budget hinder you or does it help you in terms of innovation?

I wanna say something about that. In hip hop, there's a budget ceiling, and I think the ceiling is set in place by racism. Record companies will not give more than $45,000 or $50,000 to make a rap video most of the time. But if you look at how quickly rap music recoups its initial investment, you'll know it's like something where they shouldn't be saying, "That's all we spending!"

What was the first video you worked on?

The first video I did was "My Philosophy" for Boogie Down Productions.

Did Kris come to you and ask you to do it or—

Uh, well, Ann Carli from Jive Records hooked that up, and I'll always be grateful to her for giving me my break. The way I got into the directing thing was, I was moving out of the painting thing—this was in the mid-'80s. I was actually getting depressed with the art world because I was moving up higher but, no Black people was coming to galleries. I was showing at Holly Solomon over on Fifth Avenue. Right off 57th street. Right across the street from fucking Trump Tower and, like, it was too boring, too calm, too quiet, too—you know—unchallenging. Everything was getting soft. My buddy Jean was exploding, Keith was exploding, everybody was always in different parts of the world; the whole downtown vibe was *over.* So I was thinking about making another record. I had done "Champs the Beat" in '82. It was pretty influential in that it was the first rap record that used a laid-back, kinda mellow groove, a simple beat like a heartbeat. It came out right after "Sucker MCs" on Celluloid. It became the most scratched independent record second only to James Brown's, of course. It became a real cult thing, and through it, everybody started knowing me.

We had started talking about the videos and "My Philosophy"—
Oh yeah, I had went out and did a lot of paintings in Cali. I had
hooked up with a real big gallery out there. Made mad dough!
Matt Dike, this white guy who used to be an assistant to Jean
Michel, was out there too running this club called L.A. Powertools,
and he had an incredible ear for music. He became one of my
tightest buddies. Matt had *crazy* underground tapes from Red
Alert and all the radio shows—all the underground shit—and
one day he said, "Look, I'm thinking about starting a label
called Delicious Vinyl." He was telling me, you know, he wanted
me to be down, to put a rap tune. But I didn't know what to rap
about. I know so much about hip hop, but like I said before I
don't consider myself a rapper. Still, I was like, "Dammit, it
would be nice to make a fucking record!" I think when you're
Black, you also gotta be versatile. I guess that's the nature of
our fucking being. We ain't got time to settle back and do one
thing. Most of the time we ain't got that privilege. It's just
inbred.

Anyhow, we was trying to work on some tracks, and around
the same time he had signed Tone-Lōc and got busy. I hooked
up with a kid named Glen Friedman who was Def Jam's liason
out there in L.A. We started hanging, talking about hip hop, and
L.L. Cool J's "Rock the Bells" was the thing then. We used to
play the tapes, then one day he said, "Yo, this the shit that Rick
[Rubin] found. Um, he's putting it out on Def Jam. Public
Enemy, Black Panthers of Rap." I was like, "What?" My father
was crazy radical when I was coming up in the '60s. He was
connected to, you know, African Liberation, just a lot of like
upper-level Black cultural and political shit. I knew all about
that, so I said, "Hmmm. Why don't I see about directing a video
for them." I started calling Russell [Simmons], Rick and everything. I already knew them, and we started talking. And that's
how I got the whole video bug. I eventually met the group—
before the album even dropped—and I had four concepts for

four different songs. But nobody could make up their minds on which song to go with. The shit never happened.

What other artists have you worked with as a director?

Queen Latifah, Master Ace, Gang Starr.

You were very influential in getting Latifah onto her label, Tommy Boy.

Right. I was tight with her producer, DJ Mark, the 45 King. I met him around the time I was thinking about getting back into music. He has this posse called the Flavor Unit out there in New Jersey: Lakim Shabazz, Chill Rob G., Apache.... Everybody was good, and Mark made beats for all of 'em. He has like a hip-hop training room out there, an incredible environment where even if you weren't good when you came in, you'd get good just being around there. It was relaxed, everybody just sittin' around drinkin' 40s and just tellin' stories. Then Mark would throw a break in and go, "You ready to box? Let's go at it." The two of us were developing some ideas for songs based on stuff I had started on with Matt Dike and them in Cali.

Oh yeah! A footnote: The whole Tone-Lōc "Wild Thing" idea came from me not knowing what to rap about. I mean I couldn't make up no fake shit, in terms of what niggers usually rap about, 'cause there I was living a relatively exciting life— travelling, the whole nine. But I had done that little cameo in [filmmaker Spike Lee's] *She's Gotta Have It:* "Yo, baby, let's go up to my crib and do the wild thing." Matt and them used to say, "Yo, man, rap about this, rap about that. Rap about the thing you said in Spike Lee's movie!"

But back to Mark. He had played a couple of beats for me to rap on. One of 'em was "School Boy Crush" by the Average White Band. I had rhymed a little bit over it and Red Alert was playing it on his show. Eric B. & Rakim had heard it, and the beat became "Microphone Fiend." I thought they had looted it, but Mark told me he was starving at the time, and he actually gave it to them.

How'd the rhyme go?

Well, part of it is on the Soul II Soul record I did on *1990: A New Decade:* "Lay your cards on the table and place your bets/I'll lay you odds this is something that you haven't heard yet/It's fine, divine like a vintage wine, best of all, yes y'all, it's genuine. . . ."

Back to hooking up Latifah.

I would get together with Mark periodically and he would play all the raw Flavor Unit tapes for me. He gave me a Latifah tape one day with "Princess of the Posse" on there. I played it for Tommy Boy A & R guy Dante Ross, and he moved on it. Fast.

Let's talk about MTV. How did that come about?

Around May 1988, the time I was directing "My Philosophy," a good friend of mine, Peter Dougherty, was telling me there were a couple of proposals to do a rap show at MTV, where he was a producer. That was something I never thought would happen because MTV still wasn't playing Black music except for Michael Jackson, Prince, what have you.

Let alone the street culture—

Let alone the contemporary, hardest shit that's going around in music. So he said [executive producer] Ted Demme had put me down to be host because I was articulate and street and I knew the whole culture. I was flattered, and months later they did a pilot with Run-D.M.C., L.L., Fat Boys hosting from the road. They had those cats intercut with videos, one of which was "My Philosophy." Then Peter called me. They wanted me to test for a regular slot. He asked me how I wanted to do it. I said, "I don't want to be cooped up in a studio—I wanna be outside—and I don't wanna be on camera too long—keep things short and sweet. He said "Great!" We shot some shit on the Williamsburg Bridge, and they liked it. They put a show together and it was on in a week. I couldn't believe that shit. And it's been on for over two years now.

So, you went from being this guy from the downtown art scene to being, like, Mr. Rap for kids in, I dunno, Omaha, Kansas— Yeah, it's like real cool. But I don't connect much with how many people could be possibly watching. I often think about the homes I might be in where people hate me.

How much influence do you think "Yo! MTV Raps" has in terms of people's record-buying habits?

I think it's been the single largest factor involved in helping hip hop move into the mainstream culture. It provided a twenty-four-hour source for the culture. But what it did that's even more important is it linked up the whole country. Radio stations are different in every city, and what we play in New York is different from what they play somewhere else. Something happening in New York used to take a long time to really hit in L.A. What "Yo! MTV" provided was, "Here's the new whomever, America . . . all in one shot!" It opened up a lot of people's ears and minds to some really mind-boggling shit. I mean, I once saw this little white girl doing the dance the Running Man. I asked her how she learned to do that. She told me, "MTV!"

INTRO

Air electric, buzzin' wit da hum of new noize; steady beat shaking da ground like an earthquake in da jungle.

On this street of tar and gravel neighborhood folks are grilling chicken legs and breasts and wings as the strong, sweet smoke rises into the air. Grown folks chatter; children scream. Reckless eyeball to the corner, where Brother J. sips Thunderbird from a paper bag and Smokey sells loose joints from a Kool cigarette package. A crew of soul brothers (Mod Squad afros, bell-bottom jeans) troops down the hill with cartons of records, speakers, two turntables, and a mixer. These are the new gangsters in town, aural outlaws controlling the public airwaves. Slammin' their equipment in front of an old street lamp, their hands move slow, hooking wire and mics and testing a Gil Scott Heron drum beat on a Technic turntable. BOOM/BLAST—"Yo, this be DJ Hollywood rockin' da turntables in da hood." Needles bounce, explode with the sound of the new urban blues. BOOM/BLAST—heavy bass riffs lifted from an ancient Stanley Clarke disc.

While Hollywood bellows into the mic', turntable assassin Lovebug Starski plays the role of Doc Magic Hands—spinnin' discs, scratchin' records, borrowing this drum beat, that keyboard riff. "All da ladies in da hood say, 'Yeah'!" Fem voices roar and the block party erupts.

Two hours pass before a police car cruises down da block. Stopping in front of Hollywood and Starski and their crew, two white cops emerge from the two-tone car: lips tight, hands

on their guns, cocky swagger. The crowd screams, "Fuckin'
pigs." The cops turn crimson and say, "If you still here when we
roll back around, we taking you to jail."

The crowd boos, but minutes later, the street is empty.

Not only was this an introduction to a new music called
Hip-Hop, it was an introduction to "outlaw culture." The term
itself embodies the media's and an uniformed public's miscon-
ceptions about hip-hop. To them the music isn't a legitimate
artform that has influenced everything from fashion design to
current slang, it's an open invitation for thugs and hoods to
break wild.

After that Black noise attack first invaded my earholes, my
eyes were open wide to the changes rap music was causing in
the neighborhood. Hiding out in front of Jose's, the local candy-
store/pinball arcade, with my homebody Darryl, both of us just
shootin' the breeze, a guy dressed in Lee jeans and unlaced
black Pumas approaches us and says, "Yo. You brothers interested in buyin' some music?" Darryl and I look at each other
and smile. "What kinda music?" I ask. Silently the brother
glares as though searching for the right words to express
himself. Then he mumbles, "Check it B., I'm selling tapes of
that new shit, that rap shit ... know what I'm sayin', B? I got
tapes of them brothers from the Bronx—ya know, Flash and
Herc and Bambaataa? Even got some of them uptown niggas
like Kurtis Blow and Spoonie G." The same way drug dealers
whisper and gesture when attempting to make a sale, that's the
way this brother was hawking tapes. I guess hustling is just in
the blood of some brothers, and hip hop was the latest hot
commodity.

Dissolve to 1979: Living in a row-house in Baltimore (the
town where Edgar Allan Poe died drunk, in the gutter) my
brother Carlos and I became friends with a dude named Walter.
Although Walt and I were about the same age, fifteen, he was
somewhat immature.

While hangin' in his basement one cool June day Carlos put the Sugar Hill Gang's "Rapper's Delight" (the first rap track on wax) on the turntable for the umpteenth time. "If you play that record again I'm gonna break it," Walter exclaimed. Never one to pay heed to minor threats, Carlos played the jam again anyway. Walter pulled the needle from the record and frisbeed it across the room. The record shattered into a million pieces against the wall. Even then rap music had the power to both entertain and provoke.

Seventy years after the Euro-artists were introduced to the theories of Italian Futurism, the first rap track was recorded in a small New Jersey studio by a group that had zero street credibility; "Rapper's Delight," released in 1979, was basically a novelty record, but it introduced the entire planet to the new noise emerging from the streets of New York.

Without a doubt hip-hop culture can be traced back to the tribes of Africa, back to James Brown sliding across the stage at the Apollo, back to the chatter of men-folk inside a barber shop, and yet, much like Futurism, hip hop/rap began as an avant-garde arts movement for the people on the street who were tired of the same-o, same-o.

Although the hip-hop creaters paid homage to past musical influences, this new noise was strictly post-modern: constructed (rather than composed) from found sounds, bass lines or guitar riffs scratched from existing texts (other records). The noise found on hip-hop tracks could be anything that bounced off the "walls of sound," from cartoon voices to high-pitched screams. As Tisdall and Bozzolla wrote in their book *Futurism*, "Noise did not mean just din and cacophony ... the wealth of sound in the world ignored by the conventions of music ranged from the primary noises of nature to the roar of life and machines in the modern city."

Although many critics of hip hop stated that the music was only a fad (a voice in da back of my mind screams "They said the same thing about jazz, rock 'n' roll and reggae!"), the hip-hop nation has gotten stronger, larger in the fifteen years since it began. In the music industry, many who dismissed rap as a brutal sound to be ignored are now signing more hip-hop artists than they know what to do with.

Fans of rap can only smile and shake their heads. When MTV finally began a rap program after years of ignoring Black music, and that program became their top-rated show; when my mother told me that she had bought a copy of M.C. Hammer's tape; when a friend's mom was blasting L.L. Cool J's "Mama Said Knock You Out" from a small tape recorder she kept in her bag, it became clear that our music had not merely crossed over, it had invaded the heart and soul of folks throughout the world.

This invasion was a slow process. For many years the major record companies and media agents made rap music and hip-hop culture into forbidden fruit: Anyone who touched or took a bite was tainted. Record companies masked their racism by stating that no one was interested in buying this Black thang. By claiming that hip hop was an underground movement whose low-income followers couldn't afford to buy records, the mainstream music industry could justify not signing any rap acts. The press was even more blatant with their race and class bashing, associating rap with gang violence, teenage illiteracy and drugs. In the eyes of white presslords, hip hop was a negative force that had to be stopped, despite evidence to the contrary: A "peace rally" held in Harlem after the slaying of a young black teenager, Yusef Hawkins, by a crowd of white toughs in Brooklyn in 1989, featured a crew of rappers that included the KRS-One and Chuck D. This event attracted thousands of hip-hop fans from every borough. But, because there were no shoot-outs or gang wars, the mainstream press failed to report this joyful event.

A bitter irony related to this situation is the Black press' treatment of rap music and hip-hop culture. While one might expect *The New York Times* or *Newsweek* to be ignorant of Black culture, magazines like *Ebony* and *Essence*, from whom Blacks have a right to expect more, showed their bourgeois contempt for revolutionary sound and style by completely ignoring rap. Only recently, after a few progressive magazines began celebrating the music, did these magazines decide the hip-hop nation wasn't about to fade away and so couldn't be ignored indefinitely.

Sadder still is the fact that once hip hop broke out of the streets and into the suites, not many Black folks were in a position to make any big money. Being in front of an audience or rapping on the mic is one thang, owning the record company or publishing rights is another; on the bizness side of hip hop, African-Americans are still a minority in their own artform. With the exception of noir visionaries Sylvia Robinson (Sugarhill Records), Russell Simmons (Def Jam), Luther Campbell (Luke Records), and Andre Harrell (Uptown Enterprises) and a handful of small labels, very few Black capitalists have invested their dollars in the production of this artform, leaving the door open for smooth operators like Tom Silverman (Tommy Boy) or Cory Robbins (Profile) to become very rich men. As Public Enemy's "media assassin," Harry Allen, once pointed out in the pages of *The City Sun*, years from now Black folks will be screaming that white enterprisers *stole* rap music, but the truth of the matter is we're giving it away.

In the long months that we took to complete this project (through sickness, writer's block, sleepless nights, computer problems, etc.), many rap records were released by many artists. It is close to impossible to chronicle the complete universe of hip hop because the music continues to evolve on a daily basis. This, combined with the unavailability of many early rap records, forced us to limit what is included here. Instead of writing a little about everyone, we decided to write in depth about the hip hop performers whose work has really made a difference and is commercially available. So, for instance, Grandmaster Flash and the Furious Five do not have their own entry here because few of their releases are in print. (Early masters like Flash and Bambaataa are discussed throughout the book, wherever we go back into rap's early days.) We also decided to review only full-length works. In its first years, hip hop existed primarily on singles, but as it has matured it has found its largest audience of LPs, cassettes, and CDs. The standout singles virtually all ended up on albums anyway, so we're able to discuss them in detail.

Our selection process has been a matter of choosing the discs we felt were fun, important, or interesting. Anyone who has listened to this amazing artform with both ears knows that it all doesn't sound the same (no matter what your parents might say). From fun guys like Heavy D and the Boys to the rebel roar of Public Enemy; from the smooth lover style of L. L. Cool J to the complex politics of KRS-One; from the pimp stance of Ice-T or Big Daddy Kane to the feminist "grain of the voice" found in Queen Latifah and Salt-n-Pepa. In writing this book we have tried to cover as many of the voices as we could, writing in as many styles and literary techniques as there are aural styles in the records.

There's a lot more to be said about how far hip hop has come—about the political messages of some bands, the pure fun of others; about the vein of misogyny that runs like a fat gold chain through some artists' work, and the rise of strong independent women performers; and about white artists ripping off the styles and accomplishments of a generation of Black artists. But that's all in the entries. It's time to let the book speak for itself.

Or, as Flavor Flav would say, "Yeahhh, boyyyy!"

A NOTE ON THE ORDER OF ENTRIES

Entries present groups and performers in alphabetical order, with a list of records by that performer or group in order of release, and including the record label. (We didn't list record label every time—only for the first record, then again if the performer changed labels.)

This alphabetical order business is complicated in a field where nearly everyone has a made-up name. In order to keep it simple, we've alphabetized everyone by the first word in the group name or individual name. So L.L. Cool J is under L, Doug E. Fresh is under D, Queen Latifah is under Q, Public Enemy is under P. The only exceptions to this rule are for the very few performers and producers who work under their real names: Neneh Cherry is under C, producer Matt Dike is under D. We think this works best and hope it isn't too confusing.

THE AFROS

KICKIN' AFROLISTICS (JMJ/RAL/COLUMBIA), 1990

From the frothy funk of "Welcome to the Terrordome," Public Enemy's Chuck D. bellowed: "Every brother ain't a brother 'cause a color just as well could be under-cover!" In the late '60s/early '70s, though, all true brothers (and sisters), from Jesse Jackson to the Jackson Five, unsurrepticiously sported wide, bushy 'dos as a symbol of allegiance to the red, black and green; and for the first time, Black folk in America were displaying their nationalism through their hair. What dreadlocks are to the Black boho chic of the mid-'80s/present, Afros were to an earlier generation raised on "Soul Train" and blow-out kits, bell-bottom pants and hair picks adorned with representations of Black power.

While the Cameo cut, popularized in the late '80s by bandleader/producer Larry Blackmon, came to symbolize Afrocentricity in hip-hop culture—its roots actually date back more than four hundred years, to African tribes in the motherland—a rap trio named the Afros clearly felt a deeper affinity toward *Trouble Man* than to B-boys when it came to coifs. As the crew's Kool Tee said, "We all were in junior high school when Afros were the thing. All our heroes wore 'em."

So, the Afros made their first public appearance at the beginning of Run-D.M.C.'s jaunty "Pause" video, vogueing pain-stakingly styled (but still freaky) black wigs. From there, these Hollis homies lensed more guest shots: Public Enemy's "911 Is a Joke," 3rd Bass's "The Gas Face." Moreover, they kept show-ing up at numerous rap gigs, clowning and whining "Afros!" in

1

The Afros. Photo by Gary Spector, courtesy of JML Records/Rush
Associated Labels/Columbia Records.

—

that bugged drawl (cf. those high-stepping, low-level hustlers
that populated '70s black filmscapes). As a result, the Afros
(including Hurricane members and DJ Kippy-O, the only group
member whose head wasn't clean-shaven) were hip-hop luminaries well before their debut LP was released, the first project
on the new label run by Jam Master Jay of Run-D.M.C. Of
course, crew member Hurricane—when he was younger he
"used to tear shit up"—had received some degree of notoriety
as the Beastie Boys' DJ in 1986, then as Davy D's rapper in
1987 (the underrated *Davy's Ride* on Def Jam). But that was
then; this is now.

Described by the band as A Funky Rhythmical Organization of Sound (Afros ... get it?), *Kickin' Afrolistics* is the
product of minds influenced by blaxploitation flicks. Besides
Afrolistics (countryfied language such as, "You tall, slinky,

punk-ass broomstick. You be not comin' over here with the *buull*shit!"), the disc is informed by lots of sexist, violent references to pimping and macking. These are playful games, though, parodies of the gangsta poses furthered by the Black film movement of the '70s.

Bopping like an uptown brother with attitude, "Feel It," the first single from *Kickin' Afrolistics*, affirms the crew's funky/jokey agenda over a thick Jam Master Jay and Davy D. track: "My main aim is to keep the people groovin'," raps Kool Tee. Later it's "It's not about violence/It's all about a fun thing." Further into the LP, the Afros offer visions of sex appeal (" 'Fros coolin'/Hoes droolin' "); some highly unlikely B-boy tales ("I remember one day when it was 199 degrees. Them Afros so cool, they didn't even sweat!") and advice ("Pull yourself off the floor/Open the door and let the sunshine in").

Not to dismiss the political implications of the hairstyle, Hurricane, Kippy-O and Kool Tee also threaten mayhem on the establishment from the pumping "Causin' Destruction." Leaving the clowning behind, they, like Afro bro's from back in the days, use visibility and rhetoric as a weapon in the struggle: "As I look in your eyes I see shock and surprise/I was underestimated/Now I'ma drop hard lyrics until you're disintegrated." An *in-your-face* lyrical *and* musical beatdown, this tune slinks, darts and throws us deep into the terrordome. Boom!

ANTOINETTE

WHO'S THE BOSS? (NEXT PLATEAU), 1989

BURNIN' AT 20 BELOW, 1990

I ntroducing herself on producer Hurby "Luv Bug" Azor's compilation disc, *Hurby's Machine,* as a sister with an attitude, hip-hop homegirl Antoinette entered the rap arena ready to generate some static. Spitting her words out through gritted teeth, she created rhymes that tunneled through booming systems like tracer bullets. And with a voice every bit as icy as Rakim's, she asserted the tough side of femalehood through a veneer of attractiveness.

Surprisingly, her eruption wasn't directed at the nasty boys from the man-made world of hip hop. Instead of articulating "women's issues" or addressing men's misogyny, she boasted over a raw break that "I'm no joke/The mic' smoker of chicks." If she were a guy, she would've been clutching her dick through this jam ("I Got an Attitude"), but the beautiful but deadly Antoinette probably just stood firm, rolling her eyes and snapping her wrists whenever she delivered especially brutal lines, like "You wanna know why I play you like that?/I don't like your face." On the strength of this cut, which devotes much of its energy to putdowns of a rival woman, MC (said to be Lyte of the First Priority Music posse), Antoinette earned the title "The Gangstress of Rap."

When Antoinette began production on her debut LP, she had escaped Hurby's machine in search of harder and higher hits. She found neither in the team of I.G. Off and Jay Ellis (primary producers of *Who's the Boss?* alongside Ultramagnetic MCs' Cedric Miller). In their minimalist mixes, Antoinette's voice

Antoinette, Gucci-girl gangstress. © Tina Paul, 1989.

shoves itself in your face, but at the same time the beats sound recessed—like they're weighted down by her thuggish stomping, meant to keep rival rappers underfoot.

Her words flow and skip with the constant suggestion of viciousness, but her ego-boosters and putdowns are not witty or powerful enough to be stretched over an entire LP. And most of Antoinette's Queens-born rhymes still focused themselves at Lyte over in Brooklyn.

Even if her track carried high wattage, moving speaker cones doesn't make it brilliant. The "Push It" knockoff, "Baby Make It Boom," is weak simply because its creators did very little heavy lifting in their mental gym, and the "Raw" sound waves they join on "This Girl Is Off on Her Own" crash limply against the shore. When Big Daddy Kane surfed them, it was a cool glide. Here, they're dullsville.

Critic Paolo Hewitt once remarked, "Funk music is an incredibly difficult music to play properly, despite what certain commentators have been telling you over the years. To get it right, you have to be sharp, tight and on the case. Otherwise, it's a mess." The same can be said for hip hop. Dope samples don't necessarily result in dope jams. It's how they're manipulated and mixed that make them either grand or bland.

So, we came to Antoinette's second LP with low expectations. With so much hip hop winking slyly from the edge, keeping things kinda hectic, who needed Antoinette & Co. treading water? But on *Burnin' at 20 Below*, Antoinette presents a new, more appealing image. The change is evident even from the LP's cover photo by Janette Beckman. Instead of the familiar around-the-way girl, clad in denim and fat gold, we're introduced to a sophisticated-lady kitten sporting a black-and-beige leopard fur, peering out from behind a fog of sexual cool.

With hip-hop internist DJ Doc Rodriguez mixing much of the material, Antoinette's days of aural illness are absent on this follow-up LP. She may have been on a tired smear campaign last time out, but here—though "The Fox That Rox the Box" (a cut that adds to the music used on "Big Daddy's Theme") asks Lyte to "save the cha-cha"—her raps are tackling a variety of more engaging subjects, including men and relationships. After being roasted for not scripting her texts or designing her own textures on her previous release, it's refreshing to see her co-producing credit on six cuts.

On the LP's leadoff track, "I Wanna Be Me," a wailing soul sister can be heard in the chorus supporting some truly independent funk: tumbling drums, thick bass notes and bright synth ejaculations carrying a rap about doing whuchu flippin' like. As one hears the lines "Has anybody every tried to change ya?/Shape ya, mix and twist—rearrange ya?/And tell ya that ya gotta gotta," one imagines a manipulated teen coming into her own, feeling the urge to be in control and, to paraphrase Salt-n-Pepa, express herself.

The voices as well as the sentiments of those Grammy-nominated dames of chat infuse the proceedings on *Burnin' at 20 Below*. In the splashy asphalt shaker "Never Get Enough," Spinderella and Pepa hook up with Antoinette to help make a statement about greedy male pups, panting and wagging tale for that sweet, lovely thang ("Guys—they play like they love you/Give 'em an inch and they think they're above you"). A double-edged sword, this cut presents Antoinette controlling her body in the grooves, while behind the gray-toned walls of Power Play Studios she was calling a few shots, too.

Kenni Hairston and Trevor Gale (who directed Sybil's club-wise "Crazy for You") took the helm for "In My House," while Mantronik (once the place where hip hop met high tech and came out confused) ran things on "Let's Take It From the Top" and "The Fox That Rox the Box." The mood is smooth and slippery in the former, a heavy-bottomed groove with shifty wah-wah guitar samples and squelching sirens. Lolloping out of a protracted silence, techno-crazed dandy Mantronik strolled into a brave new world of hip-hop madness and made a startling discovery—simplicity. Antoinette's words flow over the minimal-ist earthquake like a wet dream, drowning the track in a wash of nightmarish braggadocio.

So, go go, jeep funk, new-jack swing, hip house and hardcore rap make up *Burnin' at 20 Below*. Though it simmers in a stew of diverse styles, things don't boil down to aural chaos, thanks to its performer's cool, more confident outlook. She sounds crisp and precise, more palatable than when she was *raw*. It's cooking on slow, simmering on low, that Antoinette's really the boss.

AUDIO TWO

WHAT MORE CAN I SAY (FIRST PRIORITY MUSIC/
ATLANTIC), 1988

I DON'T CARE—THE ALBUM, 1990

The musical careers of Audio Two—brothers Milk Dee, eighteen, and Gizmo, twenty—started in their parents' living room. They, however, ended up in the basement. As youngsters, the pair used to perform in living-room talent contests under the guidance of their grandfather, former vaudeville piano player Leslie Walters. This was their first exposure to show biz, and eventually, in 1984, they formed a rap crew and recorded a long-lost twelve-inch called "Christmas Rhymes" for the Brooklyn-based MCM label. They felt misunderstood by these outsiders, so they subsequently developed the First Priority Music label with their father/manager, Nat Robinson Sr.

The group proceeded to create for themselves (and, later, others, including MC Lyte) a raw style known as basement flavor. It's the sound of the streets that stems from their use of nothing more than a four-track recorder and a mixer. They introduced it on the single "Top Billin'," a scratchy, skeletal beat with whiny, arrogant rhymes by Milk Dee. Even at their most confusing, they were always on target: "Yes, I'm down— down by law/I get the girlies out on the floor/G is D—down is G/To the at the top is where he'll be/At is us/Call us Aud/Girls come in you won't be bored."

Many females took Milk up on his invitation, but a few of them charged Milk with sexism for the line "If your girl's actin' up give your girl a slap." These sentiments sparked a minor controversy, but it didn't prevent "Top Billin'," co-produced by Stetsasonic's Daddy-O, from ruling the minds of homefolks in, primarily, Cleveland, Philadelphia and New York. Back in '88, had one kicked any of these homefolks the refrain, "Milk is chillin'/Giz is chillin' "—boom!—they would've retorted with the tune's next line, "What more can I say?/Top Billin'!"

The acceptance of "Top Billin' " (originally the B side to another Daddy-O collaboration, "Make It Funky") was surprising since it was one of the first releases by this fledgling independent label. Moreover, hip hop at the time was becoming more fleshed-out musically, the product of elaborate forty-eight-channel mixes. But the back-to-basics leanness of "Top Billin' " is precisely what gave it its deadly novelty edge.

Audio Two went on to release *What More Can I Say?* using the minimalist-type beats that made "Top Billin' " such a hit. While nothing else really equals it, "I Don't Care" and "The Questions" come close. The former, in which the groove from the Isley Brothers' "Between the Sheets" and a horn lick from Earth, Wind & Fire's "You Can't Hide Love" get together with a stark, implosive beat, is a three-minute tirade lashing out at the group's critics. The latter, jittery but smooth, is all about Milk.

The detailing of Milk's disposition continued with *I Don't Care—The Album*, from a pictorial representation of a wrecked Mercedes-Benz on the cover to hardcore texts about fat pockets, sexual conquests and Milk's bugging. Even a song about the dangers of drug use is injected with a dose of humor. But the bopping "Get Your Mother Off the Crack" isn't all stupid. Its intent is to break down the "Just say no" hypocrisy some adults engage in, to encourage parents to become better examples to their kids. "Whatcha Lookin' At?," on the other hand, has no socially redeeming value. In this loopy narrative Milk endorses so-called fag-bashing: "What's the matter withcha, boy? Are you guy?/Yo! I hope that ain't the case/'Cause gay mothers get punched in the face!" On an otherwise cute album that also includes a chorus line–type rap featuring MC Lyte and Positive K, "Whatcha Lookin' At?" is an ugly remark. Reckless.

HURBY "LUV BUG" AZOR

SEE ANTOINETTE, HURBY'S MACHINE, KID 'N PLAY, SALT-N-PEPA.

BEASTIE BOYS

LICENSE TO ILL (DEF JAM), 1986

PAUL'S BOUTIQUE (CAPITOL), 1989

". . . he [Elvis] is bragging, selfish,
narcissistic, condescending, materialistic
to the point of insanity." Greil Marcus, *Mystery Train* (1985)

"Elvis was a hero to most, but that's
beside the point/A Black man taught him how to sing
And then he was crowned King."
Living Colour, "Elvis Is Dead" (1990)

And so came down on Planet Pop: where the mock-sinister mug of Vanilla Ice is sniped on the cheap plywood walls of local construction sites, where the Products of the Environment beige-boys (a local street gang) stalk the gritty boulevards after dusk wearing outdated Timberland boots and torn jean jackets with airbrushed illustrations of Pete Nice and

MC Serch, blaring 3rd Bass tapes from the crackling speakers in their souped-up Volkswagens. A few blocks down a winding road, a bell tolls from the Church of Elvis, an ivory temple that stands on the same site that once housed the home of hits, Motown (sold for a coupla trinkets and coins). A wrinkled Memphis bluesman humbly sits on its marble stairs, strumming a tattered guitar, begging for loose change. Inside, the organist plays a gospel version of "Heartbreak Hotel" as stained-glass visions of Sam Phillips, Colonel Tom Parker and Elvis in a white Las Vegas jumpsuit shine multicolored lights on the patrons. And the Reverend Marcus forcefully delivers his closing words: "Brothers and sisters, as you leave the pearly gates of the Church of Elvis, I want you to remember that he sees all ('AMEN'), he hears all ('AMEN'), he knows all ('AMEN') and he ain't nothin' but a hound dog when you put other gods before him. Go in rock. Go in peace."

Back on earth I'm sitting within the post-apocalypse decor of the famed CBGB's—graffiti (band names) scrawled on its walls, the stench of urine seeping in from an overflowing bowl in the basement bathroom. As he tunes his guitar (with da Keith Haring design painted on da side), dread-headed rocker Vernon Reid eyes my copy of *The World Examiner* (headline screams ELVIS SEEN IN SHOPPING MALL). "Ya know what bothers me so much about all this Elvis stuff?" Vernon asks. "I'm worried about the *true kings* of rock like Little Richard and Chuck Berry." He pauses. "Where will they rate when the final history book is written? Those cats might be nothing but footnotes."

Later, cooling in my book-cluttered room, I throw on the DEF and dumb Beastie Boys debut disc, *Licensed to Ill*. The music is screaming/pounding as images of white boys rejected from the downtown post-punk scene, now stalking the stage with B-boy swagger (go-go dancers clad in miniskirts dancing in cages), spraying the audience with shook bottles of Budweiser (a beer no self-respecting B-boy would be caught dead with) and laughing their asses off, fill my head. Francine, my ebony lover of the moment, opens the paint-chipped door, her face as serious as a heart attack. "Why are you listening to that shit again?" she asks. "Because I like it," I retort, having heard her anti–hip-hop criticisms more than once. "I think it's one of the best hip-hop albums ever produced. What you got against the Beasties anyway? This shit is flye!"

"I don't have anything against them *now*," Francine huffs. "But don't be surprised if they become the Elvis of hip-hop and in twenty years they're crowned the Kings of Rap. Think about it. . . . L.L. Cool J just might become another footnote."

Thinking about the Beastie Boys in retrospect—five years have passed since their first album was released—it becomes somewhat difficult to assess their importance in the world of hip hop, to mystify their stance as the first white artists to crash the racial color bar (read: YOUNG, MALE & BLACK ONLY) of the rap nation. In most of America's Chocolate Cities, there have always been sprinkles of vanilla, those white folks who either couldn't afford to or just plain refused to move, who have lived on our blocks. Like my Harlem-bred homeboy White Mike, who shot hoops in the Battlegrounds and chilled with the fellas in front of José's candy store on those blazing summer days; whether we were checkin' out karate flicks in the rat-infested Roosevelt Theater over on 145th or playing the gangster role on the uptown IRT, White Mike was in e.f.f.e.c.t. Last I heard, my man was doing time upstate 'cause he was living large as a stick-up kid. And yet, in musing about the Beastie Boys, I can't help but think . . . if beige-boys were gonna start crossing over to the booms of the beatbox, the soundtracks of the ghetto, then White Mike would've been the most popular white rapper in America, if only for the mere fact that he knew and understood the real deal of surviving in these mean streets.

Instead we got the Beastie Boys: three geeks raised in Jewish, upper-middle-class backgrounds who began their teenage rebellion stage act as part of the lower Manhattan post-punk collective. After the dusk of New York's punk revolution (Richard Hell, Patti Smith), CBGB's once again became the home to crews of badly dressed youngsters seeking an alternative to their parents' mainstream existence. While uptown Black teenagers were clad in clothes that signified a high-life imagination, middle-class white teenagers dressed in dirty, torn jeans and T-shirts as part of a low-life romantic. Adam Yauch (MCA) and Michael Diamond (Mike D.) started out in a group called the Young and the Useless before joining forces with Adam Horovitz (King Adrock, son of playwright Israel Horovitz). Jumping from one youth-oriented subculture to another, these three soul mates began riding the hip-hop bandwagon to the edge of town—da other side of da tracks. Joining forces with future wolfboy, bearded beige-boy Rick Rubin—who acted as DJ Double R for a year—the Beasties cut their first hip-hop single, "Cookie Puss," a joke on ice-cream king Tom Carvel.

And then came *Licensed to Ill*, produced by the great white hope of hip hop (damn, da man useta run Def Jam out of his NYU dorm room). Rick Rubin was the perfect groovemaster for this bratty trio, as he played the George Martin role to the Beasties' rude Beatles. Having once jammed in two punk bands, the Pricks and the Hose, as well as introduce the rap world to the white noise of heavy metal via Run-D.M.C.'s triple-platinum *Raising Hell*, Rubin was familiar with the art of sonic excess, of taking two distant musical genres and forcing a collision of style and sound. Opening with John Bonham's drums before a layering of electric guitar, the whiny nasal voice of Adrock erupts from an ironic track called "Rhymin & Stealin." Yeah, they're rhymin', but one is inclined to wonder what it is the Beasties are bragging about stealin': Is it the sampled music or the spirit of Black culture that these aural pirates are thieving? Perhaps this is what Chuck D. had in mind when he screamed, *"Who stole the soul?"* With this one song, the Beastie Boys sum up their entire horny/wild-in-the-streets philosophy: from random violence to "housin all girls from city to city," from smoking (angel) dust to gulping bottles of Brass Monkey. Yet no matter how one might feel about white boys rappin', it's somewhat impossible to resist the sheer brutal force that sucks one into this vortex of sound.

Unlike other hip-hop crews who dressed in designer gear and had personas of ultracoolness, the Beasties' entire wardrobe (plaid shirts, ugly T-shirts and goofy jeans) looked like their moms ordered the damn things from the K-Mart catalog; and as for personas, theirs resembled the Revenge of the Nerds on Benzedrine. "If I played guitar I'd be Jimmy Page/The girlies I like are underage," Adrock says on the appropriately titled "New Style." If you think this ain't, then tell me the last time you heard an MC *brag* about listening to Led Zeppelin, eating White Castle burgers or smoking crack. Perhaps it was their association with the kings of rap, Run-D.M.C. and Public Enemy, or just the fact that Def Jam (at this point the hottest label in rap) had the vision to sign them, but the Beastie Boys exploded with crazy-large credibility within the Black community. Their "Fight for Your Right (to Party)" became the battle cry for the Video Music Box generation. And hearing Adrock, MCA and Mike D. playing verbal tag, exchanging lines on "She's Crafty," is one of the album's bright spots. Over programmed drums, these ivory B-boys bounce rhymes off one another as they reminisce about their blonde-booming system: "The girlie was def and she wanted to gooo!" The babe liked to dance, had a pretty smile and sticky fingers—honey stole everything in the room.

In his book *The Death of Rhythm & Blues,* former *Billboard* Black music editor Nelson George wrote: "Yes, the rap/hip-hop world has maintained its rebel status and integrity, and probably will until a Hall and Oates of rap appears—which, by the way, the Beastie Boys are not. The white rappers from New York are charged with exploiting rap and making it safe for white suburbia. As I see it, the Beastie Boys are a historic departure. There was no question that there would eventually be a white rapper." Yeah ... let's pause for a moment and wait for the violins to stop. Although a lot of Blacks grooved to their beats, an equal number were offended by their stance. And although I once considered the record to be a masterpiece of obnoxious flavors and crazy music, I could not help but feel that their entire act was a parody of Black style. Unlike Def Jam's later white hip-hop band 3rd Bass, who grew up in hip-hop culture, hung out with cats like Clark Kent and Slick Rick before anybody was Anybody, the B.B.'s were like Jerry Lewis Goes to Harlem Fest and makes millions 'cause folks think he's funny.

Let's put it this way: In 1986, this record played so much on my turntable that my girl threatened to move and the neighbors called the police. In 1991, I find this record slightly amusing, but no longer a masterpiece. It overstayed its welcome; no one informed me that masterpieces could become so boring so fast.

Go west, young man ... go!: After two years of wreckin' Holiday Inns, of attacking one journalist (Chuck Eddy) with buckets of ice water (and taping the event on their Camcorder, then releasing the footage on a compilation reel), of driving one female writer to tears after she admitted not hearing the famed— more than four million copies sold—*Licensed to Ill,* the Beasties had become hip hop's *Hammer of the Gods* as they sped on the road of excess, leaving behind a trail of empty beer cans, broken hearts, rejected go-go dancers, flared tempers, bruised egos, hash pipes and misplaced dime bags of skunk weed. And then, like a lead zeppelin, the bottom fell outta the Boys' traveling circus. I'm not sure who's to blame, but somewhere along the line, some claim, Def Jam forgot to pay the Beastie

Boys about two million dollars. Or the group forgot to record their follow-up album fast enough. Whatever ... the Beasties just loaded up their Volkswagen and journeyed to the land of earthquakes and street gangs, Scientologists and mass murderers: "See da sign on that hill," MCA screams, Adrock steering the tattered bug, *"We's in HOLLYWOOD!"*

As luck would have it, this motley crew started chillin' on the scene, hangin' in all the right places. One was a local dance dive called Enter the Dragon, owned by future Tone-Löc and Young MC producer Matt Dike. The next thing ya know, Dike and his studio gremlins the Dust Brothers (what a cool fuckin' name!) are working on the Beasties long-awaited follow-up album. As The Rickster's (Ricky Powell) Winsor McCay-esque sleeve photo suggests, *Paul's Boutique* is a funky, surreal pop fantasy that makes no sense the first two times you listen to it, but it soon seeps into your bloodstream like nerve gas. A year before Deee-Lite grooved into America's heart wearing platform shoes and other '70s threads, the Beastie Boys were prancing through their "Hey Ladies" video (the album's first single) in big-ass furry hats, leopard-skin maxi-coats and walking sticks— and Ice Cube had the nerve to ask, "Who's the Mack?"

After somewhat dissin' the Beasties in the beginning of this critique, I gotta admit my dancing feet were swayed to their "new" sound. I'm sure I wasn't the only brother who expected them to repeat themselves, take the lazy way out and record *Still Illin' After All These Years.* Yeah ... psyche your mind. On the road to Cali, the boys must have traded their crate of Led Zeppelin, Black Sabbath, the Sex Pistols and other heavy headbangers for Curtis Mayfield, Jean Knight, Funky Four Plus One, the Wailers and a bunch of soul stirrers and their wah-wah guitars. When they snatch the intro from the "Superfly" theme and quote Public Enemy for the goofy track "Egg Man" ("Humpty Dumpty was a big fat egg/He was playin' the wall and then he broke his leg/Tossed it out the window 3 minutes hot/Hit the

Rastaman—he said, 'Bloodclot' "), a tale of drive-by shootings with egg guns, one realizes that these cats aren't playing with a full deck. Funky and crazy as hell.

Paul's Boutique also works as a catalog of American pop culture as they name-drop Chuck Woolery (my fave game-show host), Fred Flintstone, Donald Trump, Alice from the Brady Bunch, Clint Eastwood movies, Alfred E. Newman, etc., etc., etc. This album should've been dubbed *Sonic Junk Culture,* as it takes aim at the highbrows. If Raymond Carver wrote K-Mart fiction, then the Beastie Boys create Salvation Army hip hop.

On one of the album's standout tracks, "Car Thief," the Beasties proclaim themselves as "... a writer, a poet, a genius, I know it," a paraphrase from Truman Capote's introduction to *Music for Chameleons* (the exact line reads: "I'm an alcoholic. I'm a drug addict. I'm homosexual. I'm a genius."). And as I was preparing to end this extended praise of three silly white boys who proved that they are also musical chameleons, my homeboy Pete "Mack Daddy" Wetherbee rang me on the H•O•T•L•I•N•E (970-FLYE) and says, "Is that *Paul's Boutique* you're spinning in the background?"

"Yeah, man ... this shit is dope as hell. I'm writing the entry for the book."

Pete chuckles and says, "Yeah. Did you mention that *Paul's Boutique* is Matt Dike's tour de force?"

"Naw, not yet."

"Well, you should.... I lost my copy somewhere. Can I borrow yours?"

"Sorry, my brother. Ya gonna have to buy your own."

BIG DADDY
KANE

LONG LIVE THE KANE (COLD CHILLIN'/
WARNER BROTHERS), 1988

IT'S A BIG DADDY THING (COLD CHILLIN'/
REPRISE), 1989

TASTE OF CHOCOLATE, 1990

No matter how narcissistic the bastard son Disco had become as he entered the room of death in the late '70s, it would be impossible not to pay homage at his throne (turntables and mixers) for introducing the world to a new civilization of sound called twelve-inch Culture. Within the darkened dancehalls of decadence that characterized a decade, the seven-inch record proved obsolete, since it left no space for DJs and remixers (the new artists of postmod dance) to experiment with various soundscapes. Within twelve-inch Culture, it was possible for those who danced at this altar of rhythmic eroticism to extend the orgasmic pleasures as the DJ pumped the sound—harder, harder.

In the early years of recorded hip hop, artists didn't think in terms of making albums—only singles. And though most rappers were more street tough than disco savvy, the twelve-inch soon became as important to rising B-boy culture as it had been in the gay dance underground. Since, as Dave Marsh comments in *The Heart of Rock & Soul (The 1001 Greatest Singles Ever Made)*, "nobody goes around humming albums," let us now recollect a brilliant rap single: Big Daddy Kane's "Raw."

As most pop fans would confess, music often acts as an aural time capsule, storing memories you think are forgotten.

Big Daddy Kane at the Apollo. © Ernest Paniccioli, 1990.

So, one Friday night while I'm cruising through Times Square—lights flashing in my eyes, the radio, tuned to Red Alert's KISS-FM show, jamming a scratchy hip-hop classic—my dented Maxima in a flash transforms into a gleaming DeLorean, speeding me back to the future of . . .

Winter 1988. Walking on the wild side, through Manhattan's Lower East Side, the streets like Berlin after World War II: empty lots where buildings once stood, decaying tenements on the verge of collapse, the smells of dog shit and rotting garbage filling my nostrils. After dark, the streets of Alphabet City are always jammed with drug dealers hawking twenties of cut speed, neighborhood wildboys gulping Heinekens, hangin' in front of some brightly lit bodega popping shit to big-booty Gucci gals passing in the moonlight; twenty-four/seven crack fiends bumming spare change, throwing dirty water onto windshields of passing cars, attempting to wash them. This freezing Sunday night in February was no exception.

Clad in bohemian black, I maneuvered through the gauntlet with Initia (Detroit blax, with Chinese eyes) on my arm, and entered a dance dive called The World on hip-hop night. *Brutal* is what this scene was dubbed—at the time, The World was one of the two venues that sponsored the street theater of rap music—and with Afrika Bambaataa rockin' da wheels-of-steel, thangs were about to become steaming hot.

After swimming through an ebony sea of B-boys (sporting thick gold chains, multi-hued Troop jackets, and beepers hanging from their starch-stiff jeans) as they whispered sweet everythangs *("Baby, do ya know what I could do wit a honey like ya?")* into the ears of some uptown flye girl, Initia and I paused at the bar for a moment. Little did we realize this was the quiet before the sonic ... BOOM!!!

"I'm coming, I'm coming!" screamed Fred Wesley (one of James Brown's horn players), before a dark cloud of blaring static, Black noise in this hour of rap chaos, invaded the ears of all gathered in this hip-hop sanctuary. Like an aural volcano in constant eruption, Big Daddy Kane's savage voice moved the crowd in this ancient ballroom as producer Marley Marl's musical lava burned the track. Hearing this record for the first time sent a shiver through me. With "Raw," Big Daddy Kane had released the first hip-hop classic of 1988. As he warned, "I'm not new to this, I'm true to this/Nothin' you can do to this/Fuck around with Kane/And come out Black and blue for this." Anything after this would be anticlimactic. Or so I thought....

After the audio beat-down of "Raw" became a hip-hop theme. Big Daddy Kane—the moniker stands for King Asiatic, Nobody's Equal—released the debut album *Long Live the Kane.* With a voice that easily transported one from tales of the dark side ("Raw") to romantic poetics ("The Day You're Mine") to fables of a hip-hop heaven that borrow heavily from '70s gospel/pop group the Staple Singers ("I'll Take You There"), Big Daddy proved to be one of the most interesting rappers to emerge in 1988. And though none of the tracks displayed the cold-blooded brilliance heard on "Raw," this album was informed with a dramatic cool that the boys in the 'hood interpreted as machoism. Yet the around-the-way girls knew the real deal. With a neo-pimp image (projected in his videos, where designer suits are in vogue), Big Daddy Kane became hip hop's first serious sex symbol. Not just another pinup fantasy lingering in the wet dreams of teenaged girls (like L.L. Cool J), Kane's regal persona appealed to *Essence* women, those Remy Martin–sipping refugees from the ghetto.

On "Ain't No Half-Steppin'," the album's second single, Big Daddy Kane seems to be aware that musical magnetism is as important as visual ecstasy. Whereas other rappers use a sonic bombast to reinforce their egocentric lyrics, Kane and producer Marley Marl covered their braggadocious canvas with soft colors highlighted with bold black lines. In short, "Ain't No Half-Steppin'" was one of hip hop's only non-noise "riffin' records." Unlike L.L., who screamed "I'm Bad!" loud enough to rip a lung, Big Daddy smoothly said, "Competition—I just devour/Like a pit bull against a Chihuahua."

With the release of *It's a Big Daddy Thing,* Kane's second album, our streetwise poet seemed to have grown weary of his melodically constructed past, choosing to experiment with the eroticism of speed. It's not that the album is devoid of grooves that sneak across the record ("Smooth Operator," the first single, which borders on self-parody), it's that the tracks that shine contain fuel-injected beats. Witness the second single, "I Get the Job Done," produced by cyberfunk kid Teddy Riley. Although hip-hop purists viewed this song as Big Daddy's attempt to escape the hip-hop ghetto for a designer-pop condo, they were very much off the mark. Riley, who redefined the world of rhythm & blues by adding elements of hip hop to its soundscape, was attempting to reverse the process with "I Get the Job Done." Even if this track is not Riley's most successful collaboration with the hip-hop nation (check out "New Jack Swing," by Wrecks-N-Effect, or "Do the Right Thing," by Redhead Kingpin & the FBI), its aggressive beats soared as though gravity didn't exist. As Kane related his tale of gigolo smooth-ness ("Let me sneak into your life like a thief in the night/ Nibble all over your ear and give your back a massage/You'll say, 'Oh, I like it!'— just like DeBarge"), T.R. was building a thick wall of Black sound for Big Daddy to tag with his lyrics.

The paradox of Kane often lies in the extreme dualism of his words. Since he is a member of the elitist Islamic sect the Five Percenters (a group whose members purport to have the knowledge to lead the remaining ninety-five percent to true wisdom), one expects (and respects) Kane's pro-Black stance. Without sounding as though he is a professor speaking to a group of students, Kane drops wisdom that every Black man in America can relate to. As "Another Victory" tumbles by, Kane saying, "Taxicabs don't even come my way/They all be afraid they won't get paid," memories of downtown Manhattan flood one's mind. After placing a microscope over urban prejudice, Kane reveals his own bias when he says, "The Big Daddy law is anti-faggot/That means no homosexuality/What's in my pants will make you see reality." Also, on this same track ("Pimpin' Ain't Easy," which features the duo Nice & Smooth), Big Daddy seems to be placing all women in the category of sluts, whose only purpose is to give up the booty.

Language like this is only part of Kane's street humor ("Jokes baby, just jokes"). But having once told journalist Barry Michael Cooper, "Words are powerful, words can change a person, change the world," he should be aware that jokes can also cause damage.

After an active year of appearing on talk shows (at Arsenio Hall's late-night gab fest, Big Daddy forced the staff to cover up the graffiti wall that had been constructed for him to perform in front of, saying that it stereotyped the music), bustin' rhymes with Public Enemy and Ice Cube on "Burn Hollywood Burn," and touring the country, Kane still managed to record and release a new album in the fall of 1990.

On *Taste of Chocolate*, he is still playing both sides of the hip-hop fence—not exactly sure if he wants pimp of the year ("A well known player, but not for the Yankees") or political activist ("That's the way my mind was poisoned/To believe that in America Blacks were inferior/So I ask myself . . . *Who am I?*"). Putting aside the Big Daddy schizophrenia theories, it's safe to say this album kicks ass with its obscure samples and Kane's pointed one-liners ("Like girls promising ya Thomas' and can't even fix toast") that would have even Eddie Murphy rolling.

After shootin' da shit wit the fellas on the corner, Kane returns to his Love Suite, where the master crooner (da man Lester Bangs once called a "molasses-voiced monument") Barry White is waiting to give Big Daddy *smoooth* lessons; and believe me, if anyone could teach a young brother how to speak the language of urban romance, it's B.W. . . . *sho's be right!* On the wonderfully warm (kinda like a bubble bath on a rainy afternoon) "All of Me," Kane drops corny lines like "The way you're standing still there/I wanna lay on the floor and make love to your shadow," but within this book of love the text is precise.

From dueting with the king of orchestral orgasms to battling the prince of comic porn (Rudy Ray Moore), Big Daddy has to be given credit for diversity. Moore is a seminal influence to hip-hop artists who saw his early-'70s films or heard his raunchy comedy albums, which were also popular during the Me Decade. Playing the dozens (bragging about yourself as you put down the other person) can be dangerous when ya doin' it with Rudy Ray, and on "Big Daddy vs. Dolemite," Kane learns the hard way to respect his elders—Dolemite verbally cuts Big Daddy down to size.

This may be the only time in the history of hip hop that a rapper has allowed himself to get dissed on his own record. But with three explosive albums to his name, Big Daddy Kane has avoided falling into any other traps that might have folks wondering if he has what it takes. Long live Da Kane!

BIZ MARKIE

GOIN' OFF (COLD CHILLIN'/WARNER BROS.), 1988

THE BIZ NEVER SLEEPS, 1989

O n *The Black Album,* one of the most popular bootleg albums ever released, His Royal Madness, Prince, throws some irreverence at the hip-hop nation. During "Dead on It" he snarls, "Rappers' problems stem from being tone deaf/Pack a hall and try to sing/There won't be no one left." On his debut offering, Biz Markie delegates singing duties to his B-boy buddy T.J. Swann, whose strained falsetto abandons melodic decorum for playful, off-key abandon. On his second offering, Biz himself sings, sliding along song lines with a child's who-gives-a-fuck feel. It should be noted that two years after his dismissive remarks, Prince himself was working with rappers T.C. Ellis and Robin Power ("New Power Generation Pt. II" from *Graffiti Bridge*) and producing tracks for M.C. Hammer. But that be another story. . . .

More than a rapper, Biz Markie can be placed in the context of Black comedians from Redd Foxx to Richard Pryor (during Pryor's early years). What these funny-men did was take everyday occurrences and make jokes about them. For example, Redd Foxx conjured up yucks by talking about someone taking a shit! Decades later such routines would influence young joke-tellers from Eddie Murphy ("It's just the fart game!") to the late Robin Harris ("I'm so horny I'll fuck the crack of dawn").

In the age of Black film, Rudy Ray Moore was perhaps the most popular funny-man on the scene. During the '70s, when all the (mistakenly dubbed) blaxploitation stars like Shaft, Superfly and the Mack were *serious* to the max, Moore entered the universe of the Black anti-hero, bringing along a humorous edge. Though without a doubt his character exploited sexist and violent themes (pimping women and shooting fellas without remorse), the nigga was funny! It was hard to take him seriously, since Rudy Ray's films seemed to be a visual satire of the genre.

Due to pressure from "proper Negroes" who did not understand the symbolic importance of *Superfly, Trouble Man* or anything featuring Pam Greir, Hollywood was forced to stop making these types of films. But not before a host of poor, young Blacks became exposed to them, thanks to neighborhood theaters that rarely paid attention to the MPAA rating system ("Under 18 not permitted"—yeah, right!). And since all artforms are a continuum, with artists being influenced by the resources closest to them, it should come as no surprise that the Black films of the '70s influenced practitioners of the fledgling hip-hop aesthetic. Not having the resources to translate their inspirations into moving pictures, they expressed them through other mediums: oral (instead of portraying gangsters on the screen, rappers like Rakim were gangsters on record; instead of panning a camera over the rubble of a ghetto block, Grandmaster Flash and the Furious Five related the scene poetically) and visual (the graffiti paintings on subways and playground walls could be said to have borrowed from the '70s Black film movement; likewise for a Superfly sort of personality like Big Daddy Kane, who once claimed half-jokingly that he watches *The Mack* every day).

But like the Yin and Yang of Chinese religion, like the theater masks created by the ancient Greeks for their humorous tragedies, every dark side has a light side. To those who view rap as religion or theater, Biz Markie is both the dark side and the comedy. He first registered his crazily inspired orientation on the sandpapery swing grooves of his first major single, "Pickin' Boogers." Revealing a slight lisp (or a tied tongue), he announced: "Now this might sound disgusting or, like, very gross." Later, he relates playful tales of booger exchange: of

The Diabolical Biz Markie. Photo by
George DuBose, courtesy of Cold Chillin'/Warner
Brothers. © Warner Brothers Records, 1989.

placing them onto his fingers before a handshake; of wiping
them onto a basketball before passing it during a game; of
flipping them into someone's school lunch back in the days. It's
one gross-out after another. But if a listener's only reaction is a
squinty-eyed, puckered-mouth gas-face, he or she probably needs
a release from the frenetic rat race of life. Or as Biz intones,
"Like, if I did som'n that was so full of shame/Yo, you *gotta*
know the name of the game!" In other words, B: Lighten up!

Based on a popular jingle for the Pathmark supermarket
chain, Biz's tag phrase from "Boogers"—the sing-songy "Hey
mom, what's for dinner?/Go up your nose and pick a winner!"—
could've been heard roaring from the mouths of those in hip-
hop's core. The jam's elastic rhythm, however, went on to
become much more universal. Having been popularized by Jazzie
B.'s Funki Dred collective, Soul II Soul ("Keep on Movin',"
"Back to Life"), it was the beat pounding through a thousand
R&B/pop/dance implosions, from Sybil's breakthrough remake
of "Walk on By" to Redhead Kingpin & the FBI's cracked-out
re-mix of "Do the Right Thing." Though labeled "the Soul II

Soul sound," it was really another example of producer Marley Marl's unsung greatness.

But back to *Goin' Off*. Along with a string of indecipherables (nonsense really), Biz barks out, "I'm the magnificent!" in the opening moments of the title track. Then, over a cascading, minimal beat (sliced through every few bars by sharp, orchestral hits), he stutter-steps through more jaunty celebrations of his vocal gift. It includes the ability to thud like a kick drum or chatter like a hambone, and the performer calls his arsenal of eccentric human noises The Inhuman Orchestra (!!).

Just like Bobby McFerrin, he can turn it out using his lips, cheeks and Adam's apple. He did so during the closing seconds of "Make the Music With Your Mouth Biz," punctuated with a sparkling piano riff. But, as he offered in "Goin' Off," he can also "rock a party with tooth decay!"

Elsewhere on *Goin' Off*, Biz paid homage to turntable art ("Cool V's Tribute to Scratching"), to an old hangout ("Albee Square Mall") and to folks who contributed to his rise ("This Is Something for the Radio"). At the same time, he invented a new street slang for payback while revealing how he and his crew got even with doomsayers from their past. Each verse in this loping track, "Vapors" (based on JB's "Pappa Don't Take No Mess"), related a now/then tale from each homeboy's life book, the first (about T.J. Swann) delivering the classic "Nigga please!/You work for UPS" line. There's joy in vindication.

But did Biz speak too soon? Would the self-proclaimed "diabolical" become a victim of his own phantasm? The answer to that question lies behind the grooves of *The Biz Never Sleeps*, his follow-up to *Goin' Off*. When word that he was producing the set himself leaked into the hip-hop nation, there was skepticism. In a *Word Up!* magazine interview, Biz said, "That's why I titled the album *The Biz Never Sleeps*. I wasn't sleeping, but people were sleeping on me. They thought I was gonna come out wack because I did this record myself. I didn't."

Instead, he came out much like before: slow and easy, fusing cool, bluesy funk froth with bugged, playful poetics. But on *The Biz Never Sleeps*, there was also a social agenda. On the cuts "Check It Out," "Things Get a Little Easier" and "My Man Rich" (a narrative about a homey done in by the forces of the violent underworld), Biz is a serious joke with serious messages: Stay in school, do drugs and you die! "I'm a comedian/message-teller," he said shortly after releasing *The Biz Never Sleeps*. "If I constantly come on too heavy, kids wouldn't listen."

Light as air, the first cut on the LP, "Dedication," floats through shout-outs to everyone from the Heavenly Father above to brothers on the boulevard below. Following this hassle-free takeoff, Biz cruises through a sea of killer one-liners, a mess of tales about girls ("She's Not Just Another Woman [Monique]," "A Thing Named Kim," "Just a Friend") and assorted B-boy goofiness. With the jingle music from an Irish Spring commercial in its introduction and coda, "The Dragon" is the silliest cut. When it talks about Tock, a smelly fella whose "underarms had bass in sensoround," it's most stoopid. The track is funny because we all know someone like Tock. Fact is, we all *are* sometimes Tock.

Being that Biz is a fan of animation—a Saturday-morning feature named "Mouthman" was supposed to be developed for Biz— it was almost no surprise that he wrote a rap about a cartoon character, too. He penned "Mudfoot," about Fat Albert's lanky pal, hoping to establish a prefab dance craze. While the step didn't catch on, I'm sure Biz is feeling satisfied (and vindicated) by the fact that one of the tunes he sang on, "Just a Friend," snapped, crackled and *still* went pop. He's probably dissing Prince with one of many mother jokes right now. Or, perhaps, he's scheming to throw Prince's own self-descriptive words (also from *The Black Album*) back at him: "That skinny mothafucka with the high voice!"

BOOGIE DOWN PRODUCTIONS

CRIMINAL MINDED (B BOY), 1987

BY ALL MEANS NECESSARY (JIVE), 1988

GHETTO MUSIC: THE BLUEPRINT OF HIP HOP, 1989

EDUTAINMENT, 1990

I made up rhymes in dark and scary places," snap-queen Arthur Rimbaud wrote in his poem "Wandering." Although this line was written in Europe during the nineteenth century, the essence of the text easily applies to the Jungle Lands of America's Chocolate Cities, the reluctantly adopted muthalands of Africa's children. These "dark and scary places" are the ghettos of the New World, with their sprawling housing projects and nodding crack heads, dimming streetlights and homeless folks sleeping in new-aged underground railroads, deserted subway stations. And yet these are the gritty Black villages (Baltimore, Philly, Oakland, Detroit, Elmhurst, Harlem, da South Bronx) that have produced the most creative styles in postmodern music—rap, house and new-jack swing. Outsiders might find it somewhat amazing that the sound of the future was first defined in neighborhoods that whites and/or buppie-class Blacks were afraid to venture into (like the playin' hi-post, redboned A.K.A. asked when she parked her average ride on my Harlem street, "Will my car be safe?" To which I replied, "Sure, there ain't no thieves around here, just drug dealers").

Living, growing up in the ghetto can be cool, but there is also a fucked-up side once the coin is flipped, a tarnished side that one wishes to avoid in the struggle of gettin' older. It would be difficult to name-check all my homies (or distant acquaintances) who were killed while trying to rob someone or who got popped by accident, who are doing time upstate or crack-noddin' on the corner. A few brothers and sisters became junkies, while others became drug dealers.

"If I don't hear someone shooting guns outside my window at night, then I think something must be wrong," Tammy O. says, her voice lacking any sort of irony. And with this statement, my memory hails back to the most brilliant hip-hop album produced in 1987, the brutal *Criminal Minded,* constructed by former Franklin Armory Men's Shelter social worker Scott Sterling and one of his "clients," Laurence Krisna Parker; as DJ Scott La Rock and Blastmaster KRS-One, this Bronx duo formed the foundation of Boogie Down Productions. An aural autobiography, this album works on several levels of awareness. "Call it a lecture, a visual picture," KRS-One informs on the album's first track, "Poetry," as he introduces one to hip hop's early years on the gritty streets of da Bronx, where King Heroin and his crazed lady Angel Dust (these were the days before their son Crack was born) roared through the trash-littered streets in a shiny pink Cadillac. While the local politicians kept their eyes closed to this modern apocalypse, buildings burned and notorious street gangs like the Black Spades and Savage Skulls battled over drugs and turf and flying colors in front of a backdrop that resembled an Iceberg Slim version of *West Side Story.* DJ Red Alert once said that *Criminal Minded* was "the nearest thing on wax to what rap sounded like back in the days. . . ."

With "South Bronx," one is transported to a place called Cedar Park and introduced to hip-hop's founding fathers, turntable master Kool Herc and microphone fiend Coke La Rock; then we are taken to a jam where Bam (Afrika Bambaataa) is rockin' the wheels of steel before gunfire scatters the crowd. KRS-One

KRS-One, rap artist as postmod thinker. © Alice Arnold, 1990.

tells us about Red Alert, Chuck Chill-Out, Flash, the Patterson and Millbrook projects and the Cyprus Boys—everyone and everything that contributed to the new wave of urban sound.

To those who think that Marley Marl and his Queens posse set the standard for this fledgling artform, KRS warns, "So you think that hip-hop had its start out in Queensbridge [projects]/If you pop that junk up in the Bronx you might not live!" One gets the impression that he ain't joking!

With *Criminal Minded,* the Boogie Down Productions crew recorded the blueprint for a new literature of crime, gangster rap ("Lookin for a style like mine, you can't find it," Kris says on the album's title track). Before the criminal imagery of Ice-T, N.W.A., Ice Cube or the Geto Boys became the subject of debate on the evening news and in the liberal press, before the FBI sent a memo to the Cali-based Niggers With Attitude in an attempt to curb their wicked ways, Scott and Kris were simply telling the world *their* side of the story. As KRS-One told writer

John Leland, of his past life: "In a shelter, unity is strength. Not too much intelligence, because the majority of the people are not intelligent. You had gangsters and criminals, murderers, drug dealers, and their idea of survival was just that: knock off the next man, sell your drugs over here, steal, gunpoint robberies."

One of the most brutal tracks on the album is "9mm Goes Bang," a delirious tale of drug dealers and gun battles that makes one's blood run cold. In the voice of a Rasta, KRS-One tells the story of a crack dealer named Peter whose posse attacks him; true to his name, the Blastmaster shoots Peter and his homeboy first: "They fell down to the floor but one was still alive/So I put my nine millimeter right between his eyes." What makes this track so eerie are the lines that follow, when DJ Scott shows up after the blood has been spilled: "But Scott is either psychic or he has a knack for trouble/'Cause Scott La Rock showed up in a all black BMW ..." A few months later, on August 26, 1987, twenty-five-year-old Scott was killed on the streets of the South Bronx when he tried to quash an argument between his "little brother" D-Nice and some neighborhood wildboys; bullets entered his head and neck.

Anyone who expected the empire of Boogie Down Productions to be buried with the corpse of Scott La Rock was sadly mistaken. No, Blastmaster KRS-One did not run for the hills and become a born-again Catholic; he did what any strong Black man would during a time of crisis—he came back "bigger and deffer." In light of Scott's bloody death, many were surprised to see KRS-One posed on the cover of *By All Means Necessary* staring out of his window holding an Uzi. With this haunting photo and the album's title, Boogie Down Productions was paying homage to Malcolm X's collected lectures and interviews, *By Any Means Necessary,* but they were both still disturbing.

"I think very deeply," a voice says at the beginning of this disc, before KRS-One begins an aural revolution that acts as a mature sequel to Boogie Down Productions' first album. In his mind, KRS-One views himself as a teacher, a street-corner scholar who preaches his philosophies to anyone who cares to listen. On "My Philosophy" he sets the stage to school us on rival hip-hop crews, crime in the streets, the dangers of eating meat ("That's suicide, self-murder") and the injustices attendant upon being a Black man in America.

Before his death, Scott La Rock told a journalist from England's *New Music Express*: "People think we're all stickup kids in the Bronx, but the government are bigger gangsters and hoodlums than we'll ever be." "Illegal Business" tells the story of police officers who take payoffs from local drug dealers. Over music sampled from Bill Cosby's bizarre "Fat Albert" cartoon series, KRS says: "Cocaine business controls America/Ganja business controls America ... Illegal business controls America." The rapper then explains that the drugs America can control (caffeine, tobacco, alcoholic beverages) are legal, but just because weed and coke are illegal doesn't mean that the government will not get their share of the profits.

Never forgetting that B-boy anthems began with brothers boasting about themselves and their crews, their neighborhoods and the art of rapping, KRS-One wrote a trilogy of songs to put other MC suckers in their place: "Ya Slippin'," "Part Time Suckers" and "I'm Still #1"; but as usual with the Blastmaster, the rhymes are more complex than mere verbal slaps. "Part Time Suckers" begins with the sounds of laughter (in ya face), as KRS says in a taunting, sing-songy style, "I want ya all to understand I'm down with BDP/I got so many styles but I'm not a MC/I'm a teacher teaching rap and of course I am back." Later, in "Ya Slippin'," which begins with a dis to former WBLS (New York) jock Mr. Magic, the Blastmaster tells his rivals, "Assume you're doomed when you walk into the room/I'll be the witch and you'll be the broom."

Though KRS-One poses on the album cover with an Uzi, there's a song on *By All Means* titled "Stop the Violence." The weapon seems to contradict the message. It could be argued that the gun is merely a symbol of the Black man's war against society, but when one hears lyrics like "When you're in a club, you come to chill-out/Not watch someone's blood just spill out/That's what these other people want to see/Another race fighting endlessly," ya get the feeling that KRS should have used a different image to represent our struggle.

Having taken his role as a teacher to heart, during 1989/1990 Blastmaster began delivering his message in universities as well as on the streets. Following the inauguration of the Stop the Violence Movement, he began lecturing at college assemblies throughout the nation, leading marches against homelessness—as someone who ran away from home at the age of thirteen, Kris knew the scoop—writing op-ed pieces for *The New York Times,* and working on a book that would record the complete history of rap. In brief, this articulate brother became the unofficial spokesman/ambassador of the hip-hop nation.

Preaching/teaching in a public forum or on television news shows is one thing, but transferring these lessons to the format of hip-hop music can be slightly tricky. If KRS-ONE is gonna assume the role of teacher, social observer and hip-hop activist, then—to be blunt—the beat's gotta be funky, like those on social protest records by James Brown, Queen Latifah, Brand Nubian or Public Enemy. Like Chuck D. said, "Ya can teach the seminar, but ya still gotta rock the boulevard!"

On the next two Boogie Down Productions albums, *Ghetto Music: The Blueprint of Hip Hop* and *Edutainment,* Blastmaster Kris stands behind the podium and educates us on African history, the failing American school system, world peace, racism and the origins of hip hop. Obviously influenced by *The Autobiography of Malcolm X,* Kris has taken the giant step from gangster to preacher. With tracks like "Who Protects Us From

You?" and "You Must Learn" (from *Ghetto Music*), he proves that he has more on his mind than rockin' the freaks walkin' down the street; both of these tracks show that Kris is well-read and intelligent, but the grooves are so minimal and raw it doesn't even matter.

A track like "Jack of Spades" (used as the hero's theme music in *I'm Gonna Git You Sucka*) is more commercial, but the message to "destroy all the stereotypes, hypes and crack pipes" works because the beat is flye. The other standout track on *Ghetto Music* is "Jah Rulez." With Baby Bam on the turntables and KRS-One's sister-in-law Harmony adding soulful singing, this song be cool runnings in the Blastmaster's minimal soundscape.

On his fourth album, *Edutainment,* a track like "Love's Gonna Get 'Cha (Material Love)"—a Jeep-boy fave—harks back to KRS-One's *Criminal Minded* days. This time, though, he explains the reasons behind the protagonist's gangster stance: Before he starts running drugs, he witnesses what the wrath of poverty does to his family; after becoming a drug dealer, his family now has a change of clothes and food to eat. His romanticization of the city streets ends abruptly when his little brother is shot and killed.

Last I time I saw my man KRS-One, he was rockin' the house at the downtown Manhattan club S.O.B.'s, recording a live version of *Criminal Minded.* The crowd was into the grooves, mouthing all the raps, and Kris's voice sounded like an Uzi blasting through the venue. Personally, I enjoyed this too-brief display better than either *Ghetto Music* or *Edutainment.*

CASH MONEY &
MARVELOUS

WHERE'S THE PARTY AT? (SLEEPING BAG), 1988

There are soulsters who'll swear the death of Philadelphia rhythm & blues occurred the night macho loverman Teddy Pendergrass smashed his ride over on the intersection of Seduction and Forlorn avenues (while a heavily painted-down transvestite sat idly by his side). Although he was paralyzed from the waist down, Teddy managed to survive this wreck; yet his career as America's numero-uno ebony love god came to a screeching halt—face it, not many gals can get their panties moist to warblings from a swoon-master confined to a wheelchair!

From 1972 to 1978, Philadelphia International became the heavenly sound that fell to earth, moving the hearts and bodies of urban America to its midnight cries of passion, its lush interpretation of a disco beat. Working out of Sigma Sound Studios, producers/songwriters Kenneth Gamble and Leon Huff crafted tunes like "Back Stabbers" and "Love Train" for the O'Jays, "Me and Mrs. Jones" for Billy Paul and "Wake Up Everybody" for Harold Melvin and the Blue Notes. But somewhere around the late '70s this hit machine also came to a full stop. In the words of Larry Gold, an arranger and musician who had worked with countless Philly soul acts, "There were times back then when this city had four or five studios running all day long making records. And all of a sudden it went from that to nothing. We ended up doing commercials. It was dead."

Now enter the new phase: with artists like Schoolly D, Jazzy Jeff and the Fresh Prince and Three Times Dope, hip hop helped revive the musical minds of Philadelphia's inner city.

In the same way that Gamble and Huff were the leaders of the '70s soul pack, the new-school groove king in the city of brotherhood is producer/studio mixer Joe "The Butcher" Nicolo; all the groups mentioned above have worked with Nicolo. Unlike the New York posse of rap producers like Marley Marl or Hurby Luv Bug, not much is known about Nicolo (I've never even seen a photo or an interview with him), but without a doubt, his studio creativity is like gasoline to the big wheels of the Philly hip-hop movement.

On Cash Money & Marvelous's debut album, *Where's the Party At?*, da Butcher is once again down with the program—this time as co-producer and engineer. On this disc's first two singles, "Play It Kool" and "Find an Ugly Woman," one can hear shades of Fresh Prince in the mix. "Ugly Woman" is a morality tale of how unattractive sisters who resemble Medusa ("It's not how she looks, it's how the girl treats ya") could be the best thing to happen to a brother. Although the story is as trite as anything found on Jazzy Jeff and the Fresh Prince's album (at the time the most popular mainstream rap crew in the nation), it's quite obvious that Cash Money & Marvelous are the supreme team in both vocal phrasing and turntable finesse—on the record's cover, Cash proudly displays his first-place belt from the New Music Seminar's Battle for World Supremacy as well as his DJ Mixing Champion jacket from an outfit called DMC. The closing wail of saxophonist Jammin' Jay Davidson pays homage to James Brown sideman Maceo Parker, but he just ain't sweatin' as hard, making his horn line less funky. And just when you thought you've entered another boring high-school boys' room—fellas talkin' 'bout their underwear that make women smile ("Marvelous Drawers") or about the girls sporting extensions in their hair ("Is It Real")—Money & Marvelous turn into aural gymnasts and cold flip on yo' ass.

With "The Mighty Hard Rocker," "Who's in the Place" and "Where's the Party At?" the M&M duo (melts in your ears, not in your hands) have sculpted three brilliant tracks that transport the listener back to the days of blazing summertime block parties on Riverside Drive, of Flash droppin' sonic bombs on the sweaty audience in the famed Audubon Ballroom (September 2, 1976) as the intensity level reached the boiling point, of Afrika Bambaataa making the mixed downtown Roxy crowd go stoopid berserk. These tracks aren't great hip-hop tracks from a Philly crew, they're great hip-hop tracks period.

From the sounds of the rehearsed rhymes on "Find an Ugly Woman," Marvelous now seems as though he's happy to be relieved of commercial burdens, just bustin' a flowing freestyle "that's rockin' your butt." As he boasts about being the baddest MC in town, screaming out neighborhood names ("Is Parkside in the house!?"), Cash Money gets deadly with dirty scratches, found sounds and funky samples that'll have you dancing solo in your chair. Or doing the freaky-deke at some hardcore jam.

Where's the Party At? is another one of those fresh yet underrated albums that proves there is no fairness in the world. While these two brothers have sailed off to the land of unsigned hip-hop crews, the Fresh Prince is bouncing around on television, clockin' dollars. For this reason alone he deserves a slap.

NENEH CHERRY

RAW LIKE SUSHI (VIRGIN), 1989

Since its origins in the concrete

    jungles of the South Bronx, hip-hop has tottered between

music gentrification and sexual decay.

    That is, rappers have enriched

the canon of pop culture while

      tearing down the image of Black women . . .

        —Charlotte Hunter, "Postmodern Divas

        and the Aesthetic of Bitches in Rap"

And here she comes rapping down da street: Ms. Cafe Au Lait, mixed not only in the blood but in the culture of musical expression; on the crossroads where punk's "no future" aesthetic encounters the beyond futurism of hip hop. LADIES AND GENTS, INTRODUCING . . .

Neneh Cherry is hip hop's first multicultural, multinational B-gal: birthed from a Swedish mother, yet spending much of her first fifteen years in New York with her stepfather, trumpet assassin Don Cherry (one of the warriors in Ornette Coleman's jazz army). Neneh recalls living on Manhattan's Lower East Side as a youth, and touring the world with Daddy Cherry, all the while observing the prince of avant-garde (Ornette) practice in his loft. It's a wonder Neneh Cherry didn't became a jazz diva, scattin' away like Billie or Ella or Sarah.

Two ideas come to mind when thinking about Neneh Cherry, the first being ... yo, perhaps critic Harry Allen was correct when he tagged hip hop the *new jazz*. The second comes in the voice of a homeboy who sez, "Hip hop is the sound of music and rap is the sound of voice." In other words, one can sing like Keith Sweat or En Vogue and still be hip hop.

In Ms. Cherry's case, she both sings and raps. Before entering the world of a thousand beatboxes, she fled the grime of New York City for the gloom of London, where she sang back-up for feminist punk group the Slits and then joined Rip Rig & Panic and Float Up Cp. Two years after the demise of Float Up Cp, Neneh transformed from post-punk anarchist to hip-hop stylist. Or better yet, Buffalo Girl.

"No money man can win my love/It's sweetness that I'm thinking of," Neneh Cherry sings on her single "Buffalo Stance." Produced by turntable wizard Tim Simenon, this track samples the neo-hip hop of Malcolm McLaren's "Buffalo Gals," embellishing the grooves with synths, crazy 808's and melodic guitar bits that whine in the mix, sounding like Bauhaus. Although her rap voice doesn't compare with hard hitters like MC Lyte or Queen Latifah, it is interesting to hear her American/Brit accent paint a portrait of the gigolo boys hanging out on her block.

On her debut album, *Raw Like Sushi* (a line from Big Daddy Kane's classic "Raw"), Neneh Cherry enjoys manipulating the art of irony: On the cover she is an exotic wet dream, posing in black lingerine like a YoBoy Toy, and yet her songs are intelligent and witty commentaries on womanhood. While most female rappers seem to view life as though they are seeing the world for the first time (and being in their teens, they just might be!), Neneh Cherry was twenty-five and had birthed two children when this album was released; these realities are reflected in her words. She transcends the surface of her characters to show real emotion.

Wearing her aural influences like a pair of Gaultier shades, Neneh Cherry swings to the grooves of Latin hip hop and South Bronx beatbox, Paradise Garage and down-home Soul. One moment her voice sounds sweet and dreamy ("Manchild") and the next minute she's spitting venom because "some back alley rat" stole her man ("Heart").

The most brilliant track on *Raw Like Sushi*, though, is "Inna City Mamma," which sounds like a female interpretation of Stevie Wonder's "Livin' in the City." In this sorrowful song detailing the life of a small-town girl who comes to da Big City looking for fame, Neneh sings, "I loved you from a distance/And your skyline made me a promise/... Now I look at you with tears in my eyes." The blues piano line heard throughout the track (and later in an elaborate solo) becomes a metaphor for angst, while Neneh's vocals are divided between womanist strength and nervous breakdown.

Although Neneh Cherry ain't exactly soul sister number one, she does have an honest realism that many artists don't usually reflect in their music. Part rapper, part singer, Ms. Neneh is a pop life daydream.

CHILL ROB G

RIDE THE RHYTHM (WILD PITCH), 1990

While a whole spate of hip-hop performers owe their fortunes to borrowing, lifting and appropriation, most of them are the initiating agents in the deals. And funky textures, not text, almost always make up the bulk of their exchanges. When, in the fall of '89, a pair of German producers named Benito Benites and John "Virgo" Garrett III sampled New Jersey resident/Queens native Chill Rob G, they took full stanzas of his rap (from the prophetically titled "Let the Words Flow"), constructing a whole new musical environment for it by way of digital technology. After renaming their track "The Power" and releasing it under the name "Power jam" featuring Chill Rob G, the former Rob Frazier—his *Ride the Rhythm* LP had been out for almost a year—finally became a hot property, a hissing star in the ever-turbulent galaxy of urban noise.

Club play and performing "a lotta, lotta shows" across America got Rob paid, but another group named Snap was also benefiting from "The Power," basically the same music with another rap. How did two very similar singles end up in a power struggle?

It all started when New York indie Wild Pitch licensed "Let the Words Flow" to Logic Records in Germany with several mixes, including an a capella one that Benites and Garrett recontextualized. Their jam became a smash all over Europe—number one in England for three weeks—and when Wild Pitch got wind of this, they demanded the record back for U.S.

distribution. They got it, but things didn't end there. BMG (parent company to Logic) had also released the song in the U.S. through another of its arms, Arista. It, however, featured a different rap (by U.S. serviceman Turbo B) and a new singer (Jackie Harris, Turbo B's cousin).

Snap's version of "The Power" subsequently sold more copies (more than 500,000—gold) and charted higher than Rob G's in the States—there's bigger and better promotion over at Arista—but Rob G had the superior rap. His "The Power" is the one around-the-way Jeep-boys cooled out to all summer long in 1989. Like Rob Base & DJ EZ Rock's "It Takes Two" the previous year, it was a burbling, tantalizing breeze over the steamy concrete jungle. Notable for its meshing together of classic disco (a gospelly passage from dance diva Joycelyn Brown's "Love's Gonna Get You"), hardcore hip hop (a pumping electro-groove that uses, among other things, the bells from Doug Lazy's "Let It Roll") and alternative noise (listen to the fuzz-toned guitar doodle used as a bridge), it pumped it up on the club and street level while, below, weaving some tribal inspiration into its flippy verses: "I'll take a page/Write a phrase and rephrase it/Treat it like a national flag and upraise it." Moreover, with its "I've got the power!" chorus (the Joycelyn Brown bite), it recalled the Rev. Jesse Jackson's motivational "I am somebody!" salvo.

Initial pressings of *Ride the Rhythm* didn't contain "The Power," credited on the single as "A Wild Pitch reconstruction of a Logic construction of a Wild Pitch production of DJ Mark, the 45 King." But there were other gems in its eclectic mix, split between a "light side" and a "dark side" and produced by DJ Mark, the 45 King.

Indeed, long before "The Power" or, even, "Let the Words Flow," Rob had "Dope Rhymes" (his first single, recorded approximately twenty-four hours after an audition in DJ Mark's basement studio in 1988). Though flittering between bragging and motivating, the rapper's brisk, syncopated words—keeping their promise of "inspiring your mind to float like that of a kite"—never loses focus, somersaulting with intense but controlled locomotive zing. In "Ride the Rhythm," he says his motion is "similar to an ocean bringing you emotions," but don't expect pastoral surges or to be altogether soothed. While cool and effortless, Rob G's voice is a deadly hardcore instrument, asserting itself glibly inside ragged, minimalist grooves that range from roughhouse hip house (the we-can-overcome statement "Make It") to neoprimitivistic freestyle ("Dope Rhymes") to utterly contemporary/chillingly relevant narratives (the socio-political "Court Is Now in Session" and "Let Me Show You"). That is genuine (sampled) funk. That is what gives Rob his "impact that's similar to a train wreck." That is the power, the glory, the world without end, ahem.

CHUBB ROCK

CHUBB ROCK FEATURING HOWIE TEE (SELECT), 1988

AND THE WINNER IS . . . , 1989

KEEP IT STREET, 1990

THE ONE, 1991

During an especially boring stretch of the 1989 Urban Teen Music Awards, Chubb Rock stormed the great stage at Harlem's legendary Apollo Theatre, delivering a big bam boom that stirred the room. Wearing a 2XL, mustard-colored sweat suit with black trim, he (along with his crew, which included a staggering mock-drunk dancer carrying a jug of ale) breezed through, shocking the house with a lively rendition of his re-mix rap hit, "Caught Up." As he flipped through its mad, stomping beat, this homeboy Barry White (he had served up a bass-toned rhapso*dis*, "She's With Someone," on his second LP) turned into an overweight Bobby Brown, reeling out clever line after clever line while doing a little dance. Folks marveled at his cardiovascular stamina (for a six-foot-three, 250-pound brother, it truly was amazing) as they egged him on: "Go, Chubb Rock!" they chanted.

Impressed with the performer's motivational skills, cutting-edge talkologist Big Daddy Kane later tapped him for an opening-act slot on his national tour. Soon afterward, mellow man Kool Moe Dee followed suit.

Definitely an entertainment bounty, Chubb Rock started out as a heavyweight ("I think I came out of my mother's womb measuring at least four foot five," he once joked). He only grew larger. Staying limber by lifting weights and playing sports (football, handball, basketball), he's been rapping since the age of twelve. Motivated by the prospect of getting girls, he per-

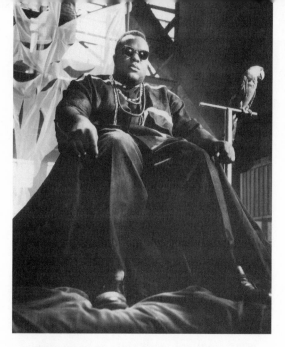

Chubb Rock. Photo courtesy of Select Records.

formed in a neighborhood group, the Sureshot 4, which also featured his cousin, DJ/producer "Hitman" Howie Tee. But eventually this crew broke up, leaving Chubbs with the unfulfilled dream of making it as a rapper.

While winning a National Merit Scholarship at age sixteen afforded him the opportunity of leaving behind the gray East Flatbush streets that dulled his glitzy vision of a show-biz career, he entered college to study pre-med. Two years later he became frustrated with that atmosphere ("I wasn't prepared for the social scene," he complained) and dropped out. After tightening up a few of the raps he had written, and seeking out production assistance from Howie Tee (who was working as Full Force protegé the Real Roxanne's DJ at the time), Chubbs landed a deal with New York indie Select, whose roster includes hip-hop businessmen/mainstream fun boys Kid 'n Play.

Sounding kind of like a Rodney Dangerfield on a sociopolitico hip-hop trip, Chubb Rock (whose real name is Richard Simpson) tried to establish himself with three singles from an eponymous debut LP: "Rock 'n' Roll Dude" (a track with a light-metal guitar sample that compared rap's rebellious edge to rock's), "DJ Innovator" (about Tee) and "Caught Up" (a narrative about meeting and then sexing "an ugly girl"). None worked.

Having finally grabbed the ears of rap's core with a re-thought "Caught Up"—it became a bright (hype) funk rave-up that threw *much* spunk onto a smooth track that mixed samples from Flavor Flav ("Rock that shit, homey!"), Inner Life (the chorus from this disco group's one hit, "Caught Up in a One Night Love Affair") and James Brown—Chubb Rock's second album was launched onto a more receptive marketplace. It contained "Caught Up (Re-mix)" as well as a number of tunes that chronicled the performer's rise from obscurity. From the opening "Stop That Train," where he's climbing aboard "the rap Amtrak . . . the success express," to "Mr. Nobody Is Somebody Now," he sounded like someone who was going places.

But *And the Winner Is . . .* isn't just the portfolio of a rap star's journey. Along with nimble funk, it's also a showcase for wit. In the chuggy "Bump the Floor," Chubbs disses a can't-dance lunkhead with the line "Gregory, you're too slow like Heinz [Hines] . . . ketchup." In the organ-happy "What a Differ-ence," he compares himself favorably to plastic sprinkled with oxide particles: "You bet/If I were a cassette/I'd be chrome/ Hard like metal . . . but never normal."

Chubbs's style (steady, forceful, buggy) weaves in lots of inside rhymes ("I pour a rhyme like wine/Yo! Canei reach the top . . . ?"), compelling the listener to constantly back up his playback whatever (compact disc, cassette or LP). It addresses distressing topics, including the social blemish of Black-on-Black crime ("Blow the Whistle") and the Grammy Awards' refusal to fully acknowledge rap's viability (the title track) in a tone that's neither pedantic nor murky.

Written in 1988, before the National Academy of Recording Arts and Sciences initiated a category for rap, the former tune begged to know just what qualifies a rapper to be in the running for a golden gramophone. Clearly, it wasn't sales or popularity, since at the time "Compton hardhead" Eazy-E, for instance, had sold well over a million units against retro-neuvo angel Anita Baker's 600,000. She was up for a number of awards that year, but to NARAS voters Eazy didn't even exist. Foul, cried Chubb Rock.

A portion of "And the Winner Is . . ." recreates the society's presentation ceremony, nominating Biz Markie, Big Daddy Kane and Chubbs himself in a category. Things become at once thought-provoking and funny when the victor is finally announced—curiously, Whitney Houston. Chubbs's deadpan tone when he mentions the plastic diva's name carries with it the weight of both racial and generational conflicts.

An institution like the Grammys is liberal enough to give a nod to a Black lady, yet their progressiveness precludes putting a gangsta-minded homie D (that's D for down in street parlance). They're regarded as hip, yet they're really very out of tune with the shifting tastes in American popular culture. The crossover dreams of rappers everywhere were being viewed by traditional artists and technicians not as genuine musical breakthroughs, but as racial nightmares.

Even the following year, when NARAS finally made plans to add a rap to its telecast, it had proposed issuing a statue to the genre's participants *before* the big show, preferring, instead, to spotlight other less-heralded (and less-commercial) categories like bluegrass. In the wake of this announcement, the hip-hop nation organized a boycott of the Grammys that was spearheaded by former Rush publicist Bill Adler. While a mixed success, the boycott sent a pointed message to the powers that be: The hip-hop nation is to be respected.

Having collaborated with R&B stars Kashif, Patti Austin, Jeff Redd and Al B Sure! following the success of *And the Winner Is . . . .* Chubb Rock (who also has a supporting role in the Warner Bros. flick *Private Times*—he plays a quasi-gangsta named Jellyroll) jumped back onto the rap scene "with a lean and a pocketful of green." As if to assure his developing core that his dabblings in non-street music didn't corrupt him, he titled the release, a five-song EP, *Keep It Street*. Coming with "no pop tunes/only rough street beats," it's a righteous thrust for street-corner respect and Black power as well as hardcore stylism.

Beginning with "Treat 'Em Right," the main single which re-creates notes from the repetoire of First Choice (the early '80s dance classic "You Treat Me Right") and James Brown (some obscure track Chubbs says he "went diggin' in the crates" for), Chubbs relates experiences he's had living in Blackland during 1989. Calling attention to spiraling drug use (crack cocaine) and Black-on-Black crime, he urges listeners to "ignore temptation set by the nation." Later, it's "Don't forget Yusef Hawkins!" —alluding to the instance of racial assault that occurred in Bensonhurst, Brooklyn. Responding to this incident (as well as others like the Eleanor Bumpers and Michael Stewart cases), the rapper proposes education and structure.

From the molasses groove of "What's the Word?" (informed by an anti-Bush speech by Nation of Islam leader Minister Louis Farrakhan, a sound bite that chants, "Impeach the president!," and reggae toasting by Chubbs's stepfather, "Robin Hood"), he paints an ill scene of South Africa's white supremacist regime. Then he encourages African-Americans to evaluate their own so-called freedoms in America: "Read between the lines/Don't recline your mind," he instructs. It's time for action; so in the next cut, the message is "Organize!" Using, among other things, a sports metaphor that could be construed as racist (he asks, "If the battle of the races were a basketball game, who'll reign?"), he sets out a plan for social and economic victory: "Frame it, aim it, name it, proclaim it."

If everything on *Keep It Street* sounds heavy, it is. "Things have gotten more serious," Chubbs laments. Still, there are light moments, like in "Keep It Street" when he complains about every rapper wanting "a Mr. T starter kit." From this same jazzy groove, our Afrocentric brutalist turns affable and invites all disciples of pop-rap to "come back and dance to a James Brown beat." Going with the flow, the next cut pays respect to "The Regiments of the Steel," those hardcore stylists from Afrika Bambaataa to Compton's Most Wanted, "who stay true." Although he didn't give himself a shout-out in the song, Chubb Rock, too, is in the pantheon. A true hip-hop heavyweight.

He was poised for bigger and defferness in 1991, as his latest album hit the racks via a distribution arrangement with Elektra Entertainment. A front-page ad in *Billboard* magazine boasted "*The One* has sold over 240,000 units in ten days." But this CD—it incorporates the EP tracks—doesn't altogether stomp into The Nation. Chubbs's raps are clear and witty, but producer Tee's tracks too often sound unfinished. He should be soaking his client's words in thicker, more dissonant mixes. For example, "Another Statistic" needs violent drama, not cool minimalism, to emphasize the "fixed 'im for good" ending to a fatal attraction. And "The Night Scene" (which discusses college cuties who hoe for dough and dread-cool fuck-ups who deal for wheels) begs for emotional rescue from loopy monotony.

But Chubbs deserves props for three of the new tracks, especially "The One" and "Just the Two of Us." The former features a *crazy* ragamuffin doodle-chant, while the latter two-steps over minor-key chords and major-league boasts on the level of "Each I'm gonna reach and teach with the speech/If you riff I'ma flip like Nadia Comanici." And if ya don't believe that Chubbs can somersault over weak-wack duds like a motherlode on a findum-fuckimup-flee spree, just ask anyone who was at the Apollo Theatre March 4, 1989, the night The Big Man shocked the house with the greatest of ease.

DANA DANE

Although he bragged and boasted, seeing himself as larger than he really was, the raps of Dana Dane's debut weren't full of ego like L.L. Cool J's. Neither were they goofy like Biz Markie's or aggressive like Run-DMC's. They engaged because they were the closest rap music came to old-time storytelling.

While L.L. "Even when I'm bragging I'm being sincere" Cool J and Run-DMC took pride in being themselves on record, Dane obviously did not. His rhymes were vividly detailed, highly unlikely scenarios spiked with unexpected twists and amusing vocal characterizations—a telephone ringing, a girl whining. His main voice spoke in an upper-class British accent, bringing some affluence to a medium that thrived on poverty—minimalist beats, down duds, cheap samples. He, in fact, was one of rap music's first *GQ*–B-boys (rappers who wear silk suits instead of track warm-ups, loafers instead of sneakers).

Layered by producers Sam Jacobs, Jr. and Sr., and, later, Hurby "Luv Bug" Azor, Dane's tracks weren't hell-raising hard. They shuffled the way '70s soul and traditional (nonbrutal) disco did. With pieces from vintage Jackson Five and Tower of Power, they emerged sleek and smooth—like gold-plated bathroom fixtures, like the lines on a Lamborghini sports car.

In "Nightmares," Dane's debut 12-inch, he chronicled his encounters with three "wack" females over recreations of "The Munsters" theme music. Here he was repulsed, tossing around dreamland to loud, licking rhythms. Then in "Delancy Street" he

Dana Dane. Photo by Robert Lewis, courtesy of Profile Records.

---

was coolly bopping around NYC, only to become involved in an action/adventure through the Lower Manhattan shopping district.

Dane's own narratives were fine, but it was "Cinderfella Dana Dane," an adaptation of the fairy tale *Cinderella*, that pushed *Dana Dane With Fame* past gold status. After buying an oversized comic book detailing Cindy's drama, he updated it "so the public today could relate to it more." In Dane's story he's the ragged-up errand boy/black sheep of his family, living in Brooklyn's Fort Greene housing projects. When he gets the scoop that a royal ball will be going down, he asks his stepfolks to put him on the list; he gets dissed.

Fortunately, his fairy godfather, played by Luv Bug, boings him into a stretch limo and some flye gear (slick silk suit, Bally loafers, argyle socks ... the whole nine) and greases him into the affair. He warns Dane to split by the stroke of twelve or else. As he jets out near midnight, he loses one of his Ballys. A few days later a princess comes a knockin', holding it. The pair disappear together and live happily ever after.

While Dane's DJ, Clark Kent, went on to other projects right after the success of *Dana Dane With Fame* (he's a producer/remixer, top party spinner and an A & R rep for Atlantic Records), Dane took nearly three years to release a follow-up LP. He blamed a busy Luv Bug for the delay, but the rapper was appearing in videos by Salt-n-Pepa and Slick Rick (a buddy from a high school group the Kangol crew), and running a successful "fresh gear" (fashion design) business (with Kid 'n' Play's Christopher Reid) in Elmhurst, NY, called IV Plai (pronounced "foreplay").

Some residents of the hip-hop nation were buying duds from the shop while Dane was out of the studio, but they were also innovating, pushing B-boyness to a higher degree. They were asserting themselves with tracks made of brutalist boom as well as laid-back layers, and their contributions make Dane's style on *4-Ever* sound outmoded.

The legendary Hurby Luv Bug directed most of *4-Ever* with his posse the Invincibles. These tracks, however, sound shrill and corny. One of them, "Dana Dane To It," makes empty promises along the order of it's "a single with a jingle that you all will be loving soon." On this egomaniacal terrain, Dane threatens MC comp with lines about this being his era and about him delivering the gospel like "the pastor or the master." Throughout the track, Dane deludes himself, like he's punchy from being knocked about by hardcore brothers like L.L. or EPMD.

There's a cut where Dane tries to compete with nasty boys like Too Short. He doesn't curse or anything like that; Dane's too classy for that. He plays a game with homepal Joeski Love, wherein he weaves scenarios full of whimsical double entendres. After pulling the rug out from under Joeski he declares, "Uhu, Joe, I knew what you were thinking!" To which Joe retorts, "Yes, you definitely almost caught me out there! All this, and a lazy track with syrupy pop gloss too!

What saves *4-Ever* from being total garbage are two Fresh Gordon productions: "A Little Bit of Dane Tonight" and "Tales From the Dane Side." Although not the shots of spunk Jeep boys like to guzzle while chasing babes doing the shake dance, the aisle between funky and booty narrows when these cuts come on. Their amusement-park flavor is contagious, and while they play, Dane's flair for tall tales with yucks sounds fresh again.

DE LA SOUL

3 FEET HIGH & RISING (TOMMY BOY), 1989

DE LA SOUL IS DEAD, 1991

C oming from Long Island (Strong Island in hip-hopspeak), this crew has its origins on the same Black Land that gave birth to Public Enemy, Rakim (but not Eric B.) and EPMD. Yet, unlike other rappers/DJ's from Long Island, De La Soul were not impressed with the fashions of the hip-hop nation of old ('70s) styled gangsters or new-age militants. With the debut of their first single, "Plug Tunin'" (as well as the grainy, arty, super-8 production video), De La Soul created an image that screamed "good-bye!" to gold chains and track suits, Troop jackets and Kangol hats. Sporting baggy pants and paisley shirts, De La Soul introduced a new style/sound movement that went beyond def, journeying into Other-Worldness that wasn't only new to hip hop but to the entire spectrum of pop culture. This was the dawning of the D.A.I.S.Y. age ("da inner self y'all"), a world of difference that would be an influence from the streets to the suites, the parks to the pop charts.

Producer Prince Paul, from Stetsasonic, who also contributed cash toward the making of De La Soul's demo, went into the studio with the three De La Brothers (Mase, Posdnuos and Trugoy) and constructed their surrealistic debut, *3 Feet High & Rising,* in little over a month. Prior to composing what some critics dubbed "rap's Sgt. Pepper," Pos and Trugoy were in a group called Easy Street, while Mase and Prince Paul had worked together on another rap project. Mase didn't meet Pos and Trugoy until the trio were all in the same summer-school class, goofing off and exchanging lyrics.

With its Day-Glo cover that highlighted colorful flowers dancing around the heads of the group, *3 Feet High & Rising* was released in 1989, quickly gaining acceptance from Black urban youth, pop critics and college radio stations. Although some observers of this postmodern funk trio tried to label them psychedelic, a more realistic term would be Blackedelic, since De La Soul are more influenced by sepia rocker George Clinton than by '60s hippies (the inner-sleeve graphics, which depict De La Soul teleporting from Mars, are a direct homage to the Pedro Bell/Overton Lloyd funkateer cartoons featured on Parliament/Funkadelic album covers).

Moving away from De La Soul's arty public image to their innovative private soundscape, one cannot help but be amazed by the strange, sonic diversity that is displayed on this disc, with a garden of samples that include French instruction records, Steely Dan, screams of passion, Hall and Oates, found sounds, Prince and dozens of other aural sources. In this vast amusement park of joyful noise, twenty-four tracks are featured as part of a game show that broadcasts throughout the record.

Although much of the lyrics are spoken in nonsense metaphors, there is also a seriousness to De La Soul that is often ignored. On "Ghetto Thang" the group details a world of teenage mothers, pimps and random gunfire. "Say No Go," perhaps the most danceable anti-drug song, speaks out against the dangers of crack. In a decade where safe sex could mean the difference between life and death, De La sing the praises of wearing "your jimmy caps" on a track called "Buddy"; this track also features Afrocentric rappers the Jungle Brothers and Q-Tip from the jazzy A Tribe Called Quest. On "Me Myself and I," the group's crossover smash, the Clinton/Funkadelic sample "(Not Just) Knee Deep" is clearly heard.

In an unusual footnote for one of the most inventive hip-hop albums of 1989, De La Soul was sued for $1.7 million by aging hippies Flo and Eddie, formerly with the Turtles, for

De La Soul: . . . and as they emerge from the Mothership, these hippy-hoppers introduce a new sound to the rap nation. © Tina Paul, 1989.

sampling the first four bars of their 1969 pop hit "You Showed Me" for "Transmitting Live From Mars." This legal matter places De La Soul at the center of the copyright/sampling controversy that has the music industry divided.

After the brilliance of *3 Feet High & Rising*, the entire hip-hop nation is quietly awaiting more bizarre soundwaves to splash upon our urban beaches. Prepare to swim or drown.

De La spent two years on the road—youthful audiences tossing flowers onto their stages, countless journalists asking variations on the "So, what's it like to be Black hippies?" question. The De La Brothers were becoming disenchanted with the image they had created, the cult of day-glo madness/hype that their label, Tommy Boy, helped build. And what better way to cease being the object of unwanted desire than to kill yourself . . . ?

With the release of *De La Soul Is Dead* (the cover art shows three potted daisies knocked over), most fans and critics had doubts that this trio from Strong Island would be able to survive in the crowded sea of hip hop without their peace signs; but, as the spider said to the fly, "You gotta another think coming." Like their suburbia homeboys Public Enemy, the De Le Gang proves that it's possible to create two sonic masterworks in a row—just gotta keep your eyes on the prize and your ear to da beat; with eighty minutes of sound to fill our potholes, they rock harder than one had reason to expect.

De La Soul Is Dead is both silly and serious, a stylish balancing act that very few hip-hop acts could pull off. Alongside "Millie Pulled a Pistol on Santa," which details the sad saga of a sexual molestation that turns into murder, are tracks like "Bitties in the BK Lounge" and "A Rolling Skating Jam Named Saturdays," two totally escapists goofs. In a lot of ways it's like *3 Feet High,* only more ghetto-ruff.

DIGITAL UNDER-GROUND

SEX PACKETS (TOMMY BOY), 1990

With images of John Travolta, the Bee Gees and Saturday Night fevers flashing through their minds like strobe lights, some cultural theorists of the decade that was the '70s would like to dispose of the entire era in the nearest dumpster. What is often interpreted by mainstream critics as the end of the Summer of Love (hippies, the Beatles, Woodstock) was actually (actively) the rebirth of America's Chocolate Cities.

After the brutal deaths of Martin Luther King, Jr., and Malcolm X, after the riots in Watts, inner-city Detroit and Harlem, which left these communities knee-deep in ashes and broken glass, the '70s was the decade that Black Americans used to make bold and innovative statements. Thirty-plus years after the zoot suit was synonymous with the Black cool of the bebop generation, Black Americans were once again standing on the edge (in high-heeled shoes, flared pants and giant Afros) of a political and artistic renaissance. From Sly Stone to John Shaft, from slogans like "Say It Loud, I'm Black and I'm Proud" to the poetic musings of Nikki Giovanni, these new noir images screamed threats to mainstream culture that slashed its Norman Rockwell painting of normality.

The chief auteur of nonconformist sound and image was a former doo-wop singer named George Clinton. As creator of the Parliafunkadelicment Thang, Clinton communicated that da funk led to the road of freedom. By making his private joys public spectacles, Clinton and Co. (a band that included four guitar players, a horn section, keyboards and a parade of other musicians/ singers) composed radical funk-operas, dressed in psychedelic style and performed with wild abandon. This was, in the words of the grand orchestrator/street poet Clinton, "one nation under a groove," and everyone was invited to the party.

Fast-forward to the late '80s, and the hip-hop nation is searching for new blood to fuel its rhythm machine. After older rappers had exhausted the entire James Brown catalog, the new breed had little alternative but to follow the natural progression of the funk train. New York rappers the Jungle Brothers, De La Soul and A Tribe Called Quest all borrowed from the P-Funk songbook, but it wasn't until Cali-based Digital Underground emerged on the scene that the essence of Clinton's goofy funk aesthetic was placed in the proper B-boy context.

With the release of their debut single, "Doowutchyalike," in 1989, Digital Underground set the tone for a new school of rappers who were less interested in being aural gangsters, more inclined to be freaky and experimental. "Doowutchyalike';' is funky yet arty, sounding like a hundred radios (all set to different stations) blaring simultaneously. "Now as the record spins around/You recognize this sound/It's the underground," lead rapper Shock G. begins this anthem of B-boy independence, before a shower of sound rains down from the heavens. From

Digital Underground, da Sons of Funkadelic. © Tina Paul, 1990.

sound effects to animation voices, bites from Clinton's "Atomic Dog" to an extended piano solo played in ragtime style (hip hop influenced by Scott Joplin!), this track introduces a crew who is serious about music, but they just happen to live in a cartoon universe. As journalist Frank Owen observed in the pages of *Spin* magazine, "This is music that goes beyond def."

Like Clinton, Shock G.'s music overdoses on science fiction and drug culture. But where Clinton was wailing through a haze of hallucinogens and soaring on spaceships with alien creatures, Shock G.'s brand of sci-fi is more cyberfunk than space-opera. Having created a complete mythology about a new drug invented by Dr. Edward Earl Cook which "is just sex in pill," Digital Underground titled their concept album *Sex Packets*.

Celebrating the music of artful orgasms (both human and instrumental), Digital Underground begins with the *Sex Packets* saga with "Packet Prelude"; with background chatter coming from the bar, a piano player performs in the semidarkness of a local jazz dive. A male voice that appears to be drowning in a dream says, "It's so real ..." And then comes the erotic femme who moans, "It is real/it is real/it is real." What follows is the title track, detailing the pleasures of taking a drug that will bring wet-dream images to whomever swallows it; with a soundscape that is both funky and melodic, this drug is highly addictive. In a society obsessed with pleasure but having to "just say no" because of the fear of diseases, one would think that the Sex Packets would be legal ... wrong.

On "Packet Man" the listener is taken on a tour of the nighttime streets of Cali, where one overhears the Packet Man convincing a "virgin" to sample his wares. He tells him that if his wife "wants to hit the sack, it's cool/Take a packet fool," Shock G. says with glee, before warning the customer, "But don't pull your money out yet, see/There's one or two narcs in this area sweating me." The irony/reality of drug addiction is placed in perspective when the customer returns at the end of the track attempting to trade his television and VCR in exchange for more packets.

The second single, "The Humpty Dance," is just a goofy song that contains more Clinton beats to promote a silly dance that rapper Humpty Hump says "makes you look like M.C. Hammer on crack." Slightly entertaining, but sort of ho-hum when compared to hip-pop gems like "Underwater Rimes" or "Freaks of the Industry."

In the mix 'n' match planet of current dance music, Digital Underground are just more youngbloods bum-rushing the gates of culture, smashing the objects and displaying the pieces as new artifacts. Or as George Clinton once said, "Hip hop has kept the funk alive."

DJ MARK, THE 45 KING

SEE CHILL ROB G, QUEEN LATIFAH

MATT DIKE
& MATT ROSS

SEE BEASTIE BOYS, TONE-LÖC, AND YOUNG MC.

DJ JAZZY JEFF
& THE
FRESH
PRINCE

ROCK THE HOUSE (JIVE/RCA), 1987

HE'S THE DJ, I'M THE RAPPER, 1988

AND IN THIS CORNER . . . . , 1989

While DJ Jazzy Jeff and the Fresh Prince's melodic mixes did little to endear them to rap's hardcore purists (whose purblind idea of rap is defiant and arrogant scratch-and-cut melanges), they scored plenty of points in the wasteland of Middle America, MTV. By spinning colorful narratives and tossing them against mostly polished (sometimes brittle) tracks with nice-guy charm, this crew from West Philadelphia and Winfield (two Pennsylvania suburbs dotted with gilded ghettos) was a hip-hop crossover story waiting to happen. Though many believed their breakthrough album, *He's the DJ,*

I'm the Rapper, was their first, it in fact was the follow-up to the ten-song *Rock the House,* originally released on Dana and Laurence Goodman's Pop Art label (at one point also the home of Juice Crew members Roxanne Shanté, Big Daddy Kane and Biz Markie). The LP yielded a hit, "Girls Ain't Nothing But Trouble," before being picked up by Jive, but the song benefited further from a subsequent video provided by the indie major. Showcasing a Good Arnold image, it paved the way for one of '80s rebel art's first mainstream success stories.

For DJ Jazzy Jeff (Jeff Townes) and the Fresh Prince (Will Smith), the passions and the suffering of the civil rights struggle weren't part of their middle-class existences coming up. Thus, instead of defiant anger, their raps are full of mundane pleasures and jokey fantasies/nightmares. Hostility is removed due in part to financial achievement by their parents and social acceptance by white neighbors not yet spooked by a so-called "tipping point." Inviting, polite and joyous, theirs is hip hop smoothed out on the bourgeoisie tip, rap that is far more tightly linked to the broader American fabric than most.

With "Girls Ain't Nothing But Trouble" (the first track on *Rock the House* as well as the first cut DJ Jazzy Jeff and the Fresh Prince ever recorded), when the Fresh Prince calls a female "toots" over a crisp (original) jack track layered with Hugo Montenegro's (orchestral) "I Dream of Jeannie" theme music, it is clear that he and his DJ partner didn't rise out from the polluted waters of Bronx River (a neighborhood in New York that pioneered hip hop; where records were made by pairing ancient [found] drumbeats with brutal street *attitude*). Though the duo listened to rough bootleg tapes by Grandmaster Caz and others for inspiration, they just couldn't rise above their Theo Huxtable–type upbringings to create a record that sounded like it came out of the ruins of hip hop's borntown. So, while Fresh Prince's flow (by turns fast-paced and smooth, but always understandable) is from Caz et al., his subject matter and tone stem from his immediate environment (a dreamland both real and imagined). While DJ Jazzy Jeff's mastery of rhythm was helped along by hip-hop producer Kool Herc's ingenious metronomic manipulations, it started developing on a set of drums bought for him by his parents.

Though "Girls Ain't Nothing But Trouble" was recorded as a joke, it revealed some serious sexual anxiety. In one of the tune's three vividly detailed episodes, the Fresh Prince is jumping out of a lover's window after being discovered by her husband. He runs home through a snowstorm dressed only in underwear, then, having left his keys in his pants pocket, is forced to break into his own apartment. Later, he develops a cold, too. All this drives him to caution fellow fellas: "The next time a girl gives you the play/Just remember my words and stay the hell away." One chuckled, but one also wondered what impact such advice had on Black male/female relationships, already threatened by crossover lust and government-endorsed castration by way of double-dipping (hiring Black females over Black males, thus satisfying two minority quotas at once) and the like. This, pilgrims, was (and still is) no laughing matter.

Included on *Rock the House* is the answer record "Guys Ain't Nothing But Trouble" by Ice Cream Tee. She should've served the sweetboys something tart, but instead of confronting them, tying them up with elastic words, she just fronts. First, Ms. Tee willingly accepts a ride with the Fresh Prince when she discovers that he has a Jaguar. Taken to his house, she encounters a pimp who informs her she'll be working Forty-second Street. She then pulls out a .357 Magnum and escapes (yeah, right!). On the cut's fade-out, Jeff and Prince wake up to their insensitivity toward the opposite sex (it's anyone's guess what convinced them) while she nods, "Can't live with 'em and can't without them." Answer records are supposed to *slam* their targets, blow them to smithereens. This one, besides having bad aim, has no power to speak of.

D.J. Jazzy Jeff & the Fresh Prince. Photo courtesy of Jive/RCA.

More confrontational and interesting is "A Touch of Jazz" and "The Magnificent Jazzy Jeff," both of which spotlight the amazing techniques that won J.J. a 1987 Urban Teen award (Best DJ) and 1986's New Music Seminar Battle of the DJs competition. The latter track is an airy, seamless collage of quasi-jazz releases by Bob James, Donald Byrd, Grover Washington Jr. and others over a break beat. The former, master of ceremonied by the Fresh Prince, is a more spirited, more blunt display, where one section of sound is manipulated to produce three distinct effects—a burp, a chirp and a whistle.

Along with human (or is it *in*human?) beatbox Ready Rock C, Jeff got more room to show off on *He's the DJ, I'm the Rapper,* hip hop's first double album. The spinner has top-billing in the act, and on this record he *really* is the star on six cuts, including one recorded live at Manhattan's Union Square in 1986. Using grooves from various *Ultimate Breaks and Beats* compilation albums as well as other myriad sources, he cold-gets-bizzy on the wheels of steel, shifting space, transforming rhythms and mutating melodies in thoroughly engaging ways. His displays are a reminder of hip hop's early years during the '70s, when the DJ was the focal point in a crew. But this is an '80s record, so its hit singles, "Parents Just Don't Understand" and "Nightmare on My Street," contained no cuts, no scratches, no sign of a DJ.

These smooth songs were more jaunts about what a hassle it is being a middle-class teenager. In the eerie "Nightmare," Prince recounts his only terror—being chased by Freddie Krueger. Then, in "Parents," he turns his attention to—uh-oh!—going shopping with Mom. It's this tune (the first single and video ripped from *He's the DJ*) that transformed their teeny tales into cross-sectional smashes. It won them a Top Ten position on the pop charts—the album went Top Five—and hip hop's first Grammy. It made the pair household names.

Naturally, DJ Jazzy Jeff and the Fresh Prince continued dishing out sitcom humor on their third release, *And in This Corner* . . . Sweetened with saxophones, flutes and trumpets, this LP (surprisingly) provided more dopicity than before (the stream-of-consciousness De La Soul knockoff "Then She Bit Me," the subtly slamming "Jazzy's Groove"). But young Black teenagers, more interested in the P-Funkology of EPMD or the sociopolitical beatboxology of Public Enemy, still dismissed it.

Meanwhile, the white fans who had accepted the crew last time out had, for the most part, moved on to another flame. This action kind of reminds one of James P. Comer's musings that go something like: Middle-class Blacks who make it in white society are playing their home games on the opponents' field. Once that field is reclaimed by whites, the Blacks are *outta* here. See ya!

D-NICE

CALL ME D-NICE (JIVE/RCA), 1990

Although Special Ed billed himself as the "youngest in charge" when he released his debut album in 1989, the moniker could've originally belonged to Bronx-bred flye boy D-Nice. After being discovered when he was fifteen by the late Scott La Rock, the baby-faced DJ Derrick Jones became one-third of one of hip hop's most influential rebels, Boogie Down Productions (BDP). With the sharp guidance of Scott La Rock and the razor-edged rhetoric of KRS-One, D-Nice went from being mildly interested in rap to one of its most active participants.

Shortly after the group produced its first album, *Criminal Minded* (a prototype of New York urban gangster style), La Rock was gunned down with two bullets to the head following a dispute on the same violent streets that inspired him. Although many observers felt the group would collapse without its mentor, it became obvious that his spirit was still guiding it. Or as KRS-One roared from more than one future BDP track, La Rock was "in here!"

A stronger (and larger) unit two years later, KRS-One and D-Nice decided to send a manifesto to the tribes of African-America: that it must reevaluate its agenda for survival, that Black-on-Black crime must cease. By recruiting hip hop's principal players, they set the stage for the Stop the Violence Movement. With a cast that included Big Daddy Kane, MC Lyte and Doug E. Fresh, its twelve-inch "Self Destruction" became the first record D-Nice ever produced. Although there were apprehensions, some participants thinking he lacked the necessary polish, he triumphed. With unburdened funk appeal, "Self Destruction" went gold and became the soundtrack for community solidarity.

Boppin' into the new-jack '90s, D-Nice decided it was time to break north and fly solo. Those who expected a sequel to the politically charged lyrics of his colleague KRS-One were a little disappointed. The majority of the raps on *Call Me D-Nice* are what some listeners might dub retro, tracks that are mostly boastful displays of sportive egomania. Which is not to say that D-Nice is totally lacking social consciousness; the bluesful track "Glory" (inspired by the Edward Zwick film) details the legacy of Black soldiers in the Civil War, while "A Few Dollars More" tells of the war on the streets of the Bronx.

With Three Dog Night and Stax samples, live rock guitar and a Roland 808 drum machine (which damn near dominates the soundscape with its BOOM!), the mix of *Call Me D-Nice* contains funk that's so smooth it's slippery. D-Nice mixes a number of styles, some that work better than others, yet they all retain a certain minimalism that reflects an old-school aesthetic that is absent in much of today's current rap product (i.e., the multi-textures found on productions by Public Enemy and Ice Cube). But it's not the rawness of the tracks that reduces this album from good to mediocre, it's the underproduced quality that is *felt*; much of this album begs for *more.*

"It's Over," a track that D-Nice co-produced with keyboard player Carl Bourelly, is one of the few exceptions. Though it uses the now formulated "new-jack swing" style made popular by producer Teddy Riley, the aggressive elastic beat (with its many layers of sound mixing rap breaks and R&B melodies) is well suited for D-Nice's mellow tenor. Relating a tale of a "once upon a time love affair" that went sour, D-Nice raps the verses with controlled anger, while Dawnn Lewis sings the choruses with angelic charm. Both voices sound as though they're trapped in a web of sound, crawling from the keyboard riffs to the guitar clashes to rhythms borrowed from Biz Markie's "Dedication."

"Crumbs on the Table" and the title track are both boastful raps that D-Nice directs to all the sucker MCs who tried to dis him during the "Self Destruction" sessions. Although not operas of egoism like those of macho-boy L.L. Cool J, these tracks each have hypnotic beats that rock.

And what back-to-roots hip-hop record would be complete without an aural pose of our B-boy hero cupping his dick with one hand, while using the other to hold a mic'? That's the stance D-Nice strikes in "Pimp of the Year," perhaps the funkiest track on the album. Using the voice of one of those Richard Pryor characters, D-Nice details a porn adventure with a girlie he meets at a party: "Guide your tongue from my crack to my feet/And then, you'll be ready for the street." Why this pose? Much rap is, of course, based on Staggerlee complexes. But nowhere else on this album does D-Nice appear to be insensitive to women.

In a recent interview, D-Nice said, "I don't really want to be a pimp or anything like that—yo, it was just a goof!" But even cock-strong gangsters like Big Daddy Kane and L.L. Cool J know that seduction, not domination, is the way to a woman's heart.

See also Boogie Down Productions.

THE D.O.C.

NO ONE CAN DO IT BETTER (RUTHLESS/
ATLANTIC), 1989

During the infancy of rap as a recorded artform, it was not uncommon for civil wars to break out over the facts of its origins: Witness the "bridge" records, where Queens production company the Juice Crew (Marley Marl and company) battled with Bronx warriors Boogie Down Productions (KRS-One and Scott La Rock); witness the infamous night when L.L. Cool J entered the popular Manhattan dance dive the Latin Quarter (decked out in gold, walking with a gangster swagger) playing the role of Suburbia's Ambassador of Hip Hop, only to be bum-rushed by a few Harlem wildboys. These were the days when hip hop was still viewed as "an eruption from the gutters of inner-city recession," before rap artists were considered pop stars or video idols.

With a complete arrogance that is common to B-boy culture, hip-hop crews didn't understand that their new urban blues, those defiant soundtracks of the street, were not just limited to their own basketball courts *or* backyards. If, as Black conceptual artist Adrian Piper says, "This country makes you [African-Americans] want to disappear yourself," then hip hop was the medium that provided both visibility and voice to young Blacks throughout the country. From the mountains of Colorado to army bases in Alaska and North Carolina (where enlisted soul-bro's blast their homemade tapes), hip hop had become a clear signpost of the new Black-power generation.

Emerging from a trunk of funk and hardcore jollies in 1989, Texas-born (and raised) rapper the D.O.C. stunned New York's hip-hop hierarchy when his debut album, *No One Can Do It Better*, outsold any other that year. After heading west to the notorious streets of Compton, D.O.C. joined the Ruthless posse (controlled by Eazy "Muthafuckin' " E.) and began working with in-house groovemaster Dr. Dre.

Although fans of the label are used to the gangsterology displayed by N.W.A. and Eazy-E records—they often forget that Dre also produced bubblegum rappers J.J. Fad and the smokey ballad "Turn Off the Lights" for World Class Wrecking Crew—the lyrics dropped by the D.O.C. do not drag the listener through violent scenes of urban bloodbaths or police brutality. But just 'cause D.O.C. doesn't project himself as a mobster guru, *No One Can Do It Better* isn't weak in the knees; if this album was a boxer, it could go twelve rounds with Tyson.

The lead track, "It's Funky Enough," drops you right into '70s Black teen-pop wonderland as it samples beats from "Misdemeanor," by Jackson Five clones the Sylvers. Using a West Indian accent ("I be visualizing things when I'm rapping," D.O.C. once said, "and I started talking Jamaican in 'It's Funky Enough" because I was imagining dreds shakin' "), D.O.C.'s voice slams into Dre's wall of noise. He sounds rough without giving the impression of pure sonic assassination. And with a voice that bangs as loud as an African talking drum, he sends messages not only in the words but also in his vocal rhythms.

With *No One Can Do It Better*, Dr. Dre has amassed a funky orchestra that includes Sly Stone, George Clinton and Marvin Gaye. On "The Formula," the D.O.C. boasts, "Each sucker [was] ready to leap up on the tip when we made it" over Gaye's classic "Inner City Blues." But as D.O.C. also says, "We gettin' hype cause Dre rockin' the instrumental ... making dope beats with rhythmic American poetry." One hears the rhythms of drums in the D.O.C.'s voice, and the poetry in Dre's music.

Unlike other Cali hip-hop artists who become comfortable with one style (be it street-tough or candy-coated), Dre is willing to experiment with different styles. Witness when D.O.C. says he's gotta "take one o' them long-ass eight-ball pisses . . . take me to a commercial." What we get is the Ruthless debut of R&B singer Miche'le belting out (with strong, churchy vocals) an urban blues track called "Comm. Blues." As Eazy-E and the boys ad-lip in drunk voices, Miche'le sings meaningless words about the D.O.C. "You should never underestimate the passion," he said on one track. (This is a statement that could also be applied to Miche'le's voice.) One should *also* never underestimate aural metaphors. Thought is thrown in to give one a brief history lesson. Without going into a lengthy discourse about the origins of big-city blues, it should be stated that in the universe of Black popular music, urban blues and hip hop are more than kissin' cousins; the pair is up on the hot, tarred roof doing the wild thang. As Larry Neal wrote in his essay "The Ethos of the Blues": "Like any artist, the blues singer has the task of bringing order out of chaos . . . the blues are not concerned with middle-class morality, black or white. This is because the audience that they address is forced to confront the world of the flesh: the body is real, the source of much joy and pain."

The last track on this album is called "The Grand Finale," and it also proves to be one the best hip-hop ensemble pieces, with Eazy-E and MC Ren throwin' down (it's also the last Ruthless track that features Ice Cube). Kickin' gangster lyrics over a Clinton break beat, this song has the energy of Saturday night on the streets of Compton. No single rapper dominates the song, 'cause like the gang of ball-busters' myth states, everyone has to be strong together.

If the D.O.C. sticks with this posse, perhaps his next album will be on the cutting edge of the new funk. But for now, to paraphrase Rakim, he's following the right leader.

See also N.W.A.

DOUG E. FRESH & THE GET FRESH CREW

OH MY GOD! (REALITY), **1985**

THE WORLD'S GREATEST ENTERTAINER, **1988**

o Doug E.! Get busy!" revelers screamed out as Doug E. Fresh pointed a silver, steel microphone at them. "Who? What?" he demanded repeatedly to a beat while flashing a wide Cheshire cat smile, the crowd's chant becoming more resonant each time. Then he busted into a human beatbox roll, finally settling into a loopy pattern that supported Milk Dee's rendition of his crew's once-upon-a-time smash "Top Billin'." He next accompanied Kool Moe Dee (on the nitro-charged "I Go to Work"), Stetsasonic member Delight (the jaunty "Sally") and even Melis'a Morgan (her early '80s rendition of Prince's grinding "Do Me Baby"). For just a few minutes at Manhattan's Town Hall, the gently heated air throbbed with the sound of lips, cheeks, gums and Adam's apple masterfully creating something out of nothing.

When Doug E. Fresh rocks a beat, his vocal kick drums sound like real ones fortified with delay; his snares sound like those generated by computer sequencers. He can imitate a telephone ringing or a computer game blip or a descending roller coaster cutting briskly through a cool summer wind. He can rock a house with just his mouth and leave the audience drooling for more. Back in the day, Doug E. became the king of the new rock (hip-hop) technology. While machinists were reveling in "Hard Times" (Run-D.M.C.'s blueprint for hip hop's extremist electro minimalism, followed closely by "Sucker MCs"), Doug Davis and crew—nasally sidekick Slick Rick (a.k.a. MC

Ricky D.) and twin DJs Barry Bee and Chill Will—were setting up a more musical agenda free from the brashness and culture shock of Def Jam's color-blind, teenage noise.

The quartet's doubly stacked debut twelve-inch, "The Show"/ "La-di-da-di," was a hit on the lips of folks who didn't even like rap. It wasn't crossover, but it presented a fundamentally pleasing sonic pastiche that knitted British accents, good-guy respectfulness and aural flashbacks into monster tunes that parents as well as their streetwise kids could understand. But let's get specific, shall we?

Though walking down the street to a hardcore beat, "La-di-da-di" displayed a B-boy image through Rick that was cool even if he used sweetboy toiletries like bubble bath and Oil of Olay and ran away from women instead of sexing their brains out just to bust a nut (Wham! Bam! Thank you, ma'am, youknowhumsayin?). He reveals his attractiveness to less than flye females, too. One episode in this narrative (whose pounding human beatbox track got ripped by Just-Ice for "Latoya") features an encounter with a "bitch" (his ex-girlfriend's mom) he can't get next to because she's so old she's got a "wrinkled pussy." If this isn't standard B-boy braggadocio, it wasn't meant to be. It's a smutty, comical tall tale designed to shock and amuse the same way kids' mother jokes ("Your mother's so old she took her driver's test on a dinosaur!") do.

While "La-di-da-di" created a new rap sexuality, "The Show" flooded hip-hop parties with good old spirituality. Over a rubbery go-go rhythm driven by a dense, eerie synth chord cluster, mouth farts, get-busy shouts and turntable cutting, Slick Rick entered to ask Doug: "Have you ever seen a show with fellas on the mic' with one-minute rhymes that don't come out right?" Without apologizing for past wackisms, Rick promises to present "the best darn rappers of the year," he and Doug. Doug crafts a how-it-all-began tale, then Rick steps in to weave a narrative about walking onto the downtown D train, then sliding over next to "a pretty girl." About to seduce her, Rick hears her roar like Tony the Tiger. Spooked, he cries out, "Oh no!/There's been a mistake/My name is Rick not Frosty Flakes!"

Not just the first glimpse of Rick's sexual anxiety (played out more fully on his *Great Adventures of Slick Rick*), or an introduction to Doug's performing gift, "The Show," according to Fresh, was designed to get a message across about God. He told an interviewer: "That's why throughout the whole record there's that 'Oh my God! Oh my God!' and a section that said, 'Six minutes, six minutes, six minutes.' Three sixes is the sign of the devil, and at the end of it all everybody was saying 'Oh my God' more than they were saying 'Six minutes.' That was showing the power of God over evil." Turning his attention to another recurring vocal snatch, the quickly delivered "Is it real," Doug added, " 'Is it real' spoken real fast sounds like Israel. It was done in the mind, so you won't really recognize it!"

The track "All the Way to Heaven" on *Oh My God!* boasted that it was "the first time in history/A rap jam is dedicated to G-O-D." Reveling in the bliss of music, a gift from the creator, Doug declares in another tune, "One DJ will rub it/The other overdub it/And I'm lovin' every minute of it." He vamps on short phrases, prolonging ecstasy and forestalling climax, and engages in happy call-and-response passages and playful ego-boosting before getting back to reciting words of upliftment and positivity. From the reggae-ish "Nuthin'," he spins admonitions against drugs. Afterward, he comes out against abortion ("If God wanted you to lose it, it would've been done") and the lifestyle of a single female constantly on the make ("Now you can have fun and not be a nun/But I don't like a girl who's on the run").

Instead of getting labeled a chewy-centered Bible thumper, Doug has always maintained a reputation as one of hip hop's most-liked figures. His religious beliefs may have helped him turn the other cheek when the Fat Boys' Buffy took the human beatbox concept and ran away with Doug's invention. Persistence overcame resistance, and instead of complaining, Doug kept maintaining. Like he said in "All the Way to Heaven," he was "on a mission."

The first single on his crew's second LP was the determinedly sure "Keep Rising to the Top," which sampled soul stirrer Kenni Burke's hypnotic tune of the same name for its main groove. Co-produced by the fellas with Bomb Squad members Hank Shocklee and Carl Ryder (a.k.a. Public Enemy's Chuck D.), this cut—spiced up in the chorus by "Ain't no half-steppin" from Heatwave's disco shuffler "Boogie Nights"—is cushiony soft like a pillow, but when amped through systems in darkened clubs and souped-up Jeeps, it suddenly seemed rough like Brillo. In another track, D.E.F. admits to always being "Crazy 'Bout Cars." With jazzy trumpet lines and tight kick drums, this car song was not the soundtrack of B-boy revelry and teenage ghetto spirit that L.L. Cool J's "The Boomin' System" turned out to be years later. Still, it was frisky enough and painted images of late-night cruising and harassing encounters with Five-O that are familiar to any young brother with wheels.

Rolling right along, *The World's Greatest Entertainer* is much less preachy than its predecessor. Its beats and tempos are more varied, with active, edgy tunes as well as bare-bones ones coming correct with ready rhymes that should've garnered Fresh and the Crew juice as well as sales. But the artist's marketing was weak and his release patterns weren't consistent; the flam "Cut That Zero," for instance, came out long after "Keep Risin' to the Top" was already a classic. "Zero," which presents thoughtfulness and sensitivity to a woman with a wounded heart ("Instead of that chicken McNugget, you know what you need, baby?/You need a Value Pack!"), is egged on by a purring bite from Levert's "Cassanova," a tune whose protagonist opts likewise for marriage over playboy shenanigans.

Ironically, the LP's wackest track is "Greatest Entertainer," meant to pay homage to the Get Fresh Crew's talent for moving crowds. Besides Fresh's verbal agility and the fact that he performs his beatbox routine through a harmonica, nothing here is really *that* interesting. Still, like the go-go style he loves so much—also check out "I'm Gettin' Ready" on the second disc— Doug E. Fresh (without ultimately slighting teasing concoctions like "The Show" and "Keep Rising to the Top") is much more convincing live and direct, a bigger and deffer attraction onstage than on disc.

See also Slick Rick.

DR. DRE

SEE THE D.O.C., EAZY-E, AND N.W.A.

DREAM
▉ WARRIORS

AND NOW THE LEGACY BEGINS (4TH & BROADWAY),
1991

Sites in New York are haunted by ghosts of jazz artists past: the Bowery Bank Building on 145th (where Dinah Washington used to rest following early morning jams), bars along 125th (where Miles and Max used to gulp drinks till dawn). Postmod innovators were never terribly tormented by these specters—until recently. After plundering their parents' record bins for years, a few of them, like A Tribe Called Quest and Gang Starr (who recorded a lost side with da Warriors), finally happened upon hard bop to pair with cool hop.

Some artists and critics viewed their efforts as a cold movement, an attempt to smother hip hop in the sort of sterile middle-brow respectability vacuum that killed jazz as a vital Black artform in the first place. But *jaz-hop* stemmed from the same lively curiosity that inspired hip hop. The same way teens discovered gritty '60s/'70s funk noize, they made the acquaintance of cats like Monk and Bird.

On the Dream Warriors's debut album, *And Now the Legacy Begins,* the listener is seduced by King Lou and Capital Q's jazzy dreams. A Quincy Jones sample bounces from the mix of "My Definition of a Boombastic Jazz Style." And although this Canadian duo uses Le Q and, "Wash Your Face in My Sink," Herb Alpert riffs, they use jazz not as a finishing step but as a guide into other areas of avant-rap.

"We never wanted people to think of us as trying to be a jazz hip-hop group, because that's not all that we're about," says lead rapper King Lou. Dream Warriors are Noir Canucks whose definition of boombastic would be arrived at by: experimenting with as many styles of Black noize as possible (as many as would fit onto a disc) and slapping them over offbeat, funky texts. From the neo-ska of "Ludi" to the sinister cyberfunk of "Tune From the Missing Channel," the experience of listening to Dream Warriors arouses more memories of Prince or Brain Eno than of Monk or Bird.

EAZY-E

R oland Barthes called the realm of gangster life "the last universe of fantasy," and America's fascination with the exotica of wildboys and urban gun slingers doesn't appear to be fading. From Edward G. Robinson in *Little Caesar* to Al Pacino in *Scarface,* screen gangsters have been accepted into society, operating as both fantasy figures and therapists (better to live vicariously through Hollywood's fake bullets than to spray up the neighborhood Mickey D's). Michael Mann brought the gangster aesthestic into vogue during the '80s with a feature film, *Thief,* then the TV series "Miami Vice." Although this colorful show was created during the ultraconservative Ronnie Raygun era, the public connected more with its stylish cocaine dealers than with its police force.

When Eric Wright turned from hustling drugs to running his own indie label, Ruthless Records, one's image of gangsters had little to do with pint-sized, jerri-curled, L.A.-Raiders-hat-wearing thugs, but as Eazy (Muthafuckin') E, Wright became a self-proclaimed America's Most Wanted, a noir untouchable in the aural daydream nation of contemporary pop music.

After swaggering into Audio Achievements Studios with his homies—producer Dr. Dre, DJ Yella, M.C. Ren and chief lyricist/rapper Ice Cube (who later went solo), in 1988—Eazy-E debuted the first in a series of ghetto operas that would change the sound of hip hop for the next few years. Although *Eazy-Duz-It* is credited as Eazy's solo debut, this album features the same crew that would later dub themselves Niggers With Attitude on the texturally richer *Straight Outta Compton.*

Eazy-Duz-It today sounds kind of limp. But as homeboy Dread Kool explained, it's a threshold thing: "Just like drug addicts need stronger hits to climax, us rhythm junkies need harder beats to get us excited. Granted, *Straight Outta Compton* and Ice Cube's solo album are better records, but *Eazy-Duz-It* was nothin' to sleep on out the box."

While New York brothers and sisters were begging listeners to give peace a chance on the star-studded "Self Destruction" twelve-inch, Eazy & Co. were spitting venom in the face of such righteous ideology. With his third-generation Staggerlee posing, Eazy was detailing varied street scenes: gang wars, Mack Daddy (pimp) boldness and drug related hits. Like a polluted ocean, *Eazy-Duz-It* overflows with debris from homophobia to misogyny to excessive violence. And yet, anyone who grew up in a housing project or any Black ghetto knows these extreme attitudes are right on target. It has been argued that hip hop should be more positive, but as Chuck D. said, "Rap music is CNN for Black people." In other words, brothers like Eazy-E are just reporting what they see.

With a sample from the Temptation's classic "Ball of Confusion" (perhaps the perfect theme for Eazy's posse and their environment), the album's opening (and title) track is like a welcome mat dotted with fresh blood stains; less than two minutes into the song Eazy has bragged about all his bitches, killed one sucker for talking shit, collected money from his ho's and sold more drugs than anyone in the neighborhood. Changing musical gears in the middle (after Eazy gets thrown in jail), it appears that Dre is trying for a Bomb Squad effect, but "Eazy-Duz-It" is too lackluster to compete.

A stronger track is the dark and moody "Nobody Move," which uses the same raggamuffin sample as on Dr. Ice's solo album, *The Mic Stalker.* Walking through a drum-heavy soundscape, Eazy details his (mis)adventures as a bank robber, reminding one of the wacky villians in Jimmy Breslin's *The Gang that Couldn't Shoot Straight:* First he blows away the guard, then what he thinks is a flye babe "wit the biggest titties a muthafucker ever saw" turns out to be a transvestite. It's somewhat surprising that Eazy gets blasted by da police at the fins of this jam; but with songs like "Ruthless Villain" and "Boyz-N-The Hood" one can rest assured that this is the last time the fuzz will pop Eazy (at least on record).

Eazy-Duz-It is far from a mature work. It's like this crew's practice game, a warm-up before the team wipes away the sweat and begins playing like true professionals. Or struttin' like true gangstas.

See also N.W.A., Ice Cube.

E P M D

STRICTLY BUSINESS (FRESH), 1988

UNFINISHED BUSINESS, 1989

BUSINESS AS USUAL, (DEF JAM), 1991

Breezing in from Long Island, the hip-hop gene pool that is also home to Public Enemy, De La Soul and Rakim's DJ, Eric B., EPMD made a cool, effortless landing in the ever-turbulent rap world in 1988. Then—in spite of sounding kind of amateurish, one of their voices revealing a boyish lisp, things like plosives entering the sonicscape—their debut LP of sensual grunge, *Strictly Business,* slinked to the top of *Billboard*'s Black LPs chart in only six weeks, leapfrogging over established hitmakers like Prince, Sade, Michael Jackson and Run-D.M.C. One month later, the record was gold, the surprise hip-hop hit of its time.

The key to the crew's fast rise lies in the curious duality that exists between middle-class suburban achievement (characterized by private houses, green lawns and shiny cars) and the chilling ghetto toughness we all experience vicariously through flicks like *Scarface* and records like Grandmaster Flash and the Furious Five's "The Message." EPMD weren't city-slick gangsters like N.W.A. but, from living in a technology-induced schizophrenia, they weren't soft either; by embracing the essence of street culture but not being part of it, they were really having fun. Charming rap's affluent new audience without alienating its harder core was the point of their game, the secret to their seemingly overnight success.

Consisting of rappers Eric Sermon and Parrish Smith along with DJ K. La Boss (later replaced by DJ Scratch), EPMD—the letters stand for Eric and Parrish Making Dollars—are about looseness over polish, feel over learned musical skill. When they debuted, some critics dubbed them the rap equivalent of a rock 'n' roll garage band, and their approach confirms this analogy. With money Smith made working in a bakery, they recorded their first single, "It's My Thing," in just over three hours. Hypnotic, swirling and splashy, it was nowhere near as pounding or screeching as a track by, say, AC/DC. But the way Eric and Parrish's raps flowed—slow and easy, like maple syrup over warm French toast—made it as frisky. This funky style was sustained throughout the ten-song *Strictly Business* mainly because Eric (the one with the lisp) can't rap any other way.

The most striking feature of EPMD's approach was their use of samples—not just a few bites here, a few snippets there, but total copyright infringement. "It's My Thing" utilized little more than the groove from a Marva Whitney tune. Propelled by the hook from Kool and the Gang's "Jungle Boogie," a follow-up single, "You Gots to Chill," glided along to a loop of Roger Troutman and Zapp's "More Bounce to the Ounce." Elsewhere on *Strictly Business* other classic '70s records (by Rick James, Steve Miller and even Bob Marley) got the EPMD recontextualization treatment, too.

Although *Strictly Business* came with a take-no-prisoners agenda, two of its songs broke from the program. "The Steve Martin" lays down the steps to "a brand new funky dance," while "Jane" proceeds to dis a skeezer with an Anita Baker haircut. The source of the gripe here is revealed by Eric in the tune's closing minutes: "She said, 'Next time you have it be bigger, stronger and much faster!'" This may not be the first time a B-boy's phallocentric drunk gets sobered by a woman, but it's one of the few cases where he admits it happened.

Diva J. shows up again in "Jane II," a track on EPMD's second gold album, *Unfinished Business*. Here the insatiable fox causes P some sexual anxiety. After picking her up at a club thinking she's someone else, he puts the make on her. During

EPMD. Photo by Michael Lavine, courtesy of Def Jam/Columbia Records. © 1990 CBS Records Inc.

intercourse he discovers her true identity, then he notices that she's removed his "jim hat." He freaks. "At first I laughed as if it were a joke," he recounts. "But then my heart skipped a beat and I lost a stroke." On another track, this experience causes him to always ask, "Whose booty?" before committing.

The reappearance of Jane isn't the only reason *Unfinished Business* is so titled. Over more laid-back, pump-beat grooves, EPMD continues their tough-minded attacks on those cynics who discounted them as early on as when "It's My Thing" came out. They assert themselves, then they go in for the kill using the same deadly combination that endeared them to everyone in the first place. In the spiraling "So Wat Cha Sayin'," for example, they talk about "waxin' suckers like Mop & Glo." Then near the tune's end, Sermon starts singing in an off-key parody of elite lover-man Luther Vandross. The language of designer soul is something EPMD's middle-class neighbors will understand; the way they speak it, from the crossroads of late '80s/early '90s Black musical expression, is what keeps them down and universally appealing.

Though they became more upwardly mobile, moving on to a major label, Def Jam, and receiving a $700,000 advance, EPMD maintained their basement flavor throughout *Business as Usual*, their third effort. Manager Russell Simmons once remarked, "You can count on EPMD doing what they do forever." To which Smith added, "So far we've had the right formula for success, so why mess with a good thing?"

Thus, *Business as Usual* walks along familiar trails instead of blasting off into fresher, unexplored stratospheres. Booties will still bump to tracks like "I'm Mad," with its loopy excitement, and "Rampage" (featuring L.L. Cool J), whose chorus sounds like "Jinglin' Baby" 's. But *Business as Usual* is too sure-fire to excite masses of most-downs the way EPMD's two previous LPs did.

ERIC B. & RAKIM

PAID IN FULL (4TH & BWAY.), 1987

FOLLOW THE LEADER (UNI), 1988

LET THE RHYTHM HIT 'EM, 1990

I n his *Village Voice* essay "Hyper as a Heart Attack," critic Nelson George stated that the music of Eric B. & Rakim would make the perfect soundtrack for Chester Himes's series of Harlem crime novels. Beginning with *For the Love of Imabelle* in 1957 and ending twelve years later with *Blind Man With a Pistol*, all were driven by two of the most brutal detectives in the genre of hard-boiled fiction, Grave Digger Jones and Coffin Ed. Admirers of '70s blaxploitation movies might be familiar with the MGM features *Cotton Comes to Harlem* and *Come Back Charleston Blue*, both of which were based on Himes's "policiers noirs." In pure Hollyweird tradition, the violent yet comic surrealism that Himes used in his eight tomes ("Harlem domestic series," as he called them) was smoothed out in these vehicles for mass consumption. The savage violence and sheer speed which stalked through Himes's texts were reduced to farce.

Like Himes, aural gangsters Eric B. & Rakim use crime as a multilayered metaphor to define a society that has relegated Black men to the bottom of the social scale since the nightmare of middle passage (one of the many crimes against Afrikans that is now defined as history). Beneath the cryptic images conjured up in the texts of both Himes and Eric & Rakim, one clearly hears the gritty screams of protest over the panic wail of police sirens.

87

"The Harlem of my books was never meant to be real; I never called it real," Himes wrote in *My Life of Absurdity: The Autobiography* (Vol. 2). "I just wanted to take it away from the white man if only in my books." In the same way that Himes created a "symbolic landscape" to explore the psyche of Black America, Eric B. & Rakim create sonic soundscapes that expose the tears and fears, pride and passions of Harlems throughout the world. When Rakim recalls his crazed younger days as a stick-up kid on "Paid in Full," he says, "I used to roll up—this is a hold up/Ain't nothin' funny/Stop smilin', be still, don't nothin' move but the money." This is the type of brutal poetics that Himes would have *killed* to have written in one of his books.

On their first album, 1987's *Paid in Full*, Eric B. & Rakim sharply defined a new noize aesthetic, one that would have a profound effect on emerging rappers and DJs who wished to explore new territories in the ever-changing sphere of hip hop. With their debut single, "Eric B. Is President" (a track that Marley Marl layered and mixed), this pair further expounded on the unwritten manifesto that Afro-Pop of the future would be a product of suburbia mind waves. As Daddy-O from Stetsasonic once related, "Fellas like Eric B. and Rakim grew up in areas where they could afford to buy all the latest records and study the tracks. So, they could make *better* jams." Hooked on this brilliant idea of sound, "Eric B. Is President" exploded in urban ears like fireworks on the Fourth of July.

"Make 'em clap to this," Rakim commanded at the beginning of this jam. But hand-clapping wasn't the only activity that this song provoked on the hot pavements of New York. "Eric B. Is President" became the perfect soundtrack for a new dance craze, the Wop, that originated on the steaming streets of Brooklyn. Jumping from the groove and onto the dance floor, one teenager compared the movements of wopping to those of Dorothy from *The Wizard of Oz* taking the Scarecrow down from his

Eric B., rollin' for a moment without da R.
© Ernest Paniccioli, 1990.

———

pole: "The way she moves is kinda like the Wop," she said. It should be noted that in African-American culture the art of movement is closely linked with the art of noize (be it blues, jazz or hip hop); the image of Black bodies swaying to "the beat, the beat" is as old as the motherland.

With Eric B. "on the cut" with riffs appropriated from disco crooner Fonda Rae's "Over Like a Fat Rat," Rakim displayed a voice that was unique to the music: a slow roar that reminded one of an angry, caged lion turned rap terrorist—still king of the jungle but not within earshot of the River Niger. With lines like "Taking off my coat/Clearing my throat/The rhyme will be kickin' until I hit my last note," some folks claimed Rakim's voice actually *scared* them into buying this disc.

Having two ready-made classics on a twelve-inch is a dream that only happens in pop utopias (hell, finding *one* good track is often hard enough). But when rapketeers swooped up the first Eric B. & Rakim single, a double dose of da nasty awaited them (like sex, two orgasms are better than one). "My Melody" proved to be the second pleasure principle of this disc. Like a cyborg in the heat of passion, Eric began this jam with dirty scratches and erotic boom before Rakim entered the soundscape to claim what was his: "Pull out your money/Pull out your cut/Pull up a chair and I'll tear shit up ..." Just 'cause he was a new rapper on the block didn't mean one could play him like a sucker, and without a doubt, Rakim's bitter tone forced the sound of apocalypse culture to bombard the hip-hop nation. Eric on the turntables pushed cult-nats even closer to the edge of destruction.

So when 4th & Bway. released *Paid in Full*, a parade of ideas stormed through my mind: "Ain't no way the duo's entire album is gon' be as flye as those two tracks!" "Who knows—perhaps it'll be a supersoulhiphopfreaky masterpiece?" There are, in fact, a coupla throwaways like "Chinese Arithmetic" and "Eric B. Is on the Cut," both tracks that should have been presented as low-budget video parodies ("How to Cut Like da E.") hosted by funny-man Chris Rock. But if ya'll wanna get serious, please turn your attention to "I Know You Got Soul" and "Move the Crowd." Prepare for lift-off ... BOOM!

On "Talking All That Jazz," Stetsasonic's pro-sampling statement, Daddy-O said, "Tell the truth James Brown was old/Till Eric and Ra came out wit 'I Got Soul' ..." But to be really honest, Eric got this sample from Bobby Byrd, one of James Brown's funky-people protegés. Still, this track marks the beginning of yet another hip-hop movement: Godfather Rap.

At once apologizing and bragging ("I shouldn'ta left you ... sorry I kept you"), Rakim seduced us over Eric's slamming beats and harsh scratches. Playing the good cop/bad cop role, Eric unleashed smacks and Rakim apologized.

"It takes me a while to write lyrics, 'cause I make sure I do it correctly," Rakim once told self-described media assassin Harry Allen. "Even before I listen to the track that I'm gonna write off, I listen to some jazz or sum'n like that. Jazz is, like ... it's like real *ill,* and even though it ain't no words to it, it'll put you in a mood." Like flye-boy painter Jean Michel Basquiat or novelists Ralph Ellison and Himes (contemporary artists who have the spirit of jazz soaring through their work), Rakim's rhythmic phrasing sounds as though Charlie Parker was whispering in his ear while he was recording. The beauty of lines like "I start to think and then I sink/Into the paper like I was ink" repeat in one's mind like one of Bird's solos.

From chasing the Bird to lettin' it loose, both Eric B. and Rakim sound as though they've been sitting in the basement listening to Cecil Taylor, smoking blunts and hallucinating while watching *Blade Runner* and *The Mack* with the volume turned down. A few days after the duo's second album, *Follow the Leader,* was released, Daddy-O dismissed it: "What is that shit? Who wants to hear that? It might be cool for some folks, but kids on the streets of Brooklyn don't wanna hear it." When asked what did the kids wanna hear, Daddy-O replied, "Stetsasonic." Well, Daddy-O might be a cool rapper, but he sure ain't no prophet 'cause Stet's second album, *In Full Gear,* got lost in da mix. With "musical forms kickin' like Kato" (the Chinese sidekick to the Green Hornet, played by Bruce Lee in the '60s television series), 1988 belonged to the fifth and eighteenth letters of the alphabet.

There are many adjectives (avant-garde, mystic, go-go gas rock!) one could use to describe *Follow the Leader*'s title track. Although Rakim might sound inaudible over Eric's beautiful noise (E. uses his sampler like an other-worldly orchestral maneuver—don't even attempt to locate the samples, they're moving too damn fast), after separating the verbal poetry from the sonic poetics, one simply marvels at Rakim's Five Percenter history lesson: "Follow me into a solo/Travel at magnificent speeds around the universe," he directs. As we follow the star called the R., the rapper letting knowledge be born and "raising ya from the cradle to the grave," Eric is throwing in scratches and bleeps and buzzes that recall a Black version of *Star Wars*. With the exception of Public Enemy, no other group has paired history and futurist visions into such a loving couple. "Follow the Leader" ends with a loud blast, like a star that has gone supernova. Or a rocket ship that has crashed to earth.

No other track on *Follow the Leader* reached the manic intensity that Eric B. & Rakim displayed on the title track, but it wasn't for lack of trying. Unlike on the first album (the one EPMD must've practiced to when they were starting out), Rakim's voice was no longer as slow as a caged animal; the lion was now free to roam the jungle.

On "Eric B. Never Scared" and "Put Your Hands Together," this dynamic duo seem somewhat obsessed with the art of hand clapping; they conjured up a passage from Zora Neale Hurston's first novel, *Jonah's Gourd Vine:* "Us don't want no fiddles, neither no guitars, neither no banjoes. Less clap!" This was a call for the instrument their ancestors brought to America in their skins. Although Eric B. & Rakim are products of the postmod/techno-crazed universe, the blood of Africa still flows through them like red rivers.

And it's this blood that damn near boils over on "Microphone Fiend." After Eric's loopy samples and jinglin'-baby bells jump-start the brain, Rakim's elaborate wordplay merges into the mix: "I was a fiend before I became a teen/I melted microphones instead of cones of ice cream." Although this track is part of the basic hip-hop tradition of boasting, Rakim adds a twist to the idea by equating his love of music, his desire to rock da mic', to a habit that just can't be helped: "I fiend for the microphone like heroin/Soon as the bass kicks I need a fix." Overall, this album proved one of rap's seminal albums of the late '80s.

And then quiet: In most forms of pop music, taking two years off can be a refreshing break from the wild life, recording studios, and constant touring through many a strange land. But in the aural factory of hip hop, the machinery is in constant motion, steadily creating new products for the marketplace. This is why rap icons like Public Enemy and L. L. Cool J often record new material for their B sides, intent on keeping their sound alive and rhymes on the tongues of the masses.

With *Let the Rhythm Hit 'Em,* Eric B. & Rakim returned from their two-year musical hiatus with the same futuristic gangster style that had made them stars, though many ears wanted to hear them do somethin' different. While Eric and Ra were away, hip-hop fans had witnessed the rise of groups like Digital Underground and N.W.A., A Tribe Called Quest and Ice Cube. The weird had become weirder and the gangsters had become harder. Exactly where Eric B. & Rakim fitted in was debatable.

On the album's title track, da E. proved he was still Dr. Strangelove on the wheels of steel, taking the music to atomic heights of ecstasy, while "In the Ghetto" has Rakim still blasting phrases like an outta-control Uzi, taking mind trips out of the bowels of urban decay, through the sorrowful eyes of South Africa, and into the arms of Mecca.

While the team was away, there were rumors that Ra was locked up on Rikers Island for selling crack; true, he *was* on an island, only it was Long Island, where he was chillin' with his wife and kids. "If I was in jail, it won't be for sellin' keys/It'll be for murderin' MCs," he intoned on "Set 'Em Straight."

Just 'cause a hip-hop group has been inactive for two years doesn't mean the public should sleep on 'em, but *Let the Rhythm Hit 'Em* shows that if one is inactive for two years, one's jams might sound a little dated (like those thick gold chains and Dapper Dan outfits) in the ever-changing minds of the public. In other words, Eric B. & Rakim should not sleep on themselves.

FATHER MC

FATHER'S DAY (UPTOWN/MCA), 1990

I t's tough having guilty pleasures. Like when you're sitting around with a bunch of Parliafunkadelicmenticized fans and one of them, Otis, blurts out, "Yo! Mike boarded the Mothership ten years late 'cause he was too busy listening to Led Zeppelin and Rush." Or when chillin' at Soul Kitchen with Bönz and a coupla cats from *The Source,* everyone discussing the brilliance of Ice Cube and KRS-One, Otis (who's been standing near the bar, close enough to hear) screams, "Yo, Mike, why don't you tell them how much you like Father MC?" The crowd suddenly becomes silent, the sea of '70s funk seems to evaporate—and everyone stares. And laughs ...

So what if Father MC's debut LP, *Father's Day,* ain't the hardcore rap that was created up in da Bronx many years past? So what if Father ain't posing on the cover in some abandoned lot, gripping an Uzi or a 9mm? (In fact, the album's sleeve photo resembles a seductive centerfold from some new Black woman's nasty magazine.) In Daddy's—I mean, Father's—first single, "Treat Them Like They Want to Be Treated," with its soul-stirring backgrounds that recall Guy lead singer Aaron Hall, the sensitive Father raps about his broken heart: "Why girls play with my feelings ... Everytime that I meet the right one, it seems that she plays with my mind." Talk about wearing your emotions on your sleeve! Father just blurts his into the mic'. This is buppie bubble-gum music. This be flye-girl wet-dream soundtracks. But this be slick as hell.

Coming from the Andre Harrell Home of Hits (the man who brought us Guy, Al B. Sure! and Heavy D. & the Boyz), this is that type of Teddy Riley/Eddie F. sound, new-jack hip hop, that rap purists swear will be the *death* of the movement, the sound that will send the holy walls of hip hop collapsing into the ocean. But hey, this ain't all smooth loverboy stuff—the brother can be almost as hard as the fellas shootin' the giph from the bar at the Apollo.

On the Fresh Gordon–produced "I've Been Watching You," Father verbally duels with female rapper Lady Kazan (the sassy female who appeared on Special Ed's first album) after he offers to buy her a drink and she retorts, "Play like Soul II Soul and keep on movin'." Ouch! Gigolo-cool homeboy continues coming on like a june-bug Billy Dee, but he just keeps getting caught in his own web of lies. Though he insists, "Like Keith Sweat said, 'I won't gas up your head!'" Honey ain't having it. In ghetto heaven, one witnesses scenes like this more often than drive-by shootings.

Over the course of eight more tracks, Father is more R&B (especially on "I'll Do 4 U" and "Lisa Baby") than hip hop, but even the most hardcore of Jeep-boys will be rockin' to the album's title track while speeding down Flatbush Avenue. As produced by Brooklyn groovemaster Howie Tee, "Father's Day" samples Big Daddy Kane ("Give me that title boy ..."), and FMC's tone rates with the best of hip hop's forceful rappers as he runs across the track in his practiced freestyle style. The other Howie Tee–directed track, "Dance 4 Me," reminds me of the stuff those stompin' masses of baggy pants/paisley shirt-clad teenagers used to rave to at the "industrial chic" Tunnel Friday nights.

One final thing, confidential to Father: Let's back a pact. You don't apologize for being on the road of rhythm & blues and I won't apologize for my guilty pleasures.

FRESH GORDON

SEE DANA DANE, FATHER MC

GANG STARR

NO MORE MR. NICE GUY (WILD PITCH), 1989

STEP IN THE ARENA (CHRYSALIS), 1991

J uly 1986. The revolving bar at the Marriot Marquis in Manhattan is packed with record-types, hangers-on and hangers-on of hangers-on. I'm sitting opposite a Black producer-of-the-moment, sipping a fresh-squeezed o.j. and challenging the assertion that the music biz is overrun with crooks, slippery assholes and frauds. I was an industry rook then, and as we spoke, thoughts of cool, fiery Elliot filled my nappy head.

I first encountered Elliot Horne when I started writing reviews in the mid-'80s. A button-down old-timer with an intense streak, he functioned as a (Black) pop publicist at the time. Yet many of our conversations dealt with jazz, his passion. He shared many amusing anecdotes and opinionated critiques of the genre, often about how youngblood pomos were dismissing it in favor of street corner ballistics.

Before his death in 1989 Elliot had placed a poem he wrote celebrating jazz's legacy with Brooklyn rap crew Gang Starr. Using the poem as stepping stone, they created "Jazz Music," the second track on *No More Mr. Nice Guy.* Rapper The G.U.R.U. (for Gifted Unlimited Rhymes Universal) Keith E performed Elliot's words over a DJ Premier track (made up of sampled horns, looped beats and live piano riffs) that was languid, totally cool.

Elsewhere on their debut, Gang Starr laid out spiritual lessons, and merely dabbled in jazz. Although the LP's hit was "Positivity," the track that landed Gang Starr Big Prop—a prominent slot on the soundtrack for *Mo' Better Blues*—was "Jazz Music." While completing that movie (about jazz in modern times), filmmaker Spike Lee happened upon the tune. He hooked up with Gang Starr, then he engineered them a meeting with saxophonist Branford Marsalis. This trio completed "Jazz Thing," which played over *Mo' Better Blues'* closing credits. In its wake Gang Starr came to a better understanding of jazz.

Step in the Arena contains bits of strafing noise and subsonic bass tones, but its grooves feature things like cymbals riding and pianos tinkling throughout. Keith E unravels rhymes (what he calls "facalities," facts about reality) that are intelligent and vivid, aggressive but restrained.

In "Execution of a Chump (No More Mr. Nice Guy, Pt. 2)," a right-hand homie betrays Keith. About to explode, this "spiritual teacher" exclaims: "I dis using fists using force of any sort/My conscience says it's nonsense." Then "Just to Get a Rep," which rubs in "stickup kids is out to tax" from Nice & Smooth's "Funky for You," shakes its head at brothers who kill for a name. Seeing that Gang Starr borrowed from Nice & Smooth, maybe they can return the favor by lending that crew some of the knowledge of jazz they picked up from Branford and Elliot. Please fellas, tell Greg Nice that Dizzy Gillespie plays the trumpet, *not the mo'fugging sax.*

HEAVY D.
& THE BOYZ

LIVING LARGE (UPTOWN/MCA), 1987

BIG TYME, 1989

PEACEFUL JOURNEY, 1991

Since the earliest days of rock 'n' roll, female fans have adored portly chanters, those curious sex objects who would've been overlooked had they been busboys or businessmen. From Fats Domino in the '50s (powerful declarations like "Blueberry Hill") to Luther Vandross in the '80s (soulful fantasies on the order of "Never Too Much"), fleshy fellas have become big-time aural seducers, giving weight to Eddie Murphy's contention that *anybody* who sings can get laid. This might have held true for pre-rap performers, but to aficionados of hip hop, fat rap in its first incarnation wasn't too appealing. Though the Fat Boys and B. Fats (the artist responsible for one of superstar producer Teddy Riley's initial smashes, "The Wop Dance") no doubt got loved by an adoring B-girl or two, they never really displayed any sex appeal. The reason for this is simple: During their fifteen minutes of fame, lovey jabbering in a rap jam was for chewy-centered suckers; no legit rapper after L.L. Cool J ("I Need Love") wanted to be perceived in that light. And besides, B. Fats and the Fat Boys were jokey slobs.

And then, straight out of suburban, money-earnin' Mount Vernon, New York, came six-foot-two, 260-pound Jamaican-born flye boy Dwight Myers. A former resident of the Bronx, he first heard rap music when he was eight years old, and at twenty, as mild-mannered, bespectacled MC Heavy D., he tramped into the hip-hop nation with his crew, the Boyz. Riding drum rolls programmed by teenaged wunderkind Teddy Riley and a richly contoured groove lifted from one of Jean Knight's chuggy Stax classics, he began his first hit, "Mr. Big Stuff," by forcefully disavowing any claims to wackness: "I'm rough and tough and all that stuff/I make you dance and prance till you huff and puff."

But underneath the battleship shenanigans, a loverboy's heart tuned to sensitivity, not doggishness, was beating. He could've easily turned "Mr. Big Stuff" into a macho metaphor for penis size (Philly gangsta Schoolly D did, via "Mr. Big Dick" back in 1988). Instead, as the song progresses, Heavy (a self-described "overweight Romeo") hints at what a gentle and adoring worshipper of the fairer sex he is. Not surprisingly, women of all ages liked "Mr. Big Stuff," citing its performer's lyrical and musical maturity. B-boys did, too, because alongside the glycerine were gritted teeth.

Like a character from a classic gangster flick, Heavy was at once a poet and a pugilist, a smooth lover and a hardrock. In the basement-flavored "The Overweight Lover's in the House," he bops up to a cutie and lays his treats out for her to sample. With a sly wink, he declares through a fourth wall: "She may try to pop that boyfriend junk/But I don't really care 'cause I know he's a punk/I'll stomp him like a roach/If he tried to approach."

While he's not quite a threat to Big Daddy Kane's position as ideal hip-hop dream date, Heavy D's commanding/understanding stance in this roaring single (horned-up and funked-down by veteran reducer Marley Marl) did much to enhance the eroticism of fat rap. Presenting himself with total refined confidence, not absolute arrogance, was Heavy's charm. "He's slick," says cuddly Dina Baby. "And he doesn't make disgusting pig noises like the Fat Boys." A young-tender named Tracy adds, "He just comes off as somebody with a nice personality. He wasn't like all those other ignorant assholes who just wanted to ride a woman's rhythm. It didn't even matter how he looked—although he did look sharp. He was someone I would let approach me."

Bounding out of a meeting room at MCA Records one day in late 1988, slim goody Nava Parker crashed into Heavy while turning a corner. "He asked me was I okay," she recalls. Shining with her usual emotional flair, she opened her arms, smiled, and responded: "Yo, Heavy! Meet the Underweight Lover Nava P." He laughed. "That was *sooo* lovable," coos Nava.

As endearing were some of the other amorous cuts on *Living Large.* The swinging "Dedicated" (which introduced pinup-boy/new-jack crooner Al B. Sure! to the world) spoke of "the obligation in a love situation, while "Don't You Know" (where Heavy talks to a long-lost love over a TR-808 drumbeat) entertains thoughts of marriage. "I'm Gonna Make You Love Me" showers an ebony princess with enough flattery to keep her wet for at least a few days. Teddy Riley was involved in all three of these cuts, and on the liner notes for *Living Large,* Heavy warned us in big bold letters about the musical beatdown T.R. was about to unleash: "WATCH OUT, HE'S COMING!!"

Within the period between *Living Large* and its follow-up, Riley's swing-beat sound had indeed taken over. The style had become refined, more intricately woven. Having collaborated with a host of chart busters from Keith Sweat ("I Want Her") to his own band Guy ("Groove Me"), the Harlem flipmaster had developed into *the* musical innovator of his generation—a result of his funky fusion of hip-hop hardness and soul smoothness. For all intents and purposes, he had arrived by the time he worked on "We've Got Our Own Thang," the first single off *Big Tyme.* Hev had, too, having recorded with Levert ("Just Coolin' ") and Janet Jackson (the twelve-inch re-mix and video for "It's Alright").

Using C.J. & Company's '70s disco classic "We've Got Our Own Thing" for inspiration, Hev's "Thang" bops and jives like an uptown dude out for fun on a Saturday night. "Yo, you ready to drop this?" Teddy asks at the top of the jam.

"Yeah," answers Heavy playfully/tunefully.

"Well, kick it for me one time."

There is a cushion of warm synth smoke riding atop a cold, elastic beat, a loopy house groove snaking around an assortment of short, frisky James Brown samples. Then Heavy D. comes in with *didleydidleydee,* a quick-tongued bit of nonsense that has become his signature line. (In an episode of NBC's "Fresh Prince of Bel Air," when the star claims Bo Jackson, famous beyond football and baseball for those "Bo Knows!" Nike commercials, really isn't aware of didley, guest sideman Heavy D. retorted, "No, it's *didleydidleydee!*" Folks across the rhythm nation cracked up.) What follows are more vocal acrobatics, Heavy performing flips like a flying Wolenda. While promoting individuality, he does more than just hang with Riley's swing; he helps push it along with his hefty, well-conditioned tone.

Riley isn't the only one to return to the Heavy D. producer fold for *Big Tyme.* He, in fact, creates alongside the same studio army as before. But while Teddy directs only one cut here, Marley Marl handles three—"Gyrlz They Love Me," "EZ Duz It, Do It EZ," and "Here We Go Again, Y'all." Crew member DJ Eddie F. (who has developed into a hit-making force, working with singers Jasmine Guy, Jeff Redd, Al B. Sure!, Ralph Tresvant and others) does the rest with the exception of "A Better Land," which the artist produced himself.

"Nobody ain't gotta worry about me being a bully or nothin'," Heavy once said. "Still, I'm not a pushover." This let's-chill philosophy informs "EZ Duz It, Do It EZ," a laid-back chugger about maxin' while relaxin'. Though it can move a crowd, it has nothing on Marley's other *Big Tyme* creation, "Gyrlz They Love Me." With subsonic bass tones that cause concussions, snares that tear away at brain cells, and (unrelenting) hip-tickling organ fills, "Gyrlz" will rock you till your walls come tumbling down— especially when that female chorus kicks in.

The same can't be said for much of the rest of *Big Tyme,* jams produced by DJ Eddie F. that are nice but safe. Using familiar beats from James Brown, Ohio Players, Grover Washington Jr. and Zapp resulted in hip jips—slamming grooves that do little to spotlight the producer's inherent inventiveness. It's when he hooks up with keyboard player Nevelle for "Somebody for Me" (which again features Al B. Sure! on vocals) that the copycat haze settles. After placing Hev's voice inside thick, bright synth lines, it proceeds to go looking for the right girl. "I want somebody to love me for me/Not because I'm MC Heavy D.," he says. "I'm looking for a love that's as solid as a rock." No luck, though. While throngs of girls fall in lust with his image projected from stages and teen-pop centerfolds ("Chile, he dress so flye and he so cute"), the chances of one of them truly *loving* him are quite slim. Being an overweight lover does have its drawbacks.

Hev manages to hook up with a river-deep giver, though, and in his cover of Third World's "Now That We Found Love" he gushes: "I'm feeling hunky-dory 'bout this thing we've found." This is the beginning of *Peaceful Journey,* which courses a path through several breezy jams on the me-in-love/me-so-horny tip. When Hev shifts his attention away from Special Lady to brothers trapped in a cage of rage and Nubian princesses everywhere "who have gone through so much pain and struggle," the surprise isn't how respectful "Sister Sister" sounds, but how closely its Marley Marl–produced track resembles those by Teddy Riley, represented here with "Now That We Found Love" and two other flippy-dippy tunes.

On "Don't Curse," which features Kool G. Rap, Grand Puba Maxwell, Big Daddy Kane, C.L. Smooth and Q-Tip, a sly pitch is made against censorship. The tune ends with the chant "Free Slick Rick! Free Slick Rick!" The crowd is probably rallying further for personal freedoms (detailed sex raps are what made

Rick the ruler): but, then again, they could be demanding that the authorities spring Rick, locked up for a July 3, 1990, attempted murder incident in the Bronx.

Throughout *Peaceful Journey* da Hevster stays true to the same persona he stepped up with on *Living Large*. This nice-guy, socially aware rapper on the smoothed-out R&B tip is cruising along on a wave others have since joined. Nothing has changed through three albums, except that Heavy's fatter (more popular in hip-hop speak). The sexy-voiced crooner, in one new song, will attest to his being as good as ever, maybe even better—and that's not just because he's now sporting a pinchhead either!

"HITMAN" HOWIE TEE

SEE CHUBB ROCK, REAL ROXANNE, SPECIAL ED

HURBY'S
MACHINE

THE HOUSE THAT RAP BUILT (SOUNDCHECK/
NEXT PLATEAU), 1988

In the aural jungle of Black pop, record producers are usually high-profile stars with reputations as performers as well as creators of radio-friendly funky noise. So, while new-jack swinger Teddy Riley can be heard and seen bopping with his own group, Guy, it is also known that his sound is the midas touch of Bobby Brown's "My Prerogative" and Keith Sweat's "I Want Her." The Black producer as superstar tag can also be applied to Jazzie B., L.A. Reid & Babyface, Terry Lewis and Jimmy Jam and on and on to the break of dawn.

In the aural jungle of hip hop, Hurby Azor, a.k.a. Hurby Luv Bug, refuses to be just another ghost in the urban dance machine. Alongside his protegés Salt-n-Pepa and Kid 'n Play, his mug is often seen peeking out at ya from album sleeves or videos. Other than head Juice Crewer Marly Marl, no hip-hop producer is as recognized by both face and sound as Hurby. But for the moment let's forget about the glossy image projected from the television and record bins and concentrate on the sound of Hurby's boomin' system.

Although Russell Simmons and Marley Marl were the first producers to introduce the world to suburbia (Queens) rappers, the sounds of Run-D.M.C. and Roxanne Shanté were still brutal enough to convince the masses that theirs was a street-tough existence. Then came Hurby. With Salt-n-Pepa and Kid 'n Play, this "supa def dope produsa" removed the grit from the grooves, creating a more intoxicating blend of funky, seductive beats and middle-class values. No, this was not a New York version of

Loose parts of Hurby's Machine. Left to right: Steeve-O, Hurb (the Supa Def Dope Produsa), Salt, Pepa, and Play. © Ernest Paniccioli, 1990.

Hammer Time, but with a Hurby group it was understood that the subject matter would have nothing to do with surviving in the ghetto or shootouts in the projects. Let Grandmaster Flash and Public Enemy preach. Like hip-hop Madonnas, Hurby's groups just want to "get into the groove" and party. The music might be funky, but the vocals are pure teen pop.

For this hip-hop compilation disc, *The House That Rap Built,* Hurby recruited producer Steeve-O (soon to lead Queens production crew The Invincibles) to help construct its B-boy maximalism. As critic Nelson George once pointed out, producers of Black pop often work best in pairs. "Why this duo-ism?" he asked. "Maybe because good Black pop demands two very different elements: strong, chromatic melodies keyed to street-corner vernacular (slang, y'all) and distinctive rhythmic innovations (fresh beats, homefolks). Four ears can really define the balance between the 'R' and the 'B.'"

Well, to make a long story short, *The House That Rap Built* is a hip-hop concept album and the only concept is hip hop. Hurby and Steeve-O had their ears to the rhythm (with one exception, the beats are slammin'), but the only blues to be gotten is from the lyrical content—which offers little autobiography and a lot of catchy slogans. The "street-corner vernacular" is mostly limited to the artists bragging about the powers of their producer ("He is the man behind the mix-board/Call Him Hurby Luv or re-cord lord," says Fabulous 2 on the reggae-fusionism of "The Fabulous") or the powers of self ("We came to rock and turn this house into a sweatbox/I am the man with the plan that can rock this land," Future Shock raps on "Just Go").

But with the exception of the Mau-Mau Clan Overlords' "Contact Sport," the homeboy posses on this disc are insignificant. In composing all the tracks on this album, Hurby gave the best tunes to his sirens of swing. Attempting to repeat the success of Salt-n-Pepa, Hurby introduced us to another set of hip-hop divas dubbed Non-Stop. With James Brown grunts, big-beat drums and jangling guitars that sound like former Smiths ax-dude Johnny Marr bum-rushing Muscle Shoals studios (where all them Stax classics were created), Hurby built the perfect pop soundscape for "Keep 'Em Steppin'." It excites on two levels: the production sparks musically while Non-Stop's cutie-pie voices speak in the perky language of hip-hop Lolitas. Listening to this track and Salt-n-Pepa's sexy "I Am Down," one hears the moaning desire of teen (wet) dream eroticism.

From "stereo porn" (Vermoel) to gangstress boogie soundtracks: Antoinette makes her debut with two tracks, "Hit 'Em With This" and "I Got An Attitude." Although the former tune buys into a male's fantasy, the latter proves that women need not be sex toys in this hip-hop jungle. If released today this hardcore would be a hit, but in 1988 folks were not ready for a strong woman with attitude.

ICE CUBE

AMERIKKKA'S MOST WANTED (PRIORITY), 1990

A t the beginning of Ice Cube's first solo album, *AmeriKKKa's Most Wanted,* we hear footsteps walking across the cold, concrete floor of a prison; the clash of bars as the jailer/executioner wakes "Cube" and marches him toward an awaiting electric chair; the chatter of strangers and the flashes from cameras can also be heard as the prisoner is strapped into the hot seat. "Got any last words?" the executioner asks, making no attempt to hide the smirk in his voice. Ice Cube sits silently, remembering his life in the city of lost angels. Flowing like urine in a dark alley, memories flood his mind. He smiles wickedly and screams, "Yeah ... fuck all y'all!"

What follows in this sound theater can be heard as flashbacks from the short life of a gangsta. What the French call *cinema verité* (filmmaking emphasizing unbiased realism) is the technique Ice Cube uses to detail his bleak visions of America's most notorious ghetto, Compton. From dealers chillin' in front of the projects to rival gangs spraying them with bullets, from the din of children roaming through the streets of shattered glass to a group of pregnant girlies gulping sweet, cheap wine in front of the local 7-Eleven. With an eye that magnifies brutal characters and violent situations, Ice Cube exposes a world that seems on the brink of exploding in the ear of the listener. This is Black Cali, 1990: Welcome to the nightmare.

As a former member/chief lyricist for N.W.A., Ice Cube is well versed in chronicling the decadence of gang life on the Left

Coast. His N.W.A. songs "Dopeman," "Gangsta, Gangsta" and the controversial "Fuck tha Police" served to create a new aesthetic in the B-boy canon. Although the myth of gangsterism was already used as an image to titillate the masses of hip-hop culture (Big Daddy Kane and Ice-T, to cite two examples), the signal was that these rappers were catering to America's romance with cartoon violence. With Ice Cube and the rest of N.W.A., the gritty tone of their voices informs that these boyz in da hood were not merely posing with their black jeans and loaded Uzis. Without a doubt, this was just a continuation of the "badder than you" stance favored by the hip-hop nation, but for the first time the myth was flavored with a sense of reality.

On *AmeriKKKa's Most Wanted*, brutality meets technology and the seamy side of life encounters the coolness of computers. Produced by the Bomb Squad (Hank and Keith Shocklee, Eric Sadler and Chuck D., founders of Public Enemy), Ice Cube's dangerous vision of L.A. is given a soundtrack of black noise that is chaotic, boldly wailing anarchy in every corner of the landscape. In this hi-tech, lo-life world, the music composed by the Bomb Squad is multi-textured funk that combines found sounds (crashing bottles, background dialogue, sirens) and live instrumentation that swings from sonic rock to laid-back jazz.

"Who's the Mack," a track that details the ways of pimps and begging crack junkies, features Vincent Henry (formerly of disco-era dance band Change) playing flute and saxophone; these instruments add a refined smoothness to the drama of Ice Cube's vocals. The album is also filled with sound bites from film and television: the racial epithets that flow from the mouth of a white character in Spike Lee's *Do the Right Thing* merge with the mock news special that serves as the preface to "Endangered Species (Tales From the Darkside)," a cut that also features P.E.'s Chuck D.

"Endangered Species" is one of the rare tracks on *AmeriKKKa's Most Wanted* that doesn't relegate women to a secondary status. Although misogyny is not new to mainstream American culture (witness the exploitation of women in other artistic mediums, and in everyday life), when applied to the artists active in the hip-hop nation, the term is used as though it were the latest social disease. In Black culture, the word *bitch* is used by women almost as much as it's used by men, though (I suppose) this gives Ice Cube no reason to use the term almost a hundred times on an album that doesn't even clock in at an hour. And Ice Cube's fear of a female planet stretches beyond a mere misplaced word, into the realm of anti-womanist rhetoric, as witnessed on "You Can't Fade Me," where he fantasizes about kicking "the bitch in the tummy" (a woman who might be pregnant with his baby), or "I'm Only Out for One Thing," where the woman asks innocently if Ice Cube will call her and he replies, "Yeah ... a bitch or a ho/After I ball ya." Since Ice Cube details the social ills of America, with racism ranked high on the hit list, the sexism found on this album is counterproductive to the goals of the struggle.

On "It's a Man's World," Ice Cube is not exactly bathing in holy water, but he does attempt to redeem himself by giving his "homegirl" Yo-Yo a forum to express her own opinions. Here Ice Cube's "debates" on the subject of womanhood are given a direct challenge for the first time. Yo-Yo's lyrics are hardly ground-breaking feminist text, but she *can* hold her own on the mic'.

In his 1964 essay on Raymond Chandler, author Lawrence Clark Powell described the works of the L.A. pulp laureate as "classical dispassion of a romantic and violent society." Perhaps this will be the legacy of Ice Cube, another chronicler of L.A.'s dark side: forever trapped in a world he didn't create, yet able to translate the disturbing scenes (like those depicted on *AmeriKKKa's Most Wanted*) with the voice of a poet.

See also Eazy-E, N.W.A., Yo-Yo.

ICE-T

RHYME PAYS (SIRE), 1987

POWER, 1988

FREEDOM OF SPEECH, 1989

ORIGINAL GANGSTER (O.G.), 1991

With a handle inspired by former pimp/best-selling ghetto author Iceberg Slim, Ice-T was the first Cali-boy rapper to gain respect from the hip-hop mecca of New York City. Born in the wild city of Newark, New Jersey, he was forced to leave the East Coast when both of his parents were killed in an auto accident; he stayed with an aunt for a while, but she too died. This is where the facts begin to turn murky: Different journalists have printed different things about Ice-T, including that he was a car thief and a member of the notorious street gang the Crips. But one thing is clear: Ice-T wanted to be a rapper from the time he attended Crenshaw High in South Central Los Angeles. "I used to read books by Iceberg Slim, a pimp who wrote street poetry. He would talk in rhyme—hustler-like stuff—and I would memorize lines. People in school would always ask me to recite them."

The journey from the parks to the charts was rough and full of false starts and broken promises. Ice made a few indie twelve-inches that did nothing for his reputation, as well as varied cameos in three trash hip-hop films: *Rappin', Breakin'* and its sequel *Breakin' II*. A few years would pass before Ice would land a recording deal with Sire Records (home of Madonna, no less).

F. Scott Fitzgerald once wrote, "There are no second acts in American lives," so Ice-T should be happy that he was able to make a follow up to his debut, *Rhyme Pays*. With songs like "I Love Ladies" (about . . .) and "Sex" (yes, say it), Ice-T's rhymes were ditzy locker-room humor over unimaginative beats/found sounds by producer Afrika Islam. If one were to listen to these tracks today one might think that Ice was sucking on whippets before moving in front of the mic'. Two exceptions to the wackness are "6 in the Morning" and "Squeeze the Trigger." With their intense grooves, both songs feature a topic Ice-T would later define himself with: living close to the edge in the criminal underground.

Impressed with this direction—he had heard "Squeeze the Trigger" while contemplating a brutal Hollywood depiction of street gang culture called *Colors*—filmmaker/actor Dennis Hopper got Ice-T to contribute the title song to his movie. Opening with the sounds of gunshots and then the spooky wash of a synthesizer, "Colors" proved to be one of Ice's best songs, notable for its restrained, floating bass line and Ice's icy tone that sounded far more powerful and dangerous than on *Rhyme Pays*. Following that track's success, Ice embarked on recording his second album. He did so in two weeks, but it doesn't show because the overall sound of this album has shocking richness and streamlined clarity.

"My heart's beating like a Saturday movie," the rapper says in one of the lesser tracks on *Power*, "Heartbeat." And the texts and textures of the LP appear to be conceived for some nonexistent blaxploitation picture. There are aural visions of pimps, hookers, hit men, flye cars and lotsa drugs. It's a cast director Gordon Parks, Jr., would be proud of.

With wah-wah guitars and numerous (Curtis) Mayfieldisms, *Power* draws inspiration from the enduring sound of '70s funk. On "I'm Your Pusherman," Ice-T moves into *Superfly* territory, borrowing from a song from that classic album. But, instead of hawking dope, Ice is selling "dope beats and lyrics—no beeper needed!"

111

Where other Cali boys (Eazy-E, Too Short) hype the lives of common street hoods, Ice-T's gangsters often have the appeal of those on "Miami Vice": hustlers, clad in finely-tailored suits, driving into the sunset in shiny new Ferraris. In "High Rollers" we are introduced to some dopeboys who make deals on cellular phones alongside their swimming pools: "They dress in diamonds and rope chains/They got the blood of Scarface running through their veins."

There's something more mature and complex about Ice-T's third release, *The Iceberg*. Although the title song and "The Girl Tried to Kill Me" are nasty flashbacks to his raging sexism (he's describing fucking a bitch with a flashlight in the title cut, a scene he details with a smirk). Having, one guesses, listened to Public Enemy and Boogie Down Productions, Ice-T decided on this album that there is more to life than pimp power, videogenic hos and automatic weapons. He used to be known for thinking with his dick and trigger finger, but now, on a track like "Lethal Weapon," a gun is a strong metaphor for his mind (which kinda recalls PE's assertion of "Miuzi Weighs a Ton" from their first effort). One can appreciate Ice-T's desire to be socially relevant, but this pseudomilitary anthem sounds more like a fascist soundtrack than an ode to King Knowledge.

It's when he performs rap poetry like "You Played Yourself" and "Peel Their Caps Back" that Ice-T is more convincing. The latter is a brutal, brilliant revenge fantasy recounted over a *most* hypnotic beat. After hearing his homeslice is dead, Ice packs real lethal weapons—enough to supply a small army—and takes his beat to the street. He details a violent gang war in a voice smooth as shattered glass: "I'm a nigger on the trigger/Madder than a pit bull," he growls. By tune's end he's dead ("All the paper's go'n read is gang murder").

He comes back to life, getting loco-wild on the hyped-up "Freedom of Speech." Over Godfather grunts and funky drums he steps to PMRC prexy Tipper Gore: "You think I give a fuck about some silly bitch named Gore?" he asks. "Yo! PMRC, here we go ... war/Yo Tip, what's the matter?/You ain't gettin' no dick?" Although his remarks were composed as serious jokes, the subject of censorship demands a more level approach. Still, with this record, Ice-T became one of the first rappers to voice an opinion on this matter of livelihood.

Ultimately, *The Iceberg* showcases a 3-dimensional Ice-T, able to at once make you laugh and think. Maybe, though, he could've left the silly sexism in the same closet where he tossed his pimp image.

After the brutal hyperactivity of Ice Cube, the Geto boys and N.W.A., one would think that America's youth be tired of the gritty soundscapes burning from the bonfires of hip-hop's ghetto infernos. And yet, in the case of Ice-T (as is often the case of living in the ghetto) some things never change. On his fourth album, *Original Gangster (O.G.)*, Ice says, "Midnight, time for a homicide/Sometime, somebody's gonna die," giving credibility to the myth that one's environment has a profound effect on the artistic soul—no matter how far away you attempt to relocate yourself.

As a follow-up to the *Iceberg* . . . , Ice T has matured as an artist, although his reference points haven't changed. With his homeboys Afrika Islam and DJ Aladdin, Ice is still detailing the misadventures of drug dealers ("New Jack Hustler"), the dangers of the jungle ("Escape from the Killing Fields") and cruising through the danger zones of L.A. ("Midnight").

Although some folks might not view Ice-T as an innovator on the level of Public Enemy or Digital Underground due to his limited subjects, his aural canvas is no less intense; his songs are confessionals screamed at dawn from a rapper who has no fear of the territory. As Ice-T told the *L.A. Weekly*, "I try to walk the edge. I'm going to tell you what you need to hear, not what you want to hear."

INTELLIGENT
HOODLUM

INTELLIGENT HOODLUM (A&M), 1990

I f Afrika Bambaataa is right, then the radicalism that stirred up America's so-called melting pot during the '60s will make a comeback in the '90s, fighting the powers that be with force, not coercion, anger, not peacefulness. And Grandpa Bam's anarchic vision suggests the following comparison: If Public Enemy are the Black Panthers of rap, combining outlaw swagger with political and social discontent, then Percy Chapman (or Intelligent Hoodlum, a.k.a. MC Tragedy) is the music's Malcolm X. Shabazz, bringing spirituality and handsome flyeboy slickness into the mix.

But Percy Chapman and Malcolm X have more in common than just style. From the shadowy concrete jungles of Black Land, Malcolm and Chapman both became victims of society's program of engineered defeat as young men; they drifted into lives of crime, selling and using drugs and stealing. When their gangster hustles landed them in jail—in 1988, Chapman served twenty months on New York's Riker's Island for robbery—they went through similar amazing transformations. By immersing themselves in books about Black culture and embracing the teachings of the Nation of Islam, they broke into more enlightened pastures. Relaying their knowledge to their still-ignorant brothers and sisters, attempting to lift them out of four hundred years of repressive conditioning, became passions for both ex-hardrocks when they reentered the general populace. Where Malcolm expressed his humanist/Black nationalist convictions through eloquent speeches, Chapman does so through sublimely forceful raps supervised by hip-hop reductionist Marley Marl.

Now nineteen, Chapman has been associated with Marl since 1983, when they were neighbors in the Queensbridge Housing Projects in Elmhurst, New York. Under the name MC Jade, the rapper released a loping single layered by Marl called "Coke Is It." When this resolutely anti-drug jam went nowhere, Chapman, who had been writing poetry since the age of eleven, became disillusioned with rhyming and a possible career in music. Throwing himself further into street life seemed his only option at the time.

Meanwhile, Marley Marl had formed the Juice Crew All Stars, with Cold Chillin' Records president Tyrone Williams and rappers Roxanne Shanté, Big Daddy Kane, M.C. Shan, Biz Markie and Kool G. Rapp. When Marl was directing the sessions for his first solo project, *In Control, Volume I,* he tapped the talents of this posse and, for two songs ("Live Motivator" and "Rebel"), Chapman.

When the album came out, Chapman was serving his time. Hearing the bopping "Live Motivator" over his FM Walkman while mopping a prison floor almost brought tears to his eyes. But instead of crying, he set out to cure what he now calls his "Black complex," ignorance of self. Relating what he's learned to his past experiences is what distinguishes the texts on *Intelligent Hoodlum* from those of most other consciousness rappers, including Boogie Down Productions' KRS-ONE and X Clan's Grand Verbalizer Funkin' Lesson.

Booming over a beat full of crispness and tension, the first voice one hears on *Intelligent Hoodlum* is that of Malcolm beckoning the Black underclass to embrace Jesus as a tool in the struggle for upliftment. "Stop thinking that you've got to exist on the low plane," he counsels. "As Jesus ascended, you can ascend!" Using this as a jumping-off point, Chapman proceeds to tell us about himself: of some of the traps he fell into coming up, of how he became a "reborn rebel," of how his rhymes are "releated to the havoc and harm." Looking behind him, then ahead, he declares, "Hoodlum is the past/Intelligent is the future."

Another cut drifts us "Back to Reality" using a melodic, sandpapery shuffle groove. Up front, the rapper boasts that his style is "smooth and a step beyond." But later he adds that it wasn't always like that. Back in the days, he was ridiculed by nonbelievers for being wack. "It took a lot of time for the skill to grow," he offers. "And it took a lot of time for my thoughts to flow." The message here is: Keep keeping on—all the way to heaven.

While *Intelligent Hoodlum* contains straight-up party jams like "Party Pack" and "Party Animal," its most booming, powerful tune—the strafingly funky "Arrest the President"—is no joke. With lines like "You can't lie/So it's time to fry," this is pro-Black explosion calling for a Black House instead of a White House. Uncompromising stuff.

JUNGLE
BROTHERS

STRAIGHT OUT THE JUNGLE (WARLOCK), 1988

DONE BY THE FORCES OF NATURE
(WARNER BROS.), 1989

Harlem, USA: Walking down 125th Street on a bright Sunday afternoon, one is often struck by the differences one notices, not only in the diverse landscapes, but also in the people. There are historical buildings like the Apollo Theatre directly across the street from postmod structures like Mart 125 (Harlem's first shopping mall). Inside this edifice of nouveau structuralism, one can purchase African jewelry in one booth, while in another a wide variety of fake fingernails and 100 percent "human hair" can be found.

Back on the street, there are similar juxtapositions of styles that include: neighborhood B-boys driving down the avenue with their booming systems blasting the latest Public Enemy track, while an immaculately dressed Muslim on the corner hawks tapes of Farrakhan speeches; a gospel choir wailing "Amazing Grace" around the bend from a skinny, tattered man selling crack beside a storefront church; a slightly decaying bar and grill entertaining lonely, sad-eyed souls with Billie Holiday out front, while in the rear, Bohemian Brothers, long dreds hangin' down their backs, are mixing Marx with their gin.

And though visiting tourists are often warned about walking through the gritty streets of this former Black Mecca, these are the same roads of artistic passage once travelled by Langston Hughes and Chester Himes; the Last Poets and Teddy Riley; James Baldwin and James Brown.

Rapper/producer Baby Bam of the Jungle Brothers.
© Alice Arnold, 1990.

———

The term *jungle* has often been used to describe Harlem
(as well as other ghettos throughout America). Listening to
Grandmaster Flash and the Furious Five's masterpiece "The
Message," one hears the aural equivalent of urban confusion in
the repeated phrase "It's like a jungle sometimes/Makes me
wonder/How I keep from going under." On their first album,
Straight Out the Jungle, the Jungle Brothers use this hip-hop
document as a blueprint for the lead (and title) track. In the
Afrocentric school of hip hop, no other group better narrates
both the joys and pains of living in "the jungle," and no other
group better translates the diverse voices heard within the Black
experience. Unlike the apocalyptic visions of Ice Cube, the
poetry of the Jungle Brothers isn't full of bitter reminiscences.
In fact, often it's a tribal call of celebration.

Critic Greg Tate has theorized that if Ice Cube were a
filmmaker, his brutal scenarios would not be such a shock to the
ears. With cinematic references in mind, Ice Cube is playing
Peckinpah to the Jungle Brothers' Scorsese. Although da Brothers are well aware of the dangers in the jungle ("You got to be

aware/You got to have the jungle eye") the Jungle Brothers' scope is not limited to pure violence. Thus, their studies are more three-dimensional.

With its raw sound—the album was recorded for a small label, for little money—*Straight Out the Jungle* is teenage meditation that encompasses serious messages and dancing in the streets. Under the leadership of Afrika "Baby" Bambaataa, the group is at once retro (check out their African clothing, knit hats, and Afrika's oval sunglasses, which make them look more like Sun Ra's back-up musicians than a contemporary hip-hop crew) and postmodern (their use of jazz samples in the sonic assemblage has influenced a parade of hip-hop artists).

The most startling track on this album merges the boundaries of the hip-hop nation with the techno-crazed universe of acid house. With "I'll House You," the Jungle Brothers became the first established hip-hop crew to load the hyper-intense music of dance clubs into the canon of homeboy culture. As Jungle Bro. Mike G. told the (New York) *City Sun.* "It was an experiment. There was a time when we didn't like house, and there was a time when we started liking house music. We wanted to make other B-boys like house, so we moved it closer to hip-hop territory." With a re-mix constructed by sonic assassin Todd Terry (king of acid house, according to the Brit press), this track moved many happy feet in dance dives throughout the U.K. and her colonies.

Moving from the dance floor to behind the bedroom door: The JB's also created seductive grooves that defined a "now-age" Afroerotic hip hop. On "Behind the Bush," instead of standing in the middle of the block holding their dicks, screaming, "Come here bitch!" they're showering a cutie with lines like "I want to be your hero/I want to be your man/I want to love you every moment I can/I want to take you back to the Motherland." Gliding over a splashy intro into a bubble bath of guitars and Fender Rhodes piano (a sound reminiscent of Barry White's

'70s love suites), Afrika sounds like he's lounging in his hut rather then sitting in front of a studio mic'.

Fast-forward, one year later: November 1989 . . .

The jungleland of New York City had been on a slow burn since the summer of Black fire that began with the media controversy over Spike Lee's *Do the Right Thing*. Things fully ignited after the brutal murder of Yusef Hawkins in Bensonhurst, Brooklyn. After witnessing prejudice from the media and on the streets, it would be impossible for Black artists not to rethink their position in society.

In one track on the JBs second album, *Done by the Forces of Nature*, Afrika "Baby" Bambaataa is questioning his place as an African-American: "Confused about where I come from/What Planet?/What channel?/What station?" Although Afrika's poetry may be overly mystical on occasion, his observations here are very much grass-roots sentiments echoed by the masses.

Whether by prophecy or coincidence, the Jungle Brothers' second minimal masterwork was released the same week that New York City elected its first Black mayor, David Dinkins. In the same way that having a Black man in City Hall might change the way politics are practiced in a major city, the JBs were hoping that their second album (their first on a major label) might change the way rap music is constructed in the hip-hop community. Yet, unlike Dinkins, whose m.o. involves mostly back-room maneuvering, the JBs are poetic nationalists with their ears tuned to the cries from the streets, exposing a grandiose world of darkness that includes ignorance, fear and negativity.

From African percussion to old-world soul, the Jungle Brothers travel freely through the vast archives of music madness, collecting funky sounds to reinforce their aural manifesto; in the minds of the Jungle Brothers, music is more on the level of a new art movement (one they've dubbed "Tribe Vibe") than regular hip hop. As the vocals on "Beads on a String" inform,

D.J. Red Alert, producer of the Jungle Brothers, with his son Li'l Red. Photo courtesy of Next Plateau Records, 1990.

"The beads are the people/The string is the vibe/The vibe is what mentally connects the tribe."

In their search for tribal authenticity, the Jungle Brothers use scratchy samples and old-school ambience on *Done by the Forces of Nature,* which gives the disc the same "raw" appeal that was heard on the first album. Yet there is still enough complexity in the grooves that one can hear a different sound after each listening. With hip-hop artists now being mass produced like this year's Chevy, it's cool to hear a group who has come to the realization that diversity can be used as a tool of power. Or as Mike G. blurts on "Beyond This World," "Lookin' out for the danger signs/Jungle Brothers bringing forth a change in times." Like the chaotic streets of Harlem, these times (tunes) are full of contrasts.

KID 'N PLAY

2 HYPE (SELECT), 1988

FUNHOUSE, 1990

HOUSE PARTY (MOTOWN), 1990

Perky, tumbling and irresistibly catchy, "Rollin' With Kid 'n Play" was a rap hit for Christopher Reid and Christopher Martin. Rolling is also an everyday occurrence for the pair, better known as Kid 'n Play. Formerly Fresh Force (which specialized in answer records), they broke through in 1987. Since then—even off-record—they've always embraced a good time. Their sweet-faced, boy-next-door personas helped bring those spooked by rap's ugly, rebellious image into the hip-hop fold.

While the music they practice may have started out near burned-out tenement buildings in the Bronx, Kid 'n Play, from Elmhurst, New York, moved it closer to more middle-class spaces where the new Black aesthetic reigns—into a house that producer Hurby "Luv Bug" Azor built.

As other auteurs of teen beat were pumping up jams with brooding breaks from the likes of James Brown and Billy Squire, Azor, influenced by Stax and '70s disco, used swift grooves that slinked and glided toward more mainstream Black values. He harnessed Marva Whitney's "Last Night Changed It All" and Chaka Khan and Rufus's "Ain't Nobody" for "Last Night," Kid 'n Play's maiden voyage, and this jolly, intricately woven narrative (about a bad blind date that ends up good) bounced around, full of teenage anxiety and playfulness. It was a crowd-pleaser, but because Kid 'n Play had no image at the time, it ended up being only a whisper in the noisy atmosphere that is Planet Pop.

With "Do This My Way," then "Gettin' Funky," the group began defining themselves for the public. These two slippery, driving raps were supported by videos that showcased nimble dancing, natural exuberance and an eraser head (Kid's six-inch Nubian crown, which became the group's unofficial logo), all of which was instrumental in jettisoning Kid 'n Play out of obscurity and into the world of commerce; they transformed B-boy art into mass-market product.

For their debut album, *2 Hype*, instead of concentrating on just one musical style, Kid 'n Play diversified, throwing Grace Jones, house, go-go and rare groove into the mix. The eager-to-please result was a clever ploy to catch as much bank as they could. While Kid 'n Play's plan was successful—*2 Hype* sold a million copies and was a Top Ten hit on *Billboard*'s Black LPs chart—it almost backfired. "2 Hype," released as a fourth single, sounded too pop, and Kid 'n Play almost became labeled sellouts. In Black music, especially hip hop, that could mean the kiss of death. But, shrewdly, the group remixed the tune and lensed a video (featuring a baby) that was too cute to hate. This was damage control in full effect.

Kid, Cosby dude/hip-hop video director Malcolm Jamal Warner, and Play. © Ernest Paniccioli, 1990.

Following *2 Hype,* Kid 'n Play began exploiting their new-found fortunes in the nonmusical arenas of movies (*House Party,* which went on to gross over $20 million) and TV (the development of a Saturday-morning cartoon series as well as a prime-time sitcom). In addition, Play, a graphic artist, opened up a fashion design business named IV Plai (pronounced "fore-play") with Dana Dane.

In light of all this, one could say that if hip hop ever went belly up, Kid 'n Play would still remain standing. Smart (Kid is a classically trained bassist) and savvy (Play used to sell his old sneakers to kids in his neighborhood), they've got a number of gifts to shoot. But the duo continues to make music.

In 1990, they dropped two albums with material of theirs. The soundtrack to *House Party* contained "Funhouse" and "Kid vs. Play (The Battle)." The former plays verbal volleyball over surprisingly clumsy beats; the latter is a frisky invitation to "do a little dance." Their second full LP, *Funhouse,* was a more focused and harder effort than *2 Hype,* an amiable attempt to steady a rocky fan base.

It's apparent that while making the second LP, Kid 'n Play took to heart how DJ Jazzy Jeff & the Fresh Prince (rap's other fun crew) lost favor in young Black America. The vapors from anger and disgust now lie over their career, and Kid 'n Play didn't want to follow them into the mainstream and then obliv-ion. Some of their raps try to balance their niceness with brashness, one warning. "Don't be fooled by the humorous image!"

While there's nothing *really* brutally blunt-spoken through-out, there are funky beats. Though they're smoothed out with catchy R&B choruses and melodic decorum, this album's B-boy. But it's also adult. In Kid 'n Play's gentrification of rap, no one gets evicted. Their *Funhouse* is a place where hip hop's old fans and new fans both can come together and be happy.

KOOL MOE DEE

KOOL MOE DEE (JIVE), 1986

HOW YA LIKE ME NOW, 1987

KNOWLEDGE IS KING, 1989

AFRICAN HERITAGE, 1990

FUNKE FUNKE WISDOM, 1991

Though the appropriation issue ("Is sampling art or is it theft?") heated up only recently, hip-hop auteurs have been biting from pop's heap of recorded history from the genre's beginnings. Quotes back in the day were snatched up not from frenetic disco titles, but from slower, more effortless sides. "Rapper's Delight" stole its soul from Chic's "Good Times," "Planet Rock" plundered the blips from Kraftwerk's "Planet Rock," and "Feel the Heartbeat" lifted from Taana Gardner's thumping "Heartbeat."

While not as notorious as the other two, the latter tune signaled the debut of an important crew from Harlem known as the Treacherous Three. In 1981, this trio of skinny teens—vocalists Special K., L.A. Sunshine and Kool Moe Dee—got spotted by Bobby Robinson, a music industry veteran (catalyst in the careers of Gladys Knight and the Pips, producer of doo-wop sides for the Orioles and the Ravens, owner of numerous R&B labels, retailer in a popular mom-and-pop shop in Harlem called Happy House) whose diverse career dates back to the early '50s. He was acutely aware of the inner workings of the music biz, yet he had an awfully hard time holding on to rappers. Like Grandmaster Flash and the Furious Five, another Robinson discovery, the Treacherous Three quickly jetted from Robinson's

Kool Moe Dee. Photo courtesy of Jive/RCA.

———

Enjoy label to rival Sugar Hill Records in search of more money and better distribution. But as they matured, the group also became disenchanted with the Hill, and disbanded when their contract expired.

In pop music, flying solo from a successful group often spells the end of one's hits, no matter how massive the originating outfit was or how significant the talent of the one who walks. Just look at the Temptations' David Ruffin (who died skinny and broke in the summer of '91), the Spinners' Phillipe Wynn (who hooked up with George Clinton and his freaky funk all-stars before *his* untimely death) or Hall and Oates' Darryl Hall. Statistics of failure are even higher in the world of rap, the Furious Five's brilliant wordsmith Melle Mel one of its many victims. As he moved through the minefield between group success and solo stardom, Kool Moe Dee—who became enchanted with rap through the poetry of *The Grinch Who Stole Christmas* and heavyweight champ Muhammad Ali—felt confident that he'd come out triumphant.

Collaborating with the boy who would be new-jack king, Teddy Riley, bolstered Kool Moe Dee's optimism, though not at first. "He sure was surprised [when he first saw me]," reports Riley, who was only seventeen at the time. "He didn't say nothing, though, because we both came from the streets and so if I did good, it didn't really matter about my age." And so this duo, along with Moe Dee's former manager, Lavaba, and two others directed the sessions for "Go See the Doctor," a twelve-inch B-boy classic whose strolling pulse and sharp, funny rhymes made it a hit for Rooftop and later Jive. Along with Spoonie Gee's Marley Marl–directed "The Godfather," Moe Dee's track was one of the rare times that an old-school performer scored among a whole new generation of hip-hop stylists. Unlike Gee, though, Moe Dee kept connecting.

On his debut solo LP, Mr. Dee used the popular "Go See the Doctor" as his jumping-off point. As a lesson in safe sex, it succeeded for a couple of reasons. First, its thick bass line and intense beat didn't rush; they both strolled like a panther on the prowl, totally cool. Second, Moe Dee's delivery beautifully showcased elements in the African-American oral tradition: a rich, commanding tone, crystal-clear enunciation, B-boy attitude and streetwise humor. The jam starts off with our man slyly tilting his head, lowering those Star Trek shades over his nose to get a better look at a sexy fox. After inviting her to treat him "like a Buddha and bow your head," he's knockin' hiney. Proud of his got-it-in-a-minute seduction, he runs outside to his posse, who are eagerly awaiting the scoop from their brother's penis ("You got it?" "How was it?"). I bet the crew got happy and started high-fiving, but three days later the joke turned deadly serious when venereal disease entered the picture.

The way Moe Dee insinuates the hook, long and whiny, and some of his colorful insight ("Now I know why her ex-boyfriend Dave/Calls her Mrs. Microwave") is the shit that brothers standing 'round drinking forties of beer taunt their homeboys with. Thanks to skillful poetics, the message in the music came across with its chumpy rag lines.

A dumb dick makes a cameo in "Go See the Doctor," then stars in another song. Over a dreary track of beefy, programmed drums, Moe Dee relates a tale about a phallocentric brother from back in the day who hated to go to school but loved to cum, a hustler by default who played himself because "his business was his pleasure." His macked-up modus operandi prompts Moe Dee to "wonder if his brain is his . . ."

What *I* thought about, meanwhile, is why did a brilliant vocalist like Moe Dee surround himself with so little music on this track and much of the rest of the LP? In the studio, a bare-bones track is a challenge to work with; what is there must constantly engage, keeping the body up, the tension of gruff B-boy attitude down. Commenting on the lean aesthetics of his state-of-the-art rap productions in 1987, Rick Rubin said, "Rap records are very minimal now, but you can't just sit down at a drum machine, like I know a lot of producers do, and say, 'Okay, this is how it's gonna go.' It's more than that."

Giving us much more is "Do You Know What Time It Is," the album's best tune besides "Go See the Doctor," where bare doesn't necessarily mean plain. Here, over a cold, unrelenting pulse beat, Moe Dee plays an aggressive dick whose sacs contain no cash: "I'm gonna run you around/Take you up and down/Turn you out and leave you in the lost and found."

If the textural richness of postmodernism (collage techniques, cutting and scratching) played at bit part on *Kool Moe Dee,* another element from the hip-hop tree's roots—competition and ego—had a supporting role in the cuts "I'm Kool Moe Dee" and "The Best." Bragging with sly inside rhymes, he asserts, "If this record was an atom I'd be the nucleus/The center of attention—Kool Moe Dee—and I'm just like the core of an apple/The priest to the chapel ..."

Nonetheless, Moe Dee wasn't offering forgiveness or salvation to brash newcomer L.L. Cool J, who he claimed ripped off his intelligent, forceful MCing style. On the cover of *How Ya Like Me Now*—a question mark is conspicuously missing from the title—his payback (a beatdown) is represented visually, with one of a Laredo Jeep's massive front wheels rolling over the newcomer's then-trademark red Kangol cap. Standing in the foreground of the shot is Moe Dee, fingering the collar of his white British Knights track suit in a cocky expression of victory.

Inside the package, verbal vanquishment awaited as well, the title track stomping through like Robocop with multilayered shards of sound (synth whooshes, swirling horns, jangly guitars, vibrating percussion) enveloping Moe Dee's unmitigated aggression, which tumbles freely like a bouncing high-tension rubber ball in an utterly convincing rap: "I'm from the old school/I used see men die for less but I'm not livin' that way/I let my mic' do the talkin' and let the music play."

When L.L. Cool J responded to "How Ya Like Me Now" with "Jack the Ripper" (the non-LP B side to "Going Back to Cali," featured in the decadent brat-pack flick *Less Than Zero*), a real war was on. Cool J hit his nemesis where it counts—in the wallet—with: "How ya like me now?/I'm getting busier/I'm double-platinum/I'm watching you get dizzier." Then Moe Dee responded with a litany of unexpurgated adjectives in "Let's Go": "L.L. stands for lower-level, lackluster/Last, least, limp lover." When, during 1989's Apollo Theatre taping of *Rapmania*, *Word Up!* magazine photographer Ernie Paniciolli captured Moe Dee and L.L. shaking hands in peace, these looked to be the final moves in a feud that had already run well over a year.

Back to *How Ya Like Me Now*. Alongside the dramatic aural snapshot of a section of Harlem called the Hill in "Wild Wild

West," a reminiscence about a peace-minded crew of homies angered by hoodlumish posses turning parks into thunderdomes, are examples of early rappinghood ("Way Way Back"), doses of mackology ("I'm a Player"), generous helpings of braggadocio ("50 Ways," "Suckers," "Rock You") and a hardrock homeboy's guide to understanding materialistic Black women ("Stupid"). Though "Wild Wild West" is *in there*, nothing, ultimately, comes even close to being as terrifically appealing as "How Ya Like Me Now."

The lesson on sackchasers continues in "They Want Money," the first single from *Knowledge Is King*, the most satisfying LP of Moe Dee's solo career. Over gurgling saxes and loopy beats, funky noises and a marvelously descending bass line, Moe Dee spills out an angry rap explaining why he chooses to be single. "Back up off me/Smell the coffee," he demands of a woman jocking him blindly. "I hear dollar signs in your careless whisper." Though this song shares the same sentiments as No Face's "Half" (inspired by a controversial Eddie Murphy routine of the same name), it's by far a much better, more intelligent record, with its fear of a female planet wrapped in a blanket so frisky, I bet even feminists couldn't resist dancing.

After jetting from a highway of screaming, pointing skeezers, Moe Dee next parks his Benz 190 on "The Avenue," attempting to find tranquillity in a splashy, percolating mid-tempo track that displays yet more of the performer's sexual anxiety. But that's not the main focus here. As it is with so many African-American males who grow up in the Jungle Land, USA, the street corner to Kool Moe Dee is a place for socializing and maxing, posing and flirting. In this arena cops represent intimidation if you're living on the wild side, but through his shades Moe Dee sees Five-O not as a threat, 'cause he's legit. With that in mind, he makes a point about racist perceptions about Black ghetto youth: "We're not only thieves 'n' thugs/And what law says we gotta sell drugs?"

From the avenue to "the Q": Moe Dee greatly expanded his performing horizons in 1989, working with popmeister/mixmaster Quincy Jones on his epic *Back on the Block* LP. What that too ambitious release attempted to do was place rap in the context of Black postwar musical achievement, pairing Miles and Diz, Ray and Chaka, James Moody and Big Daddy Kane. But if the thought that rap wasn't a legitimate gig still lingers in your mind after hearing "Back on the Block" or Jones's new interpretation of Josef Zawinul's "Birdland," then check the revved-up "I Go to Work" on *Knowledge Is King.* Here Moe Dee, a college graduate in communications, compares what he does to a doctor (it's like he puts ideas and sounds together surgically), an architect (Yo! he constructs a rhyme piece by piece), and a boxer (homeboy's poetry bobs, weaves and jabs); he expands this pugilistic theme in "I'm Hittin' Hard," saying he'll "make a skeptic look epileptic." In another cut, "The Don," he probably was inspired by the story line in *The Godfather* trilogy; with lines like "My territory spans from New York to Hollywood/The whole country's my neighborhood," Moe Dee's saying he can always be counted on for putting out a hit . . . record, that is.

After lending his support to the Stop the Violence Movement's "Self Destruction" twelve-inch (a sample Moe Dee line: "I never had to run from the Ku Klux Klan and I shouldn't have to run from a Black man"), a deeply sociopolitical cut just had to be on *Knowledge Is King.* "Pump Your Fist," which borrows part of its tense, tough beat from Manu Dibango's funk classic "Soul Makossa," counsels unity in the face of strife, awareness in the midst of media confusion. "Voice (loud)/Black(proud)/Truth(vowed)/No sellouts allowed," it intones.

The maxi-single (four songs) *African Heritage* includes "Pump Your Fist" and the propulsive "Knowledge Is King," as well as two new songs whose lumbering rhythms defeat their purpose as potent teaching tools. Messages to "stick together and keep a positive mind" don't connect because these tracks—

one of them, "God Made Me Funke," sports three mixes—don't rate as menacing hip hop. Without Riley in his studio posse, the don misfired. He could've gotten rubbed out for being sloopy, thus ending his reign as hip hop's only old-school new-jack, a forever-fresh B boy-of-the-moment for any moment. Instead he came back fighting, using an unprecedented number of loops (from such sources as George Clinton, James Brown, Sly & the Family Stone and the Average White Band). They're all too uninspiring. L.L. Cool J taunted Moe in "To the Break of Dawn" then "Mama Said Knock You Out" (the line "*Blaaw*—how ya like me now?"). On "To the Beat, Y'All" and "Death Blow," from *Funke Funke Wisdom*. Harlem boy steps back into the ring, Riley again in his corner, slinging new bundles of rapid-fire beatdowns. When he asks "Tell 'em how you fell, L," someone scratches in "Hard as hell," from "Rock the Bells." One may smile slightly, but by now isn't this feud between two gifted talkers kinda tired?

In "Rise 'n' Shine" Moe Dee is demanding deeper social consciences alongside KRS-One and Chuck D. In another song he's moaning "I Like It Nasty" and bragging, but another bragging/sex song "Mo' Better," turns out to be only 57 seconds long. New batches of young-stud poets are constantly firing off in rap-land. This kinda makes one wonder: How long can Kool Moe Dee keep his hardcore-rap life up?

L.A. STAR

hrough the eyes of a woman, rapper L.A. (Lisa Ali) Star examines both the interior and exterior of ghetto life. From South Bronx playgrounds to tenement bedrooms, she has observed both the street games and the sexual politics of the urban experience. And although her press photos and album cover display her as a sex kitten (Marilyn Monroe on the hip-hop tip), her rhymes are full of brutal, honest snapshots of street scenes drawn from personal observations, of good time/ bad time scenarios: hangin' in the Bronx parks, learning the art of hip-hop from old school MC's and DJs; becoming an unwed mother at the age of fifteen (the baby's father was later killed); driving limos for uptown drug dealers and downtown hookers.

With the hardcore rhymes of her debut album *Poetess,* L.A. Star displays no desire to change the world, yet she does want mainstream culture to have an accurate portrait of her life in urban America. As L.A. said during a recent conversation, "People talk about the violent messages of Eazy-E and N.W.A., but what folks don't understand is these fellas wouldn't be talking about this stuff if it wasn't true. What I'm doing is giving the woman's viewpoint of hanging in the neighborhood, watching their men selling drugs, seeing them going to jail or getting killed. These women can't even dream 'cause their man might be dead tomorrow. You've gotta be strong or you'll perish."

On her first single "Fade to Black," L.A. Star's tone is both gritty and fragile. It sounds as though it might shatter under the strain of her words. As she relates a tale of a young street hood who becomes involved with the neighborhood drug posse, L.A. uses the film term fade-to-black whenever she shows a scene from the protagonist's lifestyle. Although this opera of urban despair sounds a bit underproduced, L.A.'s strong pipe give it the realism it needs—all the way to its bloody finale.

Because it features the work of various producers, *Poetess* has a schizophrenic sound. For example, the new-jack swing love song "Do You Still Love Me?" (complete with joyful girl-group backup singers and a Luther Vandross soundalike) is followed by the reggae-flavored "It Takes a Real Woman," which has L.A. Star rapping in a Jafakecan (fake Jamaican) accent. Ambition is a good thang, but so is continuity.

"It's hard to be a rebel when you're a girl," rival rapper Salt said in 1987. In 1990 L.A. Star offered, "A lot of dudes think because you're a female rapper you're real hard, a dyke or something. I want people to know that just because I'm street doesn't mean I'm not feminine." With her second single, "Swing to the Beat" ("Whole posse and I/Dressed to impress, stoopid flye"), L.A. Star raps over a slow groove that conjures up images of countless house parties—when the lights are low and a sweaty body clings next to yours. With a deep-throated voice that goes beyond sexy and into the realm of aural seduction, L.A. recounts her conversation with an H.Y.T. (handsome young thang) she met at a local jam. "Where is your man?" he asked in a cool voice. "At home, outta town, away or upstate/And if he is, we can have a date." Needless to say, our femme fatale is blown into a wondrous dream—if only for a moment. With this track's use of melodic guitar (the same sample Big Daddy Kane used in "Smooth Operator"), and L.A.'s smooth delivery, there is more passion heard here than on a thousand Madonna singles.

Ain't go'n lie and say *Poetess* is the dopest hip-hop album ever recorded, but it is a successful outing for this new jill on the block. While L.A. Star vindicates the emotions of ghetto girls, her music is sure to excite the boys in the 'hood too.

L.L. COOL J

RADIO (DEF JAM), 1985

BIGGER AND DEFFER, 1987

WALKING WITH A PANTHER, 1989

MAMA SAID KNOCK YOU OUT, 1990

Defining himself as "the mic' dominator, best of all time" on *Radio,* seventeen-year-old L.L. Cool J swaggered briskly into hip-hop prominence, wielding an ego many times bigger than the massive (at least twenty pounds) Conion-Technosonic boombox pictured on the jacket of his debut album. Working against chilled-out, minimalist beats, he further insinuated that his "literature is above Shakespeare" and that "the great Edgar Allan Poe couldn't write this good!"

As the first artist released under Def Jam's landmark six-figure distribution deal with Columbia (now Sony Music), Cool J was going for the greatest asset there is to live for in hip-hop country—to be the acknowledged dopest B-boy of all time (in "Rock the Bells" he rhymes: "I'll inject into your ears a new concept/Conceived in silence to be unveiled/To the Cool J phenomenon all must hail"). Though this self-proclaimed rap master is from the same neatly trimmed Hollis neighborhood as then-rulers of rap Run-D.M.C., though he was/is managed by the same Rush Productions company, he insisted that he had his own style—"more literate and tough." He didn't sing the way deposed "King of Rap" (by this time riding the back of the old-school bus, jherri curls dripping from the heat) Kurtis Blow sometimes did " 'cause I just don't do that!" The ten tracks on his LP, "reduced" by beefy heavy mentalist/Def Jam co-owner Rick Rubin, was devoid of the sing-songy pop slickness favored by platinum "pied pipers of rap" Whodini.

L.L. Cool J standin' in a Tyson Pose. © Tina Paul, 1989.

Although his initial rude-boy singles, "I Need a Beat" and "Dangerous" (unleashed while Def Jam was still being operated out of Rubin's cluttered New York University dorm room, which he occupied several weeks following his graduation in 1985), were pumping bass on portable sound systems throughout New York City for months, much of the remainder of America didn't hear them. The first piece of L.L. aural dynamite to blow up in their faces was "I Can't Live Without My Radio," included in the B-boy morality flick *Krush Groove*, supervised by Michael Schultz, the Black director who handled the blaxploitation-era classic *Cooley High.* This film, which starred Prince spin-off Sheila E. as a rapper/love interest (help me, I'm still laughing) was *supposed* to chronicle the rise of hip-hop culture in New York. But though it failed in totally telling it like it *really* was, one scene rescued it from being complete fiction; when the sunny-faced, Kangol-crowned L.L. entered the offices of Rush Productions—they were looking for new artists—and blared "I

Can't Live Without My Radio," things got brutally real. In one theater along Manhattan's colorful/dank Times Square (where audiences are wilder and tougher than anyplace else), posses stood up and cheered at this glimmer of an urban universe that also existed in their backyards and on their stoops. Following his few minutes of screen time, everyone knew that the lanky James Todd Smith would be a star.

This teenager was a human cyclone, huffing and puffing with megalomanic force and clear enunciation words that essayed a manual for a new hip-hop era. This was the genre's first fat record, employing shrill drums of doom, fortified with generous helpings of electronic delay and "gating." Stuffed inside their barren musical void—molded into a verse/chorus structure by varying patterns and textures—was the rapper's clawing voice, trapped in his S-E-L-F but also revealing the spirit and values of its immediate surroundings. Any lingering doubts one may have had about an entire album of pure steamrolling beats (the ones L.L. asked for in "I Need a Beat," which sold more than 100,000 copies with virtually no airplay) propelled only by L.L.'s intoxicating desire for omnipotence were quickly erased by *Radio*'s sound waves.

The leadoff track, "I Can't Live Without My Radio," puts the drums up against hip hop's antisocial impulses ("I don't mean to offend other citizens but I kick my volume way past ten") as it revels in the reasons behind such finger-waving. As a social document, "I Can't Live Without My Radio" is a reaction to bougie aesthetics, and L.L.'s box also functioned as a status symbol that attracted girls and (along with a new pair of sneakers and a thick gold rope) helped gain him respect among the fellas.

While he dropped inspiring braggadocio, L.L. also had quite a way with a putdown, dissing a hopelessly bad dancer ("You Can't Dance"), a compulsive liar, played with fierce hilarity by his fast-talking superstar manager, Russell Simmons

("That's a Lie"), and a neighborhood hussey ("Dear Yvette"). His rap tracks were brutal, accentuated with roughhouse turntable scratching by Cut Creator—the hit "Rock the Bells," besides a go-goey timbale figure, also employed what sounded like a jagged bite from some heavy-metal disc. Still, he managed to create one of the closest things to balladry rap music had ever produced. With its thick, ballsy drum-machine program, accented by a percussion pattern that resembles rain dancing, "I Want You" delivered passionate poetry to one of his ex-babysitters. But this was not a dewy-eyed appeal, his first words of seduction being, "Yo baby, wanna come to my crib—have some doughnuts and milk?"

On his second album, *Bigger and Deffer* (*BAD*, y'all), L.L. took the concept of rap ballads to another level—he elevated them to schlock status. After informing us that he is "badder than Napoleon, Hitler or Ceasar" ("The Breakthrough"), L.L. glides into another one of his sensitive moments: "Romance, sheer delight ... how sweet/I gotta find me a girl to make my life complete," he says in a honey-voiced whisper that is supposed to pass for sincerity. "I Need Love" became L.L.'s breakthrough single, the track that made him less of a B-boy idol and more of an ultra-homeboy sex symbol. Although this track almost set hip hop back two hundred years (perhaps a slight exaggeration, but who cares?), "I Need Love" seemed to pave the way for other street heroes to record their own dodgy soul ballads (i.e., Big Daddy Kane) in the hopes of crossing over and becoming pinup kings to the teeny-boppers who enjoy taking baths in honey-filled tubs.

Thankfully, "I Need Love" is the only ballad on this album, though its not the only "bad" song. With "The Do Wop," L.L. displayed his ambition to spread the wings of hip hop by appropriating a genre of Black music that faded away sometime during the late '50s/early '60s (it could be argued that doo-wop is hip hop's distant cuz). While L.L. raps ("Woke up at nine-thirty on a Saturday morn, hit my remote control, turned my stereo on/Then I reached for a brush, since I don't use a pick/And the floor was kinda cold so I put on my kicks ...") the Moonglows—perhaps—are smooth, street-corner doo-woppin' in the background. As Al Pacino screamed in *And Justice for All*, "In theory it's great, in practice it sucks!"

On much of *Bigger and Deffer*, L.L. spends his time stroking his ego ("I'm the baddest, taking out all rookies/So forget Oreos eat Cool J cookies," he says on the title track) more than most folks stroke *anything*; but rarely has anyone so arrogant been so cool. Still, I like when a rapper steps outside of himself to share a glimpse of his surroundings, which L.L. does masterfully on "The Bristol Hotel." One night, after midnight, homegirl Michelle V. was driving me to the train station when we passed this decaying brick building that seemed to attract short-skirted hookers and dime-store pimps like moths under a nightlight. As I gawked from the window, I asked Shelly the name of this joint on 89th Avenue and 161st Street. "It's the Bristol," she replied coldly. And so, when I heard L.L. Cool J's raw track of the same name—a pounding drum and his voice are the instruments heard—I was amazed. The images that he conjures ("I seen her standing there, slutty as can be/Offering the pudie for a itty-bitty fee") were so realistic, one can almost hear the voices of these nocturnal creatures. "The Bristol Hotel" goes on to relate an amusing story of one customer discovering his wife working this fleabag brothel, then L.L. cold flips in the middle of the song, bringing the subject of prostitution to a deadly reality when he tells about a dude who caught AIDS.

Round Three: In interviews and on records, L.L. Cool J often compares himself to popular sports figures, droppin' names like Michael Jordan and Bo Jackson as human metaphors to explain his own swiftness on the mic'; but it is the name of Mike Tyson that L.L. uses more than any other to express his methods of ruthless aggression (the concept of being the boldest and the best) in the studio. As L.L. once explained to an interviewer, "The thing that the best rappers and the best boxers have in common is not their color or whatever. It's poverty. They're all broke, and there's no money. So, everybody's hungry. I mean you wanna be the best!"

In the universe of L.L. Cool J it often seems that the only subject that matters is ... well, L.L. Cool J. The paradox of this is the fact that no matter how loud he boasted, not many folks were listening. After breaking through to Middle America with "I Need Love," masses of urban (i.e., Black) posses turned their backs on the brother. Although *Walking With a Panther* is a much better album than *Bigger and Deffer* (whose L.A. Posse production sytle couldn't compare with their East Coast counterparts), this album would prove to be L.L. Cool J's knockout punch. As his homeboy Iron Mike proved when he stepped into the ring with Buster Douglas, even the best fighters can be knocked down.

Back in 1989, while most of the hip-hop nation had (in both sound and image) gone back to Africa or joined the Black Panther Party, L.L. was posing on his album cover with three *Jet* centerfold girls, chilled bottles of Moet, a portable phone and a *stoopid* gold cable ("thick enough to tow cars or beat elephants") hanging from the neck of a very real panther. In the minds of the "real" Black brothers and sisters, this was a portrait of a materialistic homeboy gone mad; and yet it would be a mistake to just dismiss L.L. as a plastic sucker without a social conscience. One of the most brilliant tracks—which, perhaps, was inspired by MC Lyte's "Not Wit' a Dealer"—is a small gem entitled "Fast Peg." Coming off like an aural Iceberg Slim, L.L. details the life of some Harlem freaky-deke ("Dressed to kill, her physique is ill/Her face belongs on a dollar bill/Her boyfriends down wit the m-o-b ..."); within seconds we are transformed to the world of Peg, where the money comes quick, champagne flows like water, and the rocks on her fingers sparkle beneath the Harlem moonlight. After her man beats her down, then jets to make another drug deal, Peg gets together with her flye-girl crew—making the scene like magazine queens, driving in a kitted-up Jetta. But everything ends abruptly when her man messes up the money and Peg has to take a fall. In a voice that's cold as a New York January, L.L. says, "They shot her in the head . . . that's the breaks."

And yet, one should not expect that L.L. has left behind his two favorite styles: boasting about the power of self and those damn hip-hop ballads. In fact, on *Walking With a Panther,* the brother finds the need to pour three pitchers of honey down our throats: "You're My Heart," "One Shot at Love" and "Two Different Worlds." The last two should have gasoline poured on them (while Luther Vandross lights the match); "You're My Heart" deserves better. From the spooky Princely electric synths in the intro to L.L.'s corny lyrics ("How could you hurt me, how could you treat me like ya never loved me/Were ya playin' a game?"), this track is as addictive as aural crack. The only question flowing through my mind is, Whose girl is L.L. talking about, his own or some other brother's? On "I'm that Type of Guy," L.L. point-blank says, "I'm the type of guy who comes when you leave/I'm doin' your girlfriend/That's something ya can't believe." After some brother gives honey spendin' money, she then bites L.L.'s "chunk," buys him a sweater, and the lil' bastard has the nerve to leave his drawers in my man's hamper. No wonder homeboys on the block wanted to see his body hanging from the nearest streetlight: *"Homie don't play that!"*

In an attempt to get back on the side of *right* (those fellas holding the noose, screaming, "Let's kill da punk!"), L.L. parks his Jeep on the corner, passes out forty-dogs of Olde English, and tells a story about the girls "wit' the bodies that were built to swing." While the brothers are gulpin' down their cold brews, Cool J. raps "Big Ole Butt," a tale bros can all relate to. From Tina ("wit da kinda legs that put stockings outta bizness") to

Brenda to Lisa, our main man L. was taking no shorts as he played the role of giga-ho supreme. With tracks like this one and "1-900-L.L. Cool J," this brother just cancelled out all that yang he be poppin' on those ballads.

1990, another summer: After standing on soggy ground in 1989, his respect level in New York so low he was booed *while* accepting a music award named for that town, L.L. Cool J decided to take off his bedroom slippers (molded so comfortably onto his feet yet still causing him to stumble) and put on a pair of Timberland boots. He, in fact, made over his entire look, replacing his Kangol with a Genie, his gold ropes with an African medallion, and his moody (some would say shitty) personality with an infinitely more ingratiating one; he immediately went out on an expedition in search of a new pop life. Unlike in the past, he didn't dip into the Left Coast's musical jukebox or rely totally on his own talents. Instead he hooked up with Queens Juice man Marley Marl, famous for his lean, funky precision. After talking with L.L. over at his weekend employer, WBLS, Marley told the artist, "Yo! If you ever need a re-mix done, give me a ring."

Remembering those parting words, when Def Jam needed "Jingling Baby" rethought, L.L. & Company suggested . . . you guessed it. After a spin by the man who L.L. later dubbed the Flipmaster, the tune emerged scratchy and ragged. That was good because it suggested things like litter and dust, poverty and urban decay; it pointed L.L. toward the streets, the birthplace of hip hop, which he had somehow started to dis. With its swirling, groovy screech, which sported party chatter deep in the mix, this track became a hit on the lips of urban guerillas everywhere. Around New York City, fellas on the prowl could be heard tossing the line "They jinglin' baby" to curvy cuties strutting sexily down the street. While the rap was supposedly talking about ear gear ("Lemme see your earrings jingle!" L.L.

directs), the hook ended up reaching out to breasts, butts and thighs as well.

From the static of "Jingling Baby (re-mixed but still jingling)," Marley and L.L. collaborated on "To Da Break of Dawn," a tyrannical dis (directed toward Ice-T and M.C. Hammer and Kool Moe Dee) riding atop a pounding, galloping beat paired with a clipped (and looped) blues-sax passage. "I'm like a shark with blood comin' out the gills," the rapper declares. Later he adds, "On your trail and I'ma cut that ponytail/You're disobedin' with the wrong ingredients." Leave it at that, since it would be ill-advised to indulge in "unhealthy" music-biz hearsay in this forum.

Anyhow, it's a fact that that jam led to Marley Marl supervising all of L.L.'s fourth album, *Mama Said Knock You Out*. With clenched fists and curled lip, sweaty chest and bristling biceps, L.L. looks ready for action on the set's cover. Its title suggests the attitude of a wounded child who wimped out running back to a bully ready to kick ass. Because the first words he roars from the title track are "Don't call this a comeback/I've been here for years!" it's fair to assume that the brother's punch drunk. But he catches his composure on the rest of this fourteen-song set, going down only once in a thoughtful but thoughtless show of friendship. "Farmers Blvd. (Our Anthem)" features running buddies from back in the day who have nothing really interesting to say. L. should have left them on the pavement and out of the studio.

Everything flows smoothly on *Mama Said Knock You Out*, L.L. easily moving from being hungry (his metaphor for horniness, best displayed on the playful "Milky Cereal," where he encounters lusty flye girls with names like Frosted Flakes and Lucky Charms) to being fully satisfied ("The Power of God" runs all through him). Its tunes skip and glide, and on a few of them, namely "Illegal Search" and "Around the Way Girl," backup vocalists kick in at the choruses. The latter, previously released tune was an underground dance hit that explores one particular incident of police overzealousness, a problem that plagues America's inner cities. The former, a springy, aerodynamic shuffler, is a respectful gesture to brown-skinned, glossily lipped hotties from the neighborhood, with extensions in their hair, bamboo earrings on their ears, a Fendi bag on their shoulders, and "a bad attitude" throughout.

"The Boomin' System," meanwhile, is directed at "the brothers that like to front in their rides." Opening with a bugged, blaxploitative drawl commanding the rapper to "kick a little som'n for them cars that be bumpin!" the tune slides into the milky bass line from En Vogue's riveting "Hold On," which displays frisky bits of two rare grooves: James Brown's "Funky Drummer" and "The Payback." Like "I Can't Live Without My Radio" years ago, this is another perfect soundtrack for ghetto spirit and teenage defiance. By coming full circle, L.L. once again became a mic' champion.

MAIN SOURCE

BREAKING ATOMS (WILD PITCH), 1991

I t's a little past 7 p.m. at Set to Run. The New York PR firm wants to wrap a long press day with Main Source, but the crew's bespectacled rhyme scientist, Large Professor, is still lecturing one-on-one from a conference room overlooking Lexington Avenue.

"All that bullshit they're putting out now ... that shit is corny," he's complaining. "A lot of people don't know what real rap is."

Now eighteen, Large Professor has been a fan of hip hop "since when Bambaataa used to throw jams." He started rapping after hearing seminal B-boys the Cold Crush Brothers and Kool Moe Dee kick it. And, from being a protegé of the late producer Paul C. (Ultramagnetic MCs, Stezo, Super Love Cee and Cassanova Rud), he earned a funky-dope staff that leads him through paths of righteous rhythms, *amen*. In other words, the soundscapes Large Professor creates for such acts as Kool G. Rap & Polo, Eric B & Rakim and (with twin DJs, K-Cut and Sir Scratch, who complete Main Source) his own group eschews new-jack swing, hip house and other distictly modernist stylisms.

Explaining the concept behind *Breaking Atoms*, Large Professor says, "We consider the rest of the rap industry an atom. What we're trying to do is break up all the atoms and not sound like anyone else." Main Source's determinedly sure and unflinching focus has produced one of the purest, most blissful hip-hop albums of recent times. Created by pairing "joints that haven't been sampled yet" with recorded breaks and live instrumentation, this be the real deal, y'all—raw, lyrically acute B-boy music to make ya shout "Yowsah!"

"I rap about everyday things," Large Professor offers. Whether discussng slimy schemers ("Snake Eyes"), boyz in the 'hood ("Just Hangin' Out"), playin'-high-post honeys ("Lookin' at the Front Door"), police brutality ("Just a Friendly Game of Baseball") ... whatever, his creamy tone boomerangs around dense walls of sound, swiftly spinning insinuating wordz of wizdom around and down from the underground. Even though "Looking at the Front Door" (wherein a loverbro jets to escape some sister who serves him "like a burnt piece of bacon") was a number 1 rap and radio hit. Large Professor's fave cut on *Breaking Atoms* is "Peace Is Not the Word to Play." Here he laments what the P-word has come to represent in homeslice slanguage: "Yo, I'm gone!"

MARLEY
MARL

IN CONTROL, VOLUME ONE (COLD CHILLIN'/
WARNER BROS.), 1988

Though pioneering rap tracks on Sugar Hill ("Rapper's
Delight," "The Message") replaced the breakbeat with
a band and the DJ with a producer, hip hop from its
inception has always relied more on feel than on learned musical skill. Whether a spinner in the park or an MC at a ballroom,
a B-boy didn't need traditional instruments to create a def jam;
all that was required was a strong knowledge of funk elements
and an ear keyed to poetic street-corner slang. And since Run-
D.M.C.'s "Sucker MCs" in 1983, rap performers have been
involved in the making of their own albums. As technology has
become more pervasive, everybody with a Technics turntable and
an Akai sampler, a golden voice and a steel microphone, has
been cutting tracks, shifting the power base of the music away
from musicians and toward sonic historians with show-biz
ambitions.

From this crowd a number of freelance, behind-the-scenes
groove specialists have emerged, with instincts far more advanced than those of their peers. DIY (do it yourself) imcompetence
has been responsible for some of hip hop's best recorded
moments, but its most significant innovations have come through
the masterworks of highly skilled producers such as Hurby Luv
Bug, Hank Shocklee, Curtis Mantronik and Rick Rubin. No one
has done as much as Queens native Marley Marl, though. That's
because no one has been around, behind the controls and on the
cutting edge, as long as he has.

Like a new-generation Quincy Jones, Marley (real name: Marlon Williams, age: twenty-eight) got a lift out of ghetto bleakness and into a shining musical utopia, parlaying early triumphs into a long career (an amazing feat in the ever-changing artist-dominated world of hip hop). Just like Q, Marley started out as a performer, became a record producer and now flitters between mediums (music, TV or radio and film).

From DJing in parks and clubs at fifteen, Marl started doing four-track productions in a corner in his mom's living room. Next, he began landing re-mixing gigs, the Aleems' break-through "Release Yourself" on indie Nia (Eric B. & Rakim's first label) being among the first. Around the same time, WBLS (New York) radio-jock Mister Magic pegged Marley as his "Rap Attack" spinner. Then, when Magic faded into obscurity, the new-jack became host (until early '91) of his own weekend hip-hop party. Besides jamming hot tracks in seamless overlays on twin turntables, Marley began working with a rotating stable of cut creators (Clark Kent, Funkmaster Flex, Pete Rock) and eventually founded his new state-of-the-art (digital, twenty-four-track) House of Hits in upstate New York. There he has never stopped fashioning seminal minimalist jams for Roxanne Shanté ("Have a Nice Day"), Biz Markie ("Pickin' Boogers") M.C. Shan ("The Bridge"), Eric B. & Rakim ("Eric B. Is President"/"My Melody"), Big Daddy Kane ("Ain't No Half-Steppin' "), L.L. Cool J ("The Boomin' System") and others, including R&B luminaries Chaka Khan and the Force MDs.

Walking down 125th Street in Harlem, one sees the visual equivalent of Marley's soundscapes. His textures are as rough and Black as this wide, asphalt boulevard traveled by international tourists, Afrocentric poets and criminal-minded gangstas, and as dirty as the many abandoned lots one encounters along the street. On many of Marley's tracks, the rappers sound like they're screaming through tin cans and not electronic transducers; static-y samples sound like they were picked up by antique gramophones, not S-shaped tonearms balanced by expensive moving-magnet cartridges connected to solid-state flying faders.

In 1988, working with Juice (the legendary unit featuring urban quasars Big Daddy Kane and Biz Markie) Marley Marl created *In Control, Volume One,* a collection featuring other performers but driven by Marl the same way Q's *Back on the Block* and *The Dude* were. Alongside guest shots by a parade of old friends (Kane, Biz, Shanté, Heavy D.), Marley introduces us to a few more of his buddies, the most memorable being Action and Master Ace, who performs three of the LP's eleven songs. "Keep Your Eye on the Prize," a swirling, fast-paced rhyme, sounds as if it was tapped into Jazzie B.'s D.A.I.S.Y.-age dream of everyone elevating their mind, freeing their soul and being an asset to the collective: "We have finally arrived and the dream has survived/But many died trying and they're the ones who paved the way/Real-life super men and women saved the day."

And so to "Freedom," a lalopping cut by M.C. Shan that recasts Grandmaster Flash and the Furious Five's glorious old-school tune of the same name. As this rootsy steal attests, nothing on *In Control* breaks much new ground; there isn't a "Raw" or a "Pickin' Boogers" in the bunch, but the set still displays a fine mixture of deep, muscular rhythms. Nothing here became a street-corner soundtrack on the order of Marley classics such as "Ain't No Half Steppin'" or "Around the Way Girl," but the let's-tip-the-scale-and-bubble pairing of Biz Markie and Heavy D. on "We Write the Songs" and the somersaulting moves performed by Kane on the chorus-line jam "The Symphony" cannot be ignored.

Though this may not have been the blueprint for a new hip-hop decade, it's far from a disappointment. In control? Yo, Marley wasn't dubbed the Flipmaster by comeback anomaly L.L. Cool J for nothing!

See also Big Daddy Kane, Biz Markie, Eric B. & Rakim, Intelligent Hoodlum, and L.L. Cool J.

M.C.
HAMMER

LET'S GET IT STARTED (CAPITOL), 1988

PLEASE HAMMER DON'T HURT 'EM, 1990

At the height of their popularity, the Beatles gave a press conference during which John Lennon (the self-proclaimed rebel of the mop-tops) deadpanned that the group was "more popular than Jesus Christ." America went crazy; headlines screamed that these Brit lads were the anti-Christ; large bonfires were erected so folks could toss their Fab Four discs into towering flames.

In 1990, a lone gent from Oakland (the Cali stomping grounds that gave us acid-soulster Sly Stone and purple poptart Sheila E.) bum-rushed the pop charts with his rap-by-numbers album *Please Hammer Don't Hurt 'Em,* making him not only America's newest rap sensation, but also the latest Black artist to slip smoothly into the country's consciousness. After Arsenio Hall's bark and Michael Jackson's plastic face, the baggy genie pants and flashy (high-stepping, stomp-happy) dancing of M.C. Hammer became another icon for the MTV generation. M.C. Hammer is everything that America desires in its pop heros: style without substance, sparkle without fire. Like the manager in a restaurant once said, "No one cares if it tastes good, as long as it looks good."

After entering a crowded elevator one afternoon last July, I heard a middle-aged woman standing behind me humming the chorus to the album's biggest single, "U Can't Touch This" (which ruthlessly rips Rick James's punk-funk classic "Super Freak"). When I turned to get a good look at her, she smiled and said, "Sorry, but that's my favorite song." Like hip-hop Muzak, this track is perfect elevator drone.

With that one single, M.C. Hammer did what very few rappers have ever accomplished—he made hip hop acceptable to the Geritol crowd. And though—with his strong religious beliefs—Hammer would never make a comment as raw as Lennon's, in 1990 this "Dancing Machine" (a mid-'70s Motown hit by the Jackson Five that Hammer also hijacked) was close to being as popular as Jesus. As *Spin* scribe Bonz Malone told me one afternoon while we polished off a 40-ounce of Colt 45, "Hammer can't rap to save his life, and his productions are messy as hell, but ya gotta respect the brother." Naw, he ain't no Rakim on da mic' and he sure nuff ain't no Bomb Squad in the studio, but for some reason we all humming his shit.

To paraphrase Andy Warhol, if hip-hop artists are the newest movie stars, then Hammer is the biggest star of 'em all.

Rewind that Back: Before "U Can't Touch This" became the perfect slogan for a paranoid decade, Hammer was just another Cali boy trying to convince the jaded New York press corps that his style of rap would be The Next Big Thang. Although his first video, "Turn This Mutha Out," was in regular rotation on the local rap show "Video Music Box" (Channel 31), Hammer still wasn't a household name. But, whereas other hip-hoppers have dreams, Hammer had a plan. Whereas other rappers can be difficult when it comes to the interview game, having writers wait for hours to be overwhelmed with their mere B(ad)-boy selves ("Let's try to beep him again," the press agent says), Hammer strolled into the New York offices of Capitol Records on time, ready to talk. Considering that he had spent that warm spring day taping a segment for "Yo! MTV Raps," one would think that Hammer would be a bit on the tired side, but this was not so. After showing the surreal video of his hip-hop tart protegés Oaktown 3.5.7 (da girlies clad in biking shorts as they dance through Wonderland or something), Hammer trooped into the conference room and began to talk at 150 w.p.m. "Yo, I rap about anything—anything that comes to mind." He then proved his point by creating a rap jingle about the Mountain Dew soda pop he was gulping.

"Being from Cali, it's surprising that your album doesn't have any tracks about shootouts or gang wars."

"Yo!" screams Hammer. "All them dudes like N.W.A. and Ice-T are friends of mine, but they can't tell me about the gangster world, 'cause I know all about that." He pauses for a minute, takes a sip of soda. "Most of them ain't never shot a gun on the Fourth of July or New Year's Eve and they perpetrating. Hell, they ain't never shot nothing, won't kill nothing and won't let nothing die." Dig that: Ice Cube and Too Short might be into Murder Rap, but Hammer is down with Life Rap. We both erupt with laughter.

"But what is it you really want to do with your music?" I ask.

Leaning back in the chair to collect his thoughts for a moment, playing with the frames of his Star Trek shades, Hammer loses his playful tone as he answers. "I want Oakland to be the next Motown." Gordyism meets Hammer time, I think now; *hell, u can't touch that!*

Happen on M.C. Hammer's *Let's Get It Started* and one will realize that everything you've heard from the hip-hop purists about Hammer's lack of creativity is not exactly true. All right, so da brother can't rap, but soundwise his first album has a guiding spirit whose ear is closer to the rhythm nation of hip hop than one might expect. Instead of recycling entire songs from other artists and calling them his own, Hammer has layered *Let's Get It Started* with inventive samples and live instrumentation that borrow from a slew of sources, from P-Funk's "Turn This Mutha Out," which Hammer uses for the high-energy title track, to B.B. King's "The Thrill Is Gone," which is recontextualized for rap's first gospel jaunt, "Son of a

King." Beginning with a small choir of falsetto tenors wailing like Black angels, this track features interesting keyboard noodling and cowbell samples.

"I'm standing proud/Hyping the crowd, running my style/I'm drivin' em wild," Hammer says on the melodically constructed "Pump It Up (Here's the News)." Not that anyone would ever mistake Hammer's music for the second coming of the Mothership, but this song does offer a few glimpses into its author's funk roots (but then, the album *was* co-produced by former Con Funk Shun member Felton Pilate). Something about this track reminds one of late '70's/early '80s groups—from the spacey sounds emerging from the keyboard to the disco chanting of "OhOhOhOhOh! OhOhOhOhOh!." Sounds like my man is caught in a time warp, but so what? It's the best cut on *Let's Get It Started*.

Part II of the Hammer saga began with him and his thirty-plus posse recording his second album in the rear of their custom tour bus. It must have been one hell of a year for this former Oakland A's batboy, who went from hawking his first independent single from the trunk of his car to being on the road with Heavy D. & the Boyz, N.W.A., Kool Moe Dee and others. The resulting *Please Hammer Don't Hurt 'Em* went on to sell over five million copies, beating out the Beastie Boys' *Licensed to Ill* as the biggest-selling hip-hop album ever sold—almost make a nigga wanna hum the *Rocky II* theme "Eye of the Tiger."

"Today's avant-garde is tomorrow's ready-to-wear," Glenn O'Brien once wrote. And perhaps that's the best way to describe the majority of Hammer's material: he be wearing other people's songs to death. It's almost impossible to write a proper critique of "Hammer's music," because, like a sonic chameleon, Hammer rarely displays his true colors. With his weakness for Motown and Minneapolis funk, my man be wearing Rick James, the Jackson Five, Marvin Gaye's "Makes Me Wanna Holler"

("Help the Children"), Prince's "When Doves Cry" ("Pray") and the Chi-Lites "Have You Seen Her" (surprise—Hammer used the same title!).

At this point, I can't help but think of pop artist Jeff Koons; if he were to present a second "Banality" show, it would feature a gold, porcelain boombox, and roaring from the Dolby surround speakers hanging throughout a gallery would be tracks from *Please Hammer Don't Hurt 'Em* (playing on a continuous loop). The entire gallery would be appalled, but everyone would leave humming the shit.

MC LYTE

LYTE AS A ROCK (FIRST PRIORITY
MUSIC/ATLANTIC), 1988

EYES ON THIS, 1989

With a blend of rawness and inventiveness, seventeen-year-old MC Lyte crashed into hip hop's air space in 1988 with the brilliant narrative "I Cram to Understand U (Sam)." Riding a fluid, bare-bones beat, her husky roar delivered the tale of a failed romance with a drugged-out bum, and caught the attention of fans and critics alike.

Produced by Audio Two (Lyte's brothers Milk Dee and Gizmo), "I Cram to Understand U" begins like just another venomous B-girl dis ("I used to be in love with this guy named Sam/I don't know why 'cause he had a head like that of a clam"). But quickly Lyte starts setting her entry in the rap race apart from the pack, weaving in colorful details of her relationship with Sam. She was introduced to him by his brother, Jerry, at Brooklyn's Empire Skating Rink. They made small talk for a few, then Sam said he wanted to do her. After telling him to chill, she became friends with him. The next day she busts him with another woman and snarls. "Who's the frog, the bump on a log?/You chump, You punk—how could you do me wrong?" Blissfulness resumes, but a month later Sam's fooling around again. A cousin tells Lyte that the name of *this* other female "starts with a 'c' and ends with a 'k.'" He's addicted to crack, and when Lyte finds this out, she decides to leave Sam.

This tune's fat beats were a pumped-up metaphor for a fat career. Its lyrical complexity displayed potential that simply *had* to be fulfilled.

In its wake, Lyte's first album, *Lyte as a Rock*, is a confrontational, spotty affair—it has its moments, but as a whole the parts don't add up. Her bass-heavy tone defines her not as a sexual object but a woman of strength. Her voice is an instrument of assault, not a magnet for male desires or fantasies. She views the promises of boys on the make as "just paper thin," and in the wonderfully cascading title track (re-mixed into one of the 1989's most hypnotic hip-house releases for twelve-inch), the rapper's lines ("Get out my face, I don't wanna hear no more/If you hate rejection don't try to score," for example) roll over young-blood Romeos like a boulder. In the springy "Kickin' 4 Brooklyn," they write off, then step on, opposing MCs: "If you think you're the one that could deal with this/Best prepare for a big, fat dis!"

The most power-packed dis on *Lyte as a Rock* is "10% Dis," wherein Lyte calls some unidentified B-girl a "hoe," a "nerve plucker" and a "rhyme faker." The former Lana Moorer wants to nuke this chick, chew her up, then spit her out. Why? And who exactly is she directing her remarks toward, anyway? Turned out to be another female rapper, Antoinette. Lyte had heard from informants that Antoinette was about to attack her in her own LP, and when Antoinette ended up devoting almost an entire LP side to verbal-blitzing Lyte, a war was definitely on. The ball was now in Lyte's court, but she called time out to tour—in January 1990, she became the first rapper to headline Carnegie Hall—and to lend her talents to two twelve-inches by others: Sinéad O'Connor's dance re-mix of "I Want Your Hands on Me" and the all-star Stop the Violence Movement's statement against Black-on-Black crime, "Self Destruction." But with the release of Lyte's second, *Eyes on This*, the fighting resumed.

Bolstered by producers Marley Marl, Parrish Smith (the P in EPMD), Grand Puba Maxwell (from Masters of Ceromony), Audio Two and King of Chill, this album is more even and more

MC Lyte at the Apollo. © Tina Paul, 1989.

———

fully realized than *Lyte as a Rock*. Though it's cleaner-sounding, it makes very few concessions to modernist stylisms. Lyte's still ego-boosting over hardcore breaks, still employing putdowns, keeping rap's exciting tradition of competitiveness alive. The cleverness and blunt bite of her attacks are extraordinary. As Roxanne Shanté mellows, Lyte is turning into rap's roughest female.

With her DJ K Rock at her side, she throws threats ("Don't turn your back 'cause this mike will be in yo' ass!") and practices intimidation ("How many times I got to warn you about the Lyte?/It'll blind your sight"). But things on *Eyes on This* get even more vicious, and halfway through the LP, Millie Jackson steps in to guide Lyte into the *really* tough stuff. "Yep, it's definitely time I get nasty," Mildred suggests. "Go'n be some shit," informs another sample. Then the brash, unrelenting "Shut The Eff Up (Hoe)" swings through, carrying linguistic bullets that should be the last shots fired in the Lyte/Antoinette feud. Lyte attacks Antoinette's talent, morality and looks in no-holds-barred terms. Then, to finish her off, she calls the self-titled gangstress of rap a "ghetto slut." Rough.

But Lyte also tackles social issues with *Eyes on This*. In the chuggy "Cappuchino," a fictional anti-drug narrative, she gets killed, caught in the middle of a deal. She returns to reality to tell "those who don't know" about addiction. "Not Wit a Dealer" is another death-from-drugs story, while "Please Understand" is counsel to adolescent girls on how not to be pushovers with guys. But with Lyte as an example, it's doubtful these 'ronis will tolerate poop from overbearing fellas—or anybody else for that matter.

MONIE LOVE

DOWN TO EARTH (WARNER BROS.), 1990

England has its share of hip-hop artists, but very few have crossed over to the youth of America. English rappers always seemed to be biting the style of their American counterparts: Chuck D., for example, influencing Overlord X.; Salt-n-Pepa influencing the Wee Papa Girls. As Brit crit Frank Owen said after listening to a Derek B. single, "English rappers should talk about something they know about—like the rain."

And though she isn't rapping about gray drizzle, the fog or the Queen, Monie Love is the first rapper to drift to the USA on the rhythm raft that sailed Soul II Soul and the Fine Young Cannibals to the strobe light of American dance culture.

After starting out in her native London rhyming in underground clubs with Mell 'O' and DJ Pogo, Monie eventually made her way into a recording studio and taped her first single, "I Can Do This," which reached only number 37 on the U.K. dance charts. It was her second single, "Grandpa's Party," that made her a cult sensation in London. Sampling the electro-funk of "Planet Rock," Monie composed this soulful rave as a tribute to Afrika Bambaataa; complete with the noise of tribal cheers and a bass-heavy Soul II Soul re-mix, this jam grooved the dancers in U.K. clubs. But if you'd asked some kid chillin' on a Harlem street corner with his boom box and Public Enemy T-shirt about "Grandpa's Party," his reply would have been, "Monie who?"

Enter Afrocentric rappers the Jungle Brothers: Monie was introduced to the crew in 1988. After one meeting she became their European road manager. The JB's are down with the "now school" of American hip-hop artists, which includes De La Soul and Queen Latifah, but they also have their roots planted in the Zulu Nation posse, which includes Grandpa Bambaataa and Uncle Red Alert. With her eyes on the hip-hop prize, and now knowing a few folks on this side of the Atlantic, Monie Love soon boarded that SST for New Jack City.

In New York the competition can be rough for a new artist. Most of the underground clubs are closed because of pistol-shooting knuckleheads. Luckily, Monie was taken under the watchful eye of popular DJ Red Alert and his informal collective known as the Native Tongues. When De La Soul asked the then-nineteen-year-old rapper to contribute vocals to the re-mix of their phallic fairytale, "Buddy," Monie had her first taste of success in the American marketplace. Her youthful face (chile don't even wear no makeup!) also appeared in the group's video.

That same year, 1989, Monie was recruited by MaMa Zulu (a.k.a. Queen Latifah) to collaborate on hip hop's first womanist anthem, the ground-breaking "Ladies First." As a celebration of femalehood, "Ladies First" featured Monie and Latifah exchanging rhymes of female solidarity—a unique idea for the hip-hop nation. The third single released from Latifah's album, this duet crashed Monie's slightly accented voice through America's anti-British hip-hop casbah. A third aural cameo from Monie can be heard on a track from the Jungle Brothers' second album called "Doin' Our Own Deng."

After a year of rapping on other folks' sessions and touring the States with Big Daddy Kane and Queen Latifah, Monie released an uneven debut album, *Down to Earth*. With four tracks produced by pop/dance seducers Andy Cox and David Steele (from Fine Young Cannibals), and eight tracks produced by the jungle man in da machine Afrika "Baby" Bambaataa (from the Jungle Brothers), one might expect a contemporary, cross-cultural fusion of Brit/New York politics and dance aesthetic. But as Flavor Flav might scream, "Don't believe the hype!"

With her accent gone, Monie sounds like any other loud-talkin' Brooklyn B-girl. On "Monie in the Middle," the album's first single, she tells her high-school sweetie that she's tired of him and is yearning for the love of his homeboy. "I ain't Keith Sweat/So don't sweat me," she says disgustedly. With a funky trumpet solo included in the mix, the music is kickin', but Monie's lyrics are like teenage scribble in a worn diary.

Although Cox and Steele are educated enough to create catchy Top Forty pop for their own group, they don't understand the complexity of hip hop; to speak the language of rap requires more than a few lazy beats and a smooth voice. As George Clinton said, "If you can't feel da funk, don't do da funk."

But to her credit, Monie knows when it's time to stop playing games and just throw down ... *on the one!* With Baby Bam directing the sessions, "Don't Funk Wid the Mo" recreates a Roger Troutman keyboard riff as Mo recalls her dealings with a dishonest producer trying to steal her material. Her voice slams as hard as the groove supporting it.

Afrika often throws in esoteric jazz beats that might fly over the heads of some B-boys, yet these breaks add tension and excitement to the music. Like on "I Don't Give a Damn," when Monie says farewell to her abusive boyfriend ("Remain a punch bag for you/Exactly what would I gain?"), Afrika mixes in "They Don't Know" (from Hendrix's Band of Gypsies project) and an acoustic piano that glides the song toward its climax. Other tracks that benefit from the jungle music of Baby Bam are the anti-pork ode "Swiney Swiney" and "Pups Lickin' Bones" (ya figure that out of yourself), where Monie warns all them trashy ho's to stay away from her man.

With its mundane spots, *Down to Earth* may not be the London/New York bridge that Monie Love envisioned when she went into the studio, but it is a all-right way to kick off hip hop's second decade ... *on the one!*

MS. MELODIE

DIVA (JIVE), 1989

Afrocentric singer/rapper Harmony proclaimed at a recent panel discussion of rap issues, "True social change cannot take place without a female touch." One of the females whose touch is making a difference is Harmony's sister, Brooklyn native Ramona Parker, or Ms. Melodie, who arrived on the music scene in 1989 intent on developing a more liberated role for females in the hip-hop nation. Already Queen Latifah was going for hers in this male-dominated world of video ho's and fantasy B-gals. While Latifah was dubbing herself microphone commando and Queen of Royal Badness, Ms. Melodie, draped in elegant (glittery) evening wear, was calling herself *Diva*, the title of her debut offering. She didn't spew rhetoric like her husband, Blastmaster KRS-One of Boogie Down Productions, yet she conveyed a charged message nonetheless. And she didn't dish out commands like Latifah ("I order you to dance for me!"), yet there was no question she was in control of her own proceedings.

"In an opera sense, diva means a very strong, assertive personality," Ms. Melodie told Great Britain's *Face*. "When people see me, they know that I am direct and strong." With tough beats, muscular tone, regal presence, and phrases like "Wiggle your hands from your head to your butt/No, not like that—like a slut," Ms. Melodie was defining womanist respectability. Instead of tearing down the manhood of misogynists with cusswords and verbal castration (Roxanne Shanté's sometimes unattractive technique), she simply offered a classy alternative for them to ponder. "I just want everybody to know that I'm a woman in my own right and in my own mind," she says.

Ms. Melodie wrote all of the lyrics on *Diva*, but she collaborated with producers Sam Sever, the Awesome Two and KRS-One to create a hip-hop album that's tuneful but not diluted. Firmly in the tradition of BDP, this is a lean and tough effort with some R&B sensibilities woven through it.

Melodie contributes credible singing to the cuts "What Do You Do?" and "Roll on Over" that could place her in the pantheon of big and beautiful divas. But because KRS-One's minimalist production throws so little into the multichannel mixing pot, these Melodie songs lack the "overpowering grandeur of emotion" that Leland alluded to. Bits of ear candy and some haunting chords could have made an I-will-survive jam like "Roll on Over" (the cut borrows bits from France Joli's disco hit "Gonna Get Over You") more revealing and dramatic.

But while the bare-bones approach doesn't fit there, it works marvelously on the two-step reggae track "B .. B .. B .. Bklyn," the best cut on *Diva*. As a thick groove slinks across the track, pounding drums and frisky dub elements sneak around like a sly fox. Melodie pays homage to her birth borough and turf, threatening to pull triggers on knucklehead outsiders. Armed with an arsenal of verbal ammunition, she offers, "Lyrics like these cannot cause wars." Then she dedicates an entire track to "Communication."

In "More," the one track on *Diva* that she produced herself, Melodie declares, "This is my life, my mind, my track and my rhyme." She voices the womanist desire for "a spot in the shade that's all mine." But she also craves companionship from brothers who can work it out. Aware that the Black man in America is constantly at war, she specifically calls out those who are missing in action: "We need your strength beside us to fight on/'Cause as a unit we can do it/There's really nothin' to it/And years from now I don't want to have to say we blew it."

JOE "THE BUTCHER" NICOLO

SEE CASH MONEY & MARVELOUS, DJ JAZZY JEFF & THE FRESH PRINCE, 7A3

N. W. A.

STRAIGHT OUTTA COMPTON (RUTHLESS), 1988

While walking through the streets of Harlem in the early '70s I would notice the hustlers gathered on the block. With their shiny Cadillacs and gaudy clothing, these characters laughed and screamed at each other and flirted with the ebony foxes that tap-tapped down in high heels and fur coats. They made rolls of cash selling drugs and fem Black bootie, but like notorious kingpin Nicky Barnes, they were at the same time investing some of the earnings back into the neighborhood. They were quite popular, and it seems only aging church ladies on their way to the holy land Sunday mornings avoided them.

There was method to their madness, a rhythm to their jive chatter. But in the eyes of some youth—the ones who had witnessed the gradual decay of their blocks—these cats were rebels with only one cause: to get paid and paid and paid. But, guided by materialism, the spiritual sons of the old school hustlers were younger and more ruthless than their middle-aged patriarchs. The reason America's ghettos became war zones reeking of cocaine fumes and dead bodies in the mid-'80s was that money rules over their conscience and thought.

Listening to N.W.A.'s (Niggers With Attitude) *Straight Outta Compton* is like sitting in the Theatre of Urban Mojo, staring at rapidly changing images of ghetto angst: the blinding flash of speeding headlights (attached to a cherry-red Benz), the nightmarish glare of a policeman's badge, the explosive din of an Uzi shot, the piercing screams of wounded victims drowning in pools of blood, the honey-voiced chatter of neighborhood Gucci Gals. From that theatre one can witness the yin and yang of America's noir lifestyles since, in the mythopoetic world of hip hop, the outlaw swagger of the performers is often a xerox of urban gangster attitude.

Although the prototype of gangsta rap was Boogie Down Productions's brutal *Criminal Minded,* after the crew's Scott La Rock was gunned down, rapper KRS-One moved toward more positive, Afrocentric values. While he was partly aligning himself with the nonviolent agenda preached by Martin Luther King, Jr., Public Enemy was embracing the enlightened militant teachings of Malcolm X. When N.W.A. touched down into hip-hop land they were playing the so-called ignorant Negro, unaware of the doctrines of Martin *or* Malcolm. Their response to a society that doomed the Black man to second-class status sounded like a roaring gut reaction. But it in fact has its roots in the myth of Staggerlee, which can be found throughout Black-American folk culture from early blues tunes by Mississippi John Hurt in 1929 to the more colorful portraits from '70s blaxploitation films. And with a nod, perhaps, to smooth cocaine dealer Priest (Ron O'Neal in *Superfly*) Ice Cube declares, in "Gangsta Gangsta," "Do I look like a muthafuckin'role model/To a kid lookin' up to me/Life ain't nothin' but bitches and money!"

Although underground hip hop has never been fully accepted into mainstream American culture ("Look at those tacky, illiterate hoods," whispers the Black middle class, echoing the

Doctor Dre, Eazy-E, and the D.O.C. of N.W.A.

———

sentiments of whites who don't understand the movement), only a few rap bands, like Public Enemy and 2 Live Crew, have had to cope with negativity as extreme as that directed towards N.W.A. From supposedly broad-minded music critics to local law enforcers to the big daddies at the FBI, the group was treated as a lethal germ that had to be killed.

The first four songs on *Straight Outta Compton* (the title track, "——— Tha Police," "Gangsta Gangsta" and "If It Ain't Ruff") sneak around darkened corners, attacking like a foursome of aural terrors. With these tracks one is sucked into the vortex of the group's obsessions and fears. Though they're relating tales from da palm tree ghetto of Compton, the frightening images they paint pertain to Black young men everywhere: Whether he be a rapper bopping down 125th Street or a designer waltzing over 57th Street, a Black male is a perpetual walking suspect.

Any law-abiding person who has seen the cold stare or heard the gruff commands of police as they cruise through Black neighborhoods can relate to N.W.A.'s fantasy of beating up and blowing away a few cops. Not to say that violence is the key to the door of ending racial harassment, but when MC Ren drops the line "taking out a cop or two, they can't cope wit me," one can hear silent cheers erupting from chocolate cities everywhere.

After the group became popular, crossing over even to young white kids (and what better way to piss your parents off than with voices of "invisible men" bellowing anarchy), law enforcement officials across the nation went bug-fuck: an agent from the FBI wrote a letter to the group's record company, an attempt to silence these angry, truthful, voices from the land of reality. A move like this is unusual, although most artists who speak against the system suspect there are secret F.B.I. files on them. And though many folks were outraged that the U.S.A. would endorse such a fascist action (*land of the free?!*), the fellas in N.W.A. were unfazed. "I didn't even see the letter," commented producer Dr. Dre. But he did see its effects; while on tour N.W.A. were hassled by cops in different cities. Group member DJ Yella shrugged off these incidents saying the cops were "wasting our time."

Perhaps after listening to "Gangsta Gangsta" one can understand why the police have such bitter feelings toward these neighborhood wildboys. Opening with the roar of gunfire, this track explores the adventures of "crazy motherfuckers from around the way." Showing no respect for *anyone*, these ruthless boys display their anger by shootin' and beating up "punk ass niggers." The beat is slamming, yet it proves difficult to show affection to a crew of "wilding" street thugs. Unlike the gangsters one views in film (who only kill their enemies), anyone can be a victim of the wildboys in these songs. Still, in some way one cannot help but become attracted to the brutal images—it's like staring at an auto accident.

On "I Ain't Tha 1," N.W.A. attempt to show the public (i.e., folks who don't live in the ghetto) the reason behind their material stance: women. Beginning with a cutie asking for dollars to get her hair done, Ice Cube goes into a long-winded rap about how he ain't givin' up no dollars. But we all know that after he impresses da fellas with his shpeil he'll sneak honey-chile the bucks she's asking for *'cause she's got the power!*

So where do they go from here?

Two years after *Straight Outta Compton,* N.W.A. (minus Ice Cube) released an EP entitled *100 Miles and Runnin'.* With these five tracks our worst fears have come true—this band is tired. Although Dr. Dre's production values have continued to increase with each project, the gangster themes that Eazy & Co. throw in on the title track and "Sa Prize (Part 2)"—basically a sequel to "——— Tha Police"—show no increased textural depth. Unlike Ice Cube, who went on to explore other sides of the ghetto on his debut album, *AmeriKKKa's Most Wanted,* N.W.A. are just showing us the same photo album we saw before. As Eazy might say, "Fuck that shit!"

See Eazy-E, Ice Cube.

ORIGINAL
CONCEPT

STRAIGHT FROM THE BASEMENT OF
KOOLEY HIGH (DEF JAM/COLUMBIA), 1988

Back in 1977 B.R. (before records), during the early years of hip hop, the boyz in da 'hood all fantasized to themselves about being DJs. Like neighborhood rock stars, the turntable artist in any popular crew had it *all* goin' on: all the beats, all the girls—DJ Hollywood had an entire posse of flye groupies that he dubbed Hollywood Girls—and all the fame. While he spun records, funking up the air with endless cuts and breaks, a naked mic' was sometimes held open for anyone who wished to shout their chillest rhymes, dropping words of ghetto coolness to a sweaty, excited crowd: "Hotel, motel, Holiday Inn . . ." Most of these early exhortations were quite simple, the rappers bellowing out their street handles, the names of their dapper homeboys, slick girlfriends, or products they could just barely pronounce (or afford!).

But a new day was dawning. When pillow-talker Sylvia Robinson literally founded the business of recorded rap, she used her label's house band to back up vocalists like Melle Mel and the Treacherous Three. The DJ became a figurehead—what did Grandmaster Flash contribute to his unit's ground-breaking "The Message"?—and the rapper started to eclipse him.

Thus, when critic Frank Owen stated in *Spin* that "the responsibility for this transformation of hip hop into rap lies with Def Jam," he was not entirely correct. One could clearly see the emphasis beginning to shift from texture to text with the release of "Rapper's Delight" by the Sugar Hill Gang in 1979; one need look no further than its title for evidence. With rare exceptions like DJ Jazzy Jeff & the French Prince or Eric B. & Rakim—many folks believed that E. was the rapper when "Eric B. Is President" was first released—DJs' names were not used in the packaging and marketing of crews in the age of rap with a hole in the middle. But while Def Jam can't take credit for refocusing the spotlight on the rap stage, they can proudly say they created a song structure for the rapper's words to exist in.

Storming out of the cool, dark and mad, mad world of his Long Island dungeon studio (illuminated only by numerous flashing LEDs and dimmed incandescent bulbs), the beefy Andre "Doctor Dre" Brown, speaking on Original Concept's debut Def Jam disk, declared, "It's colorful, eclectic B-boy insanity. Some people will call it a funky record. Some will call it a bluesy record and some will call it a rock 'n' roll record. Actually, it's just a reflection of our madcap personalities."

Besides Brown, this rollicking comedy act is T-Money, Easy-G Rockwell and The Rapper G. They met one another in 1977, at Westbury (New York) High, and, as the Concept, started DJing at school gigs, house parties, dance clubs, strip bars—anyplace that welcomed their appetite for sonic deconstruction. From there, they became Original Concept and began working with other groups. They brought Public Enemy to the attention of Def Jam, and for a while Dre toured with the obnoxious-as-they-wanted-to-be Beastie Boys as their DJ. After doing so much for their buddies, this posse decided to construct an album of their own. The quartet recorded forty-five finished tunes, working off and on. Two and a half years later, they decided on the eighteen cuts released on *Straight From the Basement of Kooley High*, the title inspired by the name of Brown's hole-in-the-ground recording space.

There is plenty that's cold-getting-dumb on this LP, executive-produced by Rick Rubin (bearded former punk rocker/present owner of Def American Records; engineer of Def Jam's successful marriage of hip hop and heavy metal via Run-D.M.C.

and the Beasties). All the decorum commonplace in Def Jam rap was slashed by Original Concept—a DJ crew—on this record, many of the cuts being nothing more than bugged B-boy chatter or chants, quirky aural collages constructed from movie sound bites, TV jingles, sound effects and pop sides laid over booming, vibrating beats that recall seismic Miami- and L.A-style productions (even though they were unleashed before those two hip-hop finishing schools were let out).

On the cusp of "Fat Lady," longtime WRHU-FM announcer Jeff Foss says to Doctor Dre, "There's a certain level of intellectual stimulation that one needs in a relationship, I'm sure. So with that in mind, what do you look for in a woman to truly excite you?" Dre sputters out "Big breasts!" before the wail of an excited elephant blows through the mix. What follows is—not surprisingly—a silly narrative about a big mama who turns out to be not so sweet. Meanwhile, in "She's Got a Moustache," an otherwise tasty tart ends up being "a little hairy in the wrong place." When this cut's chorus spits out some shots of locker-room ragging over a synth line from Flash & Five's "Birthday Party," it could've become sophomoric and dense. Instead its deep and slow thrusts prove nothing less than brilliant.

Ostensibly these guys don't wax real intelligent; neither do they appreciate companions who do. During *Straight From the Basement*'s biggest popular hit, "Pump That Bass" (a track that rocked urban dance dives at least two years before the LP was released), Original Concept encourage listeners to "get a little stupid," too. Further down the road, another playful cut directs us to "Get Stupid ... *Again.*"

But Original Concept is a tangled web of contradiction. They'll go out of their way to present themselves as disrespecting, unconcerned clowns whose only enemy is boredom, yet they in fact do have social consciences as well as serious opinions on issues ranging from the arms race to numbers running. They'll drop antihoodlum doggerel ("Jonnie Wuza Gangsta") and erupt colorfully about how wack bigotry is ("Prejudice"). That's def, but, truly, who gives a flunk? Hip-hop saviors Boogie Down Productions, with KRS-One's piercing lead voice, is the place where one expects to find blazing theories about inner-city angst or global concerns. On an Original Concept record one looks to get dumb, to bug without worrying about Armageddon. Interest shifts back to a time when the eroticism of beatboxes and the hammering of breaks rocked jams on the boulevard *without* treating them like seminars.

PM DAWN

OF THE HEART, OF THE SOUL, AND OF THE CROSS:
THE UTOPIAN EXPERIENCE (GEE STREET/
ISLAND), 1991

When De La Soul crossed over in '89, a whole lotta hip-hop hopefuls took heart, altering their street images into decidedly more arty and bizarre ones. As members of De La's Native Tongues unit, A Tribe Called Quest and the Jungle Brothers were initiated enough to contribute twists to Pos, Dove and Trugoy's eccentric da inner self y'all movement. But groups like KMD and Stereo MCs came off like straight-up posers who did nothing to further hippycat stylism. So in 1991, as they traded in their beads and peace signs look for a back-to-burn hardcore persona, De La declared: "The D.A.I.S.Y. age is dead!"

It would be an injustice to call rapper Prince B and DJ Minutemix (known collecively as PM Dawn) the new De La Soul, but more than a few critics and fans will as they gaze at their beatnik shades and way-cool naps. They're blood brothers from another planet, New Jersey, who seem geniunely impressed with lyrical and sonic abstraction. In other words, they're not frontin' weirdness; *they really are weird.*

"Reality used to be a friend of mine," velvet-voiced Prince B says on a tune of that same name. The proclamation begins an exodus into PM Dawn's strangeland, a universe populated by creatures with cartoon voices, sound effects and transmissions from a station with an eclectic mix: '60s psychodust trips, '90s acid journeys.

Stepping "to the rhythm of the left" these Black bohos sample the sugar-pop of the Monkee's "Pleasant Valley Sunday" in one of the few tracks that features Prince B singing *and* rapping, combining melody and hardcore over Minutemix wildness. Then, on "Shake," they ride one of Todd Terry's lesser strobe-lite beats to the last rave of the decade. Cool, bopping tracks like "Paper Doll" and "Set Adrift on Memory Bliss" (a title Samuel R. Delany might have used for one of his science fiction novels) work better than Todd's sonic madness. His studio maneuvers have a numbing effect outside of a club: all science and no fiction. PM Dawn work best when left to their own quirky devices.

POOR ■ RIGHTEOUS TEACHERS

HOLY INTELLECT (PROFILE), 1990

Who's Otis Redding?" the young girl asks innocently. At fourteen, Aisha is a tall, soft-spoken teenager with Shirley Temple curls, fond of flye clothes and dirty jokes. On this chilly December night, sitting in New York's City Center Theater, about to view the glitter of Alvin Ailey's dance troupe, she flips through the slick playbill, coming on to the page that lists "Suite Otis (A Tribute to the Late Otis Redding)." As the lights slowly dim, the silken curtain opens to graceful ebony dancers gliding through a cloudy P.A. mix of Otis's "Just One More Day," which slides into five other classics by the dock-of-the-bay soulman.

First thought of Aisha's question sends my mind reeling back to one of boxing promoter Don King's statements (in the short film Spike Lee directed on Mike Tyson): "Elvis has made more money in death than he made in life. Young white folks know who Elvis is." Second thought of Aisha's question sends my mind crashing through the Steely Dan track "Hey Nineteen," where the adolescent babydoll doesn't remember "the Queen of Soul," Aretha Franklin. And the third thought raging through my brain is a Twilight Zone fantasy of the year 2010, Aisha sitting in the same theater with her daughter, silken curtains opening, the dancers bopping through a tribute to the sound seducers of hip-hop music. As choreographed by Rosie Perez, the former Flye Girl posse leader, the set will open with sonic bombast crashing through the speakers. The troupe will begin by doing the wop to Eric B. & Rakim's "Eric B. Is President,"

175

then spin into the James Brown dance as Big Daddy Kane's "Raw" comes blaring. After Running Man through the streetlight fantastic of Ice Cube's "Once Upon a Time in the Projects," Run-D.M.C. "Sucker MC's" and Digital Underground's "Doowutchyalike," there will be a brief pause before the finale begins . . . the women dressed in Kente cloth gowns, the fellas clad in baggy jeans and Polo jackets, the sound system slamming Poor Righteous Teachers' second single, "Rock Dis Funky Joint." Everyone—the audience, the dancers—will begin to sway as lead rapper Wise Intelligent's voice comes bubbling out like a shaken bottle of champagne. Aisha will smile, memories dancing in her mind. Her daughter will lean over to her and whisper, "Who's Poor Righteous Teachers?"

Back in the present, 1990: In the year that spat out M.C. Hammer and Vanilla Ice (homeboy theorists swear that they're the same person—hey, ever seen 'em both in the same room?) into the eyes of anybody watching a video program, a few of the year's best groups were forced to ride the back of da bus—Tribe Called Quest was one, Poor Righteous Teachers another.

On their first album, *Holy Intellect,* these homies from Trenton, New Jersey (a state more known for its booming house systems, less for its hip-hop crews), git da party started with their off-kilter voices spinning verbal puzzles into hardcore rhymes. As the drums of "Rock Dis Funky Joint" echo over the roofs of the brutal Donnelly Houses (the low-income project that da fellas call home), this trio of urban blues artists be rockin' the streets while displaying the beauty of Black America—this is the music of basketball games in the battlegrounds, of jungle cowboys shooting guitar strings at full moons, of Dominican drama queens strolling down Broadway and 151st Street clad in tight jeans or noir miniskirts, of walking through Times Square at midnight—exciting and dangerous. As Poor Righteous Teachers build twin cities of sonic bliss from a blueprint of underground noise and Islamic teachings, one is reminded that hip hop is street (block parties, basketball courts) music constructed from the "grain of the voice," contained within the pipes (and turntables) of Wise Intelligent, Culture Freedom and DJ Father Shaheed. If video killed the turntable star, then Poor Righteous Teachers' mission is to breathe life into our dying memories, flashing snapshots of beatbox culture—the days of bopping down Broadway, balancing a heavy radio on one's shoulders.

"Make like a wino and swig it," Culture Freedom says on the opening track, "Can I Start This?," drunk from the rhythms of the moment. "You go Rambo, I go Predator, competitor, editor, creditor and much better than a quacker rapper who thinks he's like Dapper Dan/Like a seal I keep him clappin' his hands," he says. This is a style that our Teachers have dubbed "Butt Naked Booty Bless," and judging from the track that shares its title, this musical metaphor describes our birth into a new world—butt naked and funky as hell. Using Manu Dibango's classic "Soul Makossa" (a popular break for old-school turntable assassins), the P.R.T. crew and producer Tony D. roar through beats and vocals at equal speeds; after taking a few swigs of rhythm wine, they give us a demo of drunk driving on the mic'.

But like my boy Rakim would say, I got a question as serious as cancer: Could someone explain why so many hip-hop artists have to dabble in the art of B-boy crooning? In most cases, like L.L.'s "I Need Love" or Big Daddy Kane's "To Be a Man," the style is slicker than a can of oil, too slick for its own good. After jivescamming on the hotties while hanging with their homeboys, all of a sudden they wanna be serious loverboys. Yo, save the drama for ya mama 'cause lover-rap makes me gasp. On "Shakilya," mush rhymes are used to describe "the queens of all queens," in a Slick Rick meets Blue Magic voice.

But this is a minor complaint, since *Holy Intellect* is more urban streets than motel suites (although both environments gives one the opportunity to be buck wildin' butt naked), more funky than the Hudson River on a summer afternoon.

PRINCE PAUL

SEE BIG DADDY KANE, 3RD BASS, QUEEN LATIFAH

PUBLIC
ENEMY

YO! BUM RUSH THE SHOW (DEF JAM), 1987

*IT TAKES A NATION OF MILLIONS TO
HOLD US BACK, 1988*

FEAR OF A BLACK PLANET, 1990

When Public Enemy marched into hip-hop country with the S1Ws (Security of the First World, their uniformed, fake-Uzi–toting sentries), the territory's residents were floating on gravity, freestyling, wopping and bobbing to escapist funk. Showcasing themselves as party bands or comedy acts—pure entertainment—most hip-hop artists were, as James Brown once rhapsodized, "talking loud but sayin' nothin'." Public Enemy wasn't having any of that. Coming from "Strong Island," they proclaimed that their mission was to champion the cause of the African-American underclass. Immediately, they rated as one of pop music's most important and controversial acts. Because of their tactic of using visibility and militancy as a threat, they became dubbed the "Black Panthers of rap."

Public Enemy doesn't deliver its text straight with no chaser, though. In the tradition of Black orators like Jesse

Chuck D. and Heavy D. © Ernest Paniccioli, 1990.

Jackson and Martin Luther King, Jr., main-voice Chuck D. uplifts spirits and stirs minds with his stentorian voice that booms with the emotional intensity these serious times demand. But alongside his strident preaching is next-voice Flavor Flav's wacky snicker and juiced up flair, which is aural as well as visual: In the studio Flav plays Chuck's one-man cheering section; on stage he becomes the freaky mutant sidekick, contorting his face and jacking his body while spewing giddy retorts (including the trademark "Yeaaahhh Boyeeee!"). Always sporting oversized neck clocks and colorful mirrored shades, Flavor is Jerry Lewis to Chuck's Dean Martin. His antics are sometimes a bit bufoonish, but he's crucial to Public Enemy's delicate balance of education and entertainment.

The man in charge of deploying PE's agenda is Chuck D., born Carlton Ridenhour thirty years ago. As the native son of ex-'60s activists and a former student in a summer teen program called "The Afro-American Experience," he knows the reality of the Black struggle: of its sung and unsung heroes, of the American system that tries to silence them, of a Bupwardly mobile middle class that distances itself from ever-escalating racial tensions.

A former college radio disc jockey, Chuck understands what members of the punk culture related in their noise manifestos: If you want to stimulate the public's minds, you've got to first move their feet. In other words, you can't bore them with intellectual jabbering. Seminal speakicians Gil Scott-Heron and the Last Poets dropped science over heady jazz. With his knowledge of rare grooves and classic funk, Chuck was able to, as he intoned from the twelve-inch "Bring the Noise," "rock the boulevard and treat it like a seminar."

Public Enemy released an album, *Yo! Bum Rush the Show*, with no macho clichés, no empty boasts—just spirited defiance from Chuck D., egged on by Flavor Flav (whose raspy tone often recalls Jimmy Durante's). D. defined himself ("I'm a public enemy but I don't rob banks/Don't use bullets and don't use blanks"), and he proceeded to drop sharp critiques of what he perceived as the potholes in Black America's pint-sized lawn: police harassment, drugs, cultural ignorance and sexual misunderstanding. The band positioned themselves as targets of the society at large, a stance perfectly embodied in their logo—a silhouetted figure between the crosshairs of a gunsight. The sighted figure represents the Black man in America, a perceived menace to an establishment bent on excluding him.

The crew, which also includes DJ Terminator X, came into hip hop riding the cusp of a musico cultural wave that fused the revolutionary teachings of Malcolm X, Kwame Toure and others with the quaking beats of L.L. Cool J., Run-D.M.C. and others. Their emphasis on brains over gold chains served as a blueprint for fans of hip hop as well as fellow rappers like KRS-One, the Jungle Brothers and Kool Moe Dee.

As the first now-school LP of "radical rap," *Yo! Bum Rush the Show* name-dropped elements from African culture's pantheon of heroes and facts. And after many years of "gettin' stoopid," Black kids once again became curious about their rich pasts. Afrocentric ideologies started taking shape coast to coast. Chuck D. once called rap the Black people's CNN. After Public Enemy swooped down in Chocolate City's broadcast studios, its channel began transmitting ever more power and pride.

Never preachy, *Yo!* was one of the most relevant, ambitious projects ever committed to vinyl. It molded bristling, active soundscapes to post-apocalypse visions which suggested that in the future, contrary to the beliefs of Brother Gil, the revolution *will* be televised. There will be a riot going on, and the entire blast will be videotaped and archived for those bleak generations who choose to stare blankly at technicolor images of burning buildings and shattered glass. It will be a time of wild-style homeboys toting Uzis in the face of injustice and prejudice ("Howard Beach!" someone screams. "Michael Stewart! Eleanor Bumpers!"), a time when Black intellectuals will smash their typewriters in frustration at their own rhetoric.

On first listen, Public Enemy sounded a little like the other rap crews on the scene, Chuck boasting about being the baddest mutha on the block, cruising down the avenue as fans cheer him and his serious '98 Olds ("Get with it—the ultimate homeboy car!" Flavor Flav offers, his raspy tone sneaking around the dense aural walls of "You're Gonna Get Yours"). Then there were sexist rhymes about flye girls on jocks "like ants on candy" and dis lines about sophisticated bitches shouted over metallic Vernon Reid guitar riffs. But as Chuck explained, "Sophisti-cated Bitch" is only attacking materialism. In "Raise The Roof" and "Riotstarter: Message to a Black Man," he praises Black culture's fairer sex. A closer listen to the LP also reveals the hostile street-warrior voice of Chuck D. blurting out militant raps that seem like remnants from the first civil rights move-ment: postnationalist bloods fighting on those urban fronts of Black towns across the fruited plain.

Public Enemy hit hard, with none of that "What's Going On" passive resistance to stand in the way of their fire-bombing urban poetics ("Put me on a kick but line up—time's up/This government system needs a tune up"). This posse meant seri-ous business with Terminator X cutting on the edge of its bum-rush.

By employing faster tempos and even more inspired sound collages (fleeting riffs layered onto scratchy loops, funky bass lines and thick beats) two follow-up singles, "Bring the Noise," and "Rebel without a Pause," presented an even more perfect B-boy blend of street and science. These tracks, produced by the Bomb Squad (Chuck D. with Hank Shocklee, Keith Shocklee and Eric "Vietnam" Sadler), were the second campaign in Public Enemy's war on the status quo. The latter jam appeared in the movie *Less than Zero,* and both were included on the next PE album, *It Takes a Nation of Millions to Hold Us Back.*

As the LP shipped, Chuck D. revealed that one of his goals was to build "5,000 potential Black leaders by the end of our recording contract." Likening life in white America to a basketball game, he said, moreover, that his lectures were about helping African-American youth (especially males) prevent "getting fouled or called out." His coaching tactics became more forceful on *It Takes a Nation of Millions.* "Everything I do will be a continuation," he remarked.

Here PE continued its attacks on the ruling class, sandwiching Chuck's tough, sinuous raps (supported by speeches from King, controversial Nation of Islam minister Louis Farrakhan and Jesse Jackson) between pumping grooves that came off frisky and varied. Their rage is directed toward news organizations ("Don't Believe the Hype"), drug dealers ("Night of the Living Baseheads"), television ("She Watch Channel Zero," which folds elements of hardcore punk into a funky, danceable mix), and the government ("Black Steel in the Hour of Chaos," "Terminator X on the Edge of Panic," "Louder Than a Bomb").

Chuck D. claims that the FBI tapped his phone lines following the release of *Yo!* If this is so, his secret file surely must have gotten thicker in the wake of *Millions.* "Black Steel in the Hour of Chaos" chronicles a jailbreak aidded by the S1Ws, while "Louder Than a Bomb" accuses the CIA of lullabying both King and Malcolm. The song claims it made no

Public Enemy (without Chuck D.). Fear of a Black . . . What?
© Ernest Paniccioli, 1990.

———

difference that these two leaders operated on divergent ends of
the political scale, since both died a violent death at the hands
of white supremacists.

PE's next full album confronted these individuals, but
before it was unleashed the crew recorded the propulsive "Fight
the Power" (which turned out to be the biggest-selling twelve-
inch in the history of Motown Records) for the soundtrack to
Spike Lee's 1989 drama *Do the Right Thing.* That song's
antiestablishment stance invoked the lines "Elvis was a hero to
most but he never meant shit to me/You see, straight out racist
the sucker was simple and plain/Motherfuck him *and* John
Wayne!" Chuck commented that he was "looking forward" to
spending the summer talking about those two icons of American
pop culture. But when his "minister of information," Professor
Griff, spewed anti-Jewish remarks to David Mills of the *Washington Times,* he instead spent the season answering for them.
He ultimately fired Griff, who went on to form his own group,
the Last Asiatic Disciples, and record an album, *Pawns in the
Game.* All this dissent revealed that the band whose very existence stood for Black unity and power, was itself discordant. But
none of Griff's detractors bothered to probe his rhetoric for fact.

Public Enemy managed to pull itself together to rage yet once more. Interspersed with snippets from talk radio, the songs on *Fear of a Black Planet* are more multilayered, elaborately constructed cross pollinations of musical fragments, found sounds and postmodernist wit. From these sonic skyscrapers, Chuck flips both his words and his tone frequently, expanding on his political and social agendas: enabling self-reliance, self-respect and knowledge of the iniquities perpetrated on the Black man.

When "Welcome to the Terrordome" ("I got so much trouble on my mind") restoked the previous summer's controversy with the line, "Crucifixion ain't no fiction/So called chosen, frozen/Apology made to who ever pleases/ Still they got me like Jesus," Chuck D. remarked: "I believe Jesus is a brother who got crucified. I made the apology [for Griff's anti-Semitic comments], and people are *still* taking me out. I said that was wrong, now let's move on."

Yet another controversial line shows up in "Meet the G That Killed Me": "Man to man/I don't know if they can/From what I know the parts don't fit." About all Chuck had to say about these homophobic sentiments was "Love between men shouldn't involve sex."

Anti-gay pronouncements are only a fleeting part of *Fear of a Black Planet.* Public Enemy spend most of their time on, obviously, being pro-Black. With Ice Cube and Big Daddy Kane, Chuck champions the Black film movement and gives the finger to stereotypical portrayals of brothers and sisters in Hollywood movies. Then, in one of two solo shots, Flavor Flav reports on the slowness with which police and ambulances respond to emergencies in African-American communities. From the album's opening statement, "Brothers Gonna Work It Out," to the closing directive "Fight the Power," Public Enemy's tradition of providing food for the brain and beats for the feet continues. With the Bomb Squad's fingers on the trigger, the band keeps on firing ammunition in their "mind revolution" against slackness.

QUEEN
LATIF

Like all genres of music in the pop spectrum, hip hop is a male-dominated force that allows few women to make contributions in sound, style or discourse. Females gathered in the hip-hop nation are viewed with sexist contempt: as rappers they are seen as novelties controlled by men (even Salt-n-Pepa, before their third album, *Blacks' Magic,* were considered as much producer Hurby Luv Bug's creation as their own); on album covers and in videos, they are seen as decoration, objects of desire, sex kittens clad in skimpy costumes, bearing flesh for the masses.

Although "Latifah" is a Muslim name meaning delicate and sensitive, Queen Latifah burst onto the hip-hop scene like a Black storm in the hour of female tranquillity. On her first single, "Wrath of My Madness," she introduced a new style of woman, one who could sincerely handle the title "Queen of Royal Badness." Whereas other female rappers often came across as mindless cutey-pies trapped in the machinery of pop, Latifah was a woman with brains and attitude. In the past, only male rappers like Chuck D. and KRS-One had spoken of education and revolution, while the women chilled on the sidelines. In Queen Latifah's tone and textures, the beginning of a revolution could be heard.

One year later (1989) Queen Latifah's second single, "Dance With Me," was released. Although the beat was almost entirely constructed from the psychedelic R&B of Sly and the Family Stone's classic "Dance to the Music," Latifah still managed to

Queen Latifah with Slick Rick. © Ernest Paniccioli, 1990.

sound fresh. "This MC stands for Microphone Commando!" she screamed to the world, before proceeding to explain how bad a sister she really was. Over the din, a crowd could be heard screaming, "Hail to the Queen!"

A few months later, Tommy Boy released Latifah's debut album, *All Hail the Queen.* And, with the possible exception of Neneh Cherry's *Raw Like Sushi,* this was the strongest debut LP created by a woman in the history of hip hop. Although the majority of the album was produced by the prolific Mark the 45 King. Queen Latifah still managed to collaborate with a tribe of like-minded producers and rappers, including KRS-One and Louie Louie Vega.

Sometimes referred to as MaMa Zulu, Latifah plays the role on the Prince Paul–produced track, "MaMa Gave Birth to the Soul Children," which features her label-mates De La Soul. On this giddy yet complex track, Prince Paul builds a wall of sound that includes party noise makers, horror-movie soundtracks and the distorted voices of the De La fellas sounding like cartoon baby chipmunks. In this funky funhouse, Latifah is in control, telling all who listen that her children were born "not from the body/But from the soul ..."

From there, Latifah fast-forwards herself back to reality as she drives down the nocturnal landscape of Brooklyn's Flatbush Avenue: past the Roti and jerk chicken joints, past the West Indian record shops blaring the latest Third World import. "I stepped into a basement party in Brooklyn," Latifah informs us in the beginning of "The Pros," a track produced by Daddy-O from Stetsasonic. With its heavy bass recalling Jamaican dub and a haunting noise lurking in the background (like a siren throughout the song), this track has tension flowing from the grooves. Latifah recalls how she and Daddy-O (who shares the vocals) are approached by weak rappers who want to duel: "If you really want to do this we can do this, fine/Take six paces and begin to rhyme/As soon as she attempted to make a sound/I ate up with the verb, broke her down with the noun." Some observers might view this scene as graphic and violent, but the only weapons used are the power of poetry and the beauty of the beat.

Nowhere is this pride and beauty (of self, of sisterhood, of poetics) more apparent than on "Ladies First," perhaps hip hop's first womanist anthem. Latifah and Brit B-girl Monie Love (who makes her U.S. debut on this track) kick wicked rhymes in a call-and-response (a form of communication that can be traced back to Africa) that is so strong, one has no choice but to stop, look and listen. "There are going to be some changes made here," a male voice says. Throwing her voice into the mix, Latifah says, "A woman can bear you, break you, take you/Now it's time to rhyme, can you relate to/A sister dope enough to make you holler and scream ..." At this point, Monie bum-rushes with her vocals.

Further into the track, the call-and-response gets stronger: "Some think that we can't flow (can't flow)/Stereotypes they got to go (got to go)/I'ma mess around and flip the scene into reverse (with what)/With a little touch of ladies first." If some B-boys view Latifah and Monie as B.W.A. (Bitches With Attitude), then they are missing the point. These women are simply asking that the men of the hip-hop nation treat all women with the same respect they would shower on their mothers, sisters and daughters.

Moving from the local to the national, Latifah drops verbal bombs on the government with a track titled "Evil That Men Do." Produced by KRS-One from Boogie Down Productions (question: How did KRS-One manage to compose a beat so dope, when his own material is often quite lame?), Latifah demands to know the answers to the "evils" destroying Black America: lack of housing, neighborhoods overrun by crack, the shortage of jobs and the decline of the education system.

In the revolutionary universe of current hip hop, there is enough room for culture critics and leaders from both sexes. If Chuck D. can assume the role of rap's Malcolm X, then why shouldn't Latifah model herself after Angela Davis?

THE REAL
ROXANNE

THE REAL ROXANNE (SELECT), 1988

Exploding like a punctured steampipe, spewing carcino-
genic remarks upon the three members of UTFO, who
had dissed a sister who shared her name, squeaky-
voiced Roxanne Shanté released the first of many answer records to the bare-bones come-on "Roxanne Roxanne" in 1984.
Snarling "Why you wanna make a record 'bout me/The R-O-X-
A-N-N-E" over a scratchy beat stolen from the instrumental B
side of UTFO's hit, Ms. Shanté inspired dozens of rambunctious
MCs, with names like Roxanne's Doctor, Roxanne the Man and
Roxanne's Psychiatrist, to record—a deluge of at least thirty-
nine twelve-inches. Many of these answer records responded not
so much to the initial smash, but to the anger and sass of this
fifteen-year-old runaway with no prior studio experience. Her
response, originally written as a joke, shot a pointed message
straight at UTFO, and in its wake I bet they wished they'd left
Rox the fuck alone.

Claiming to be the girl who had truly inspired UTFO in the
first place, the Real Roxanne recorded a less explicit "official"
challenge. "I just had to do something," she told the New York
Daily News. While Shanté's rhyme was cured in vinegar, this
one was lightly salted. With producers Full Force in control
here, it was clear how she arrived at her seal of legitimacy.

Immediately, though, the genuineness of The Real Roxanne was challenged. Seems the vocalist who recorded the
album wasn't the same one who tracked the single. Discovered
by Full Force's Paul Anthony while she was waitressing in a

Manhattan diner, this flashy Roxy (Joanne Martinez) came up knowing more of clubland than of hip-hop country and got slammed as fake. Though her look is always hot, her voice never really sizzles, and she has since been regarded as a hip-hop imposter—despite her name.

Reporting about Latin dance music in the *Village Voice*, Carol Cooper wrote: "A pretty face, cooing vocals and a cute pair of legs constitute novel entertainment after a steady diet of Kurtis Blow and Run-D.M.C." Perhaps, working with Lisa Lisa & Cult Jam ("I Wonder If You Take Me Home"), clouded Full Force's vision, making them forget that rap standards are altogether different; they should've searched for a harder-edged Roxanne—a better combination of flesh and tone.

Like Shanté, Martinez (a.k.a. Dimples) managed to outlive the Roxanne cycle. Recording a tasty follow-up single, "Bang Zoom (Let's Go-Go)"/"Howie's Teed Off," and an album, the Real Rox rocked on. On the twelve-inch, which arrived on the heels of "The Real Roxanne," it's (appropriately) the producers and DJ who dominate. Roxanne is more like Lisa Lisa in "Howe's Teed Off," throwing her honey-smacked singing against a thick bass-and-drum combo. She sounds utterly girlish and bland. It's when she glowily commands, "Give it to me, Howie!" that things take on a more seasoned sparkle. Backspinning on his twin turntables, "Hitman" Tee drops in cuts and slices in breaks that send the song into space.

Though its title suggests that a similar trip through the stratosphere is imminent, with its madly shifting textures "Bang Zoom (Let's Go-Go)" sounds like the odyssey has already occurred. From freestyle rap to snatches of Isley Brothers songs, '40s swing beat to timeless Bugs Bunny jabbering, this 5:55 polyrhythmic jaunt is no-holds-barred fun. Still, if the song doesn't tickle your fancy, its looney coda no doubt will: It's a digital sample of Bugs and sidekick Elmer Fudd dancing wildly through the merry-melodied "The Rabbit Kicked the Bucket" from one of their Warner Bros. cartoon shorts.

Following these two collaborations, Martinez and Full Force were no longer one big happy family. Assorted accusations and writs flew from both parties, and for over a year, Dimples's career wasn't all that cheeky. When she returned to the racks with *The Real Roxanne* `LP, it came with a hodgepodge of producers that included Tee, Jam Master Jay (Run-D.M.C.), the L.A. Posse (L.L. Cool J) and Andy Panda (the Cover Girls). The two Full Force–directed faves were also included.

Looking at the LP's credits, one is impressed by the fact that Rox had a hand in writing all of its (thirteen) cuts. That's something neither MC Lyte nor Antoinette can boast. Roxanne tackles raps of confrontation, infatuation and motivation, but with her paper-thin restraint, she sounds misplaced in songs from the latter context. This includes the flippy "Don't Even Feel It," which marks Special Ed's debut (as a co-writer, not as a rapper). Still, with an implosive beat and an inviting cameo ("Yeah, come on!") by a digitally trapped Flavor Flav, this track's title certainly shouldn't sum up one's reaction following its fade; it should move you. Other grabby grooves can be found on the minor-key quiet-storm smoothie "Infatuated" and the Jeep-shaking funker "Her Bad Self."

The languid chugger "Early Early" contains the album's best vocal performance. Deliberately hushed, Rox reads its text like a short story: "I wake up ... what a very nice day/But I'm going back to sleep anyway/But wait—I can't do it like that/ Gots to go the studio and bust some raps ..." If they're all going to be this subtly expressive and haunting, then get a move on, Rox!

See also Roxanne Shanté.

REDHEAD KINGPIN & THE F.B.I.

A SHADE OF RED (VIRGIN), 1989

These days, nineteen-year-old Redhead Kingpin wears his striking carrot-colored fade proudly, like a shark's fin: As he enters a room, the idea is to make hearts pump faster, sucker MCs scatter. When he was younger, things were a little different. His coif was the object of constant teasing and bewilderment; he hid it.

Back then, Redhead, whose real name is David Guppy, also read a lot—novels by Poe and Dickens; comics by Stan Lee and Steve Ditko. A character in the latter pair's "Spiderman" series inspired the Kingpin portion of the performer's hip-hop moniker. But it was the output from Sugar Hill Records and several local rap crews that made this Englewood, New Jersey, resident want to rap in the first place. In 1986, he was signed briefly to Sugar Hill. When things didn't work out with the label that had pioneered recorded rap and B-boy scandal (the firm had reportedly ripped off its artists), sheer happenstance led him to an old camp counselor named GSD. He helped Redhead make a tape of two songs, "Scram" and "Speaking on Everything." GSD—who later became a part of the F.B.I. (For Black Intelligence) Tribe with DJ Wildstyle, right-hand man Lt. Squeak and dancers Bo-Roc and Buzz—took the tape to producer/manager Gene Griffin (Guy, Today, Wrecks 'n' Effect), whom he had gotten to know through bodyguard work. A deal was struck, and Redhead embarked on creating his debut LP, *A Shade of Red*, which was mixed cleanly and crisply by Teddy Riley.

Redhead Kingpin, new age Teddy boy.
© Ernest Paniccioli, 1990.

The title track is a chilling musical experiment: whips crack hard, voices wail woefully, a stentorian voice announces, "No one can stand up to the power of the Kingpin." It threatens mental meltdown. Another cut, "Do the Right Thing," proposes something far less dangerous—racial harmony. It was supposed to be soundtracked for Spike Lee's third joint but wasn't. That's a shame since, as the first single from *A Shade of Red,* it got overlooked generally. Constructed with rubbery beats, glimmering synth lines, and a sample from KC & the Sunshine Band, it was one of 1989's best summer records.

While "Do the Right Thing" has an R&B base, "Kilimanjaro Style," which uses Dillinger's "Melting Pot," has its roots in reggae. "Do That Dance," with its loopy bass line, is for clubheads. "We Rock the Mic," booming and slow, is for the Jeep-boys. And "Pump It Hottie," one big electric romp with some high-powered freaks, is for the Cali crowd. Such diversity screams for wider attention. And uptown or downtown, East Coast or West Coast, Redhead Kingpin is on the prowl in search of it.

TEDDY RILEY

SEE HEAVY D. AND THE BOYZ, KOOL MOE DEE, REDHEAD KINGPIN & THE FBI, THE WEE PAPA GIRL RAPPERS AND WRECKS 'N' EFFECT.

ROB BASE & DJ E-Z ROCK

IT TAKES TWO (PROFILE), 1988

ROB BASE

THE INCREDIBLE BASE, 1989

Eccentric rock vocalist David Lee Roth once commented about music industry hype, "You might feel like God, but you'll only be God for a year." And you better believe that while you're God your parade will be rained upon by a shower of rumors. But exactly where and how do rumors start? Someone once reckoned that there was a firm in SoHo called Rumours Inc., which spreads hearsay about anyone for a fee. How much? you might ask. Well, the amount exchanged is unknown, but the price is usually a damaged reputation. At any music industry party, the rumors flow as freely as the drinks from the open bar: "Does Big Daddy Kane really have AIDS?" "Did Al B. Sure! actually rape someone?" "Is it true that [fill in the blank] is gay?"

In 1988, rapper Rob Base, whose single "It Takes Two" was voted best single of the year by *Spin* and first runner-up by the *Village Voice*, was the subject of more than a few rumors, such as "Rob Base got this girl around the corner from me pregnant" or "Rob Base died from a heart attack while smoking crack." What always makes rumors so pervasive is that folks be spreading them without even wondering about the source; those writers at Rumours Inc. must be pretty sneaky.

Before Rob Base was the subject of anyone's flights of imagination, he was part of a fifth-grade rap crew called the Sureshot Seven. After a few years its members started falling off, and by high school only Rob and DJ E-Z Rock remained. They decided to pursue a recording career as a duo, and cut "DJ Interview" and "Make It Hot" for entrepreneur William Hamilton's independent World to World Records. These "were nice records," says Rob, "but they didn't get the right push."

When Hamilton secured a distribution arrangement with Profile Records for Base's next twelve-inch, "It Takes Two," the rapper got the boost he was looking for. That tune became a record that just wouldn't die. The summertime (talk about hot fun) jam started out rockin' neighborhood booming systems and late-night dance dives with its blizzard of thunderous bass tones and furious sexy yelps. Sampled from "Think" by former James Brown back-up singer Lynn Collins, these shouts became even more volatile through their mating with the hyperactive beat from Strafe's underground club classic "Set It Off."

And through the flickering and pounding road Base, dropping truncated phrases that were scrumptiously light and fluffy: "I wanna rock right now/I'm Rob Base and I came to get down/I'm not internationally known/But I'm known to rock a microphone ..." The song's slide from verse to chorus (Collins cooing "It takes two to make a thing go right/It takes two to make it outta sight") coursed a narrow but sinewy path of musicality that's unusual for a jam that accompanied the Jeep patrol through ghetto heaven. This was a record that was progressive, but its roots were firmly planted in the rare-groove soil

*Rob Base, cold gettin' busy at the
New York Music Awards.*
© Ernest Paniccioli, 1990.

———

cultivated by hip-hop pioneers Kool Herc and Afrika Bambaataa.
From the streets and clubs, it made a steady climb to the top,
stopping first at Black, then pop, radio stations.

While "It Takes Two" can be called an evolutionary hip-
hop disc, its follow-up, "Get on the Dancefloor," expanded the
audience. It was part of the first phase of hip-hop releases
whose bedrock wasn't funk—a sample from Sly, James or even
the O'Jays; instead, it was a jam that drew more from the '70s
downtown world of strobe lights and decadence than from the
uptown streets of fire and desire. But, though not from the core,
"Get on the Dancefloor" (recorded and mixed in less than five
hours) was still hard. The title command, which came atop the
splashy groove from cellophane superstar Michael Jackson's

"Shake Your Body Down to the Ground," mixed in aerodynamic stirs from a Todd Terry project and rigid, loopy machine beats that all together battered millions everywhere into submission.

With testimonial singing from neighborhood buddy/"Showtime at the Apollo" victor Omar Chandler, "Joy & Pain" (the other massive cut on *It Takes Two*) was similarly inspiring. Though it constructed its own slinky groove for this title first used by Maze featuring Frankie Beverly, its chorus/hook bit the words of that silky soul fave. (This didn't sit too well with Beverly, and he sued Base et al. for shares in the track.)

The mid-tempo "Times Are Gettin' Ill" used live rhythm guitar and samples from the Steve Miller Band to underscore Rob's now trademark clipped-phrase style of rapping. Though the song's goal was to spotlight society's serious tendencies toward random violence and inner-city drug abuse, lines like "He missed/I hit/And that's the end of it" were almost laughably simple. But its sane outlook made it a tune that could be taken to heart.

Taking the rumors about himself to heart, a concerned Rob Base said in 1989, "I really don't know who could've been saying these things about me." In the Gap Band–inspired "Outstanding" on his second album, *The Incredible Base,* he asserts, "Forget about the rumors/They ain't true." From the cut titled "Rumors," he tosses a vicious assault at those who have been "talkin' junk" about him, and under some swift beats, the rapper sounds genuinely disgusted and more aggressive than he did on *It Takes Two.* This hyped-up atmosphere extends throughout *The Incredible Base,* which is very understandable (the boy's got a right to be in a rage!), but it's also very exciting.

With this E-Z Rock-less follow-up LP (the DJ, according to Base, "ran into some personal problems"), Rob Base came up with another funky concept. Above more happy (even higher-charged) grooves and rhythmic melodies, Base brings the sugar to make any jam sweeter. His ambitions may be modest compared to those of MC Tragedy or Public Enemy, but partying is as much a part of the African-American heritage as the civil rights struggle. So, while a track by Trag chants "No Justice, No Peace," the first single from *The Incredible Base* yells, "Go! Go! Go! Go! Go! Go! Go, Base," as vocalist Rick Kimbo Harris scats and encourages the rapper to "make the people scream and shout."

To carry his pleasure-soaked rhymes, Base and co-producer William Hamilton build original rhythms, resurrect hip-hop classics (Grandmaster Flash and the Furious Five's "Freedom" on "Get Up and Have a Good Time") and remodel R&B jams. In his commentary on hip-hop rivalries, Base recasts Edwin Starr's "War." Like Shinehead's "Come Together" and Boogie Down Productions' "Stop the Violence," the cut begs rappers everywhere to stop calling themselves God. Unlike those other peaceful B-boys, though, Rob Base knows firsthand the price of such top billing.

ROXANNE SHANTÉ

**BAD SISTER (COLD CHILLIN'/
WARNER BROS.), 1989**

After joyriding through the B-boy ghettos of the late
'70s, female MCs started falling off one by one, casu-
alties of either bad management, the casting couch or
centripetal force. The hip-hop nation once again became a
male-dominated society, where hard beats and hard penises
ruled over "bitches," "skeezers" and "whores." It turned into an
oppressive place for women.

A sassy fifteen-year-old named Lolita Gooden fell into this
hip-hop world by accident in 1984. While walking along a dim
stretch outside the Queensbridge (New York housing projects,
she spied three men riffing about how UTFO had canceled out
of performing at a show they were promoting. As the Pyramid,
backers of a late-night hip-hop show on New York's WHBI, the
trio—Tyrone Williams, Mister Magic and Marley Marl—were
instrumental in breaking the amusing, bare-bones "Roxanne
Roxanne," in which UTFO calls a cutie "stuck up, devious and
sinister" simply because she ignores their advances. The group
had owed the Pyramid a favor. It defaulted.

Hungry and unsure of her future, Gooden—a teenage runaway with an uncanny ability to freestyle—offered to make a rap
dissing UTFO. After proving she could deliver, she escaped with
Marley Marl for a few hours and returned with "Roxanne's
Revenge," a tumbling, stream-of-consciousness rap that established Marley as a producer and Gooden as Shanté, queen of
independent flye-girl badness.

Roxanne Shanté, chillin' in da crib. © Tina Paul, 1989.

The track, recorded in the relaxed surroundings of Marley's family room with the aid of just four tracks, a microphone, a sampler and a mixer, is—perhaps—best remembered for its brutal grit and casual spunk. It stood out, in stark, funky contrast, against more polished cuts by hitmakers Kurtis Blow, Whodini and the Fat Boys. And Shanté's vicious, profane style caught even the toughest rap customers off guard.

She started off "Revenge" by bragging, in breathless, squeaky-voiced tones, about how effortlessly she could rock a jam. Then, over a sample stolen from the instrumental mix of "Roxanne Roxanne," Shanté got nasty, directing Kangol Kid, Educated Rapper and Doctor Ice ("He don't really know how to operate!") to, among other things, "Suck my bush." She was out to define a respectable place for women in hip hop, and her pointed rhyme cut through all the misogyny and sexism associated with the artform. Not just another B-girl honey, Shanté cold-cocked all the skeezoids and, on rap's battleground, she became a force to be reckoned with. She moreover blazed a trail for a new breed of female MCs, including Salt, Pepa, MC Lyte and Antoinette.

"Roxanne's Revenge" was a hit even before it was out on vinyl. After Magic and Marley first aired it from a reel-to-reel, the jam got embraced by ravers in playgrounds, record execs in suites and DJs in crowded, darkened nightclubs. Even major radio stations, deluged with requests for the record, started rocking Roxanne. But there wasn't a record!

A Philadelphia-based label named Pop Art eventually pressed the song into a single (one of the company's principals, Laurence Goodman, heard it over the FM airwaves). What followed was an unprecedented avalanche of 102 more Roxanne answer records, most of them responding to Shanté's buffalo stance more than to UTFO's original. Maybe that's why UTFO threatened to sue Shanté for biting their b-side. But instead of filing writs, they settled out of court, after which Shanté recut "Roxanne's Revenge" using a new (but not totally original) track. Unfortunately, the tune's serrated edges became worn down in this switch.

Following the success of "Roxanne's Revenge" (and the movement it inspired), Shanté could've easily ruled the world of recorded rap. She chose instead to take to stages, where she proceeded to put more fresh-boys in their place, using lines like "See that guy right there? ... Always wanting the pussy but ain't got no dick!" Her banter effectively quieted hecklers, but it also moved the rest of the crowd to heights of frenzy.

To sustain her touring activity, Shanté teased fans with two Big Daddy Kane–penned gems: the polite dis "Have a Nice Day" and the pumping, get-busy "Go on Girl." In addition, she got down on "Loosey's Rap," a smooth, perky gesture by Rick James (an idol), and "Wack Itt," a buoyant (fun) electro-breeze on producer Marley Marl's *In Control, Volume One*. According to Shanté, this tune paired "the wackest, wackest beats with the wackest, wackest rhymes." In actuality, it just placed Gooden's Shanté-ishness on ice for a little over five minutes.

Her attitude returned on *Bad Sister,* released in 1989. This, Shanté's first album, is so funky and assertive, so tart and frigidified, it's a near-perfect statement of authority. Much of it sounds cleaner than her previous efforts, and her voice, though still compellingly abrasive, is smoother, more mature. But Shanté is still capable of body-slamming an offending MC or dusting off an overzealous toy boy at the drop of a dime. Even at the break of dawn—her eyes full of sleep, her head swimming with dreams—she's game for a battle with other MCs: "A lot of MCs today rap to please/But I gave birth to most of those MCs/So when it comes around to the month of May/Send me your royalty check for Mother's Day."

That's how Shanté deals with MC underlings. When it comes to boyfriend/lovers who play around on her, she's a whole lot meaner. In "Fatal Attraction," over a slapping horn- and organ-driven groove, she tells about a married man who strung her along, always promising to leave his wife. After nearly a year, Shanté says that's it. She fixes him for good. "One day they might feel a tingle between their legs/And when they look down and check—aagh! Surprise! ... /Look near or far/What you lookin' for is somewhere in a pickle jar!"

Certainly, Shanté is not a woman to trifle with or ignore. In the ugly world of hip hop, she chose the hard road. After six-plus years, she's still rolling along, spilling lyrical venom and bounding through tragic loops. A bad sister, indeed.

See also the Real Roxanne.

RICK RUBIN

SEE BEASTIE BOYS, L.L. COOL J, AND RUN-D.M.C.

RUN-D.M.C.

RUN-D.M.C. (PROFILE), 1984

KING OF ROCK, 1985

RAISING HELL, 1986

TOUGHER THAN LEATHER, 1988

BACK FROM HELL, 1990

Novelist Linsey Abrams once wrote, "Style is never simply a technical choice, but envolves from how a writer sees the world." The same could be said for the image of the first hip-hop pop group, Run-D.M.C. Although they were products of suburbia (the neatly trimmed, upwardly mobile neighborhood of Hollis, Queens), Run-D.M.C. were raised under the influence of television and movie super-heroes like Kojak and Shaft, a part of the Black middle class that was able to romanticize the images of destruction and chaos: nodding heroin addicts, bombed-out buildings, trash-filled streets. This was, in the rushed words of rap mogul Russell Simmons, "the difference between fantasy and reality. In Queens you could hang out on the corner, but there was safety in the house; in Queens, one could be part of a gang, but it was just part of a growing-up process—in the ghetto it's a lifestyle."

Although hip hop began as urban music with acts like Grandmaster Flash and the Furious Five, Kool Herc and Kurtis Blow, the ill sounds of the city, with its brutal realism, didn't always appeal to the listeners who were living in these surroundings. "I remember one night at the [Disco] Fever up in the Bronx," Russell exclaims. "My man Junebug was rockin' the turntables with Flash's 'New York, New York' when this dude runs up to the DJ booth, smashed the record, then put a gun to Junebug's head, sayin', 'If ya play that record again, I'm go'n kill ya. I don't wanna come in here *ever* and hear that record or you're dead.' Junebug asked the brother if he was mad at Flash or something, and the dude said, 'No. I'm just tired of hearing that ghetto shit.' This is how these records were affecting some brothers." After pausing for a moment to catch his breath, Russell continues, "The early rappers were from the ghetto, so their stories reflected their lives, but it was important when rap began coming out of the suburbs 'cause these niggers had something else to talk about."

The origins of these "B-boy gangsters" from the land of backyards and mowed lawns, of America's first crossover posse, began in the mid-'70s when Joey Simmons's older brother, Russell, began promoting shows in local Harlem night spots and the Hotel Diplomat. Back in the day, before rap became a recorded artform, these live shows were the few outlets where neighborhood youth could enjoy this new music; once the hip-hop crews realized there were mucho dollars to be made (popular groups made about $150 per set), the street and park shows became limited.

Impressed by the buckets of ducats that Russell was making on the rap scene, young Joey began practicing his DJ skills in the attic of his parents' house; in time, li'l-bro Joey became quite accomplished on the wheels of steel. As Russell told author Bill Adler in *Tougher Than Leather: The Authorized Biography of Run-D.M.C.*, "We called him DJ Run because he

D.M.C., Van Silk (promoter), and Run. © Ernest Paniccioli, 1990.

cut so fast. He could catch air on 'Good Times'! Just the breath and then nothing!" In 1977, Run was nicknamed "Son of Kurtis Blow" when he became the DJ for the (then) King of Rap Kurtis Blow. As party-boy Kurt knocked off his rhymes, Joey would move the crowd with his cuts 'n' scratches. After a while Run began bustin' his own rhymes under the spotlight: "I'm DJ Run, son of a gun/Always plays music and has big fun/Not that old, but that's all right/Make all other MCs bite all night." Having known Darryl McDaniels (a.k.a. D.M.C. for "Darryl Makes Cash" or "Devastating Mike Control") and Jason Mizell (Jam Master Jay) since they were kids in school together, Run would play his tapes for his two homeboys; at the time, Jay was the DJ for a neighborhood crew called Two-Fifth Down.

As time passed, these three hip-hop brothers perfected their skills in front of the wild (and often cruel) audiences of the Manhattan/Bronx/Queens nightclub circuit. After graduating from high school in 1982, Russell took Run and D.M.C. (Jay wouldn't be down until a little later, although he is featured in early photos) to Greene Street Studios with producer Larry Smith, and the team recorded "It's Like That/Sucker MCs," a disc that was released on Profile Records in March of 1983.

One cold morning in November of the same year, I met Russell Simmons for the first time. The Fearless Four (first rap group signed to a major label, Elektra) were filming their video for their single "Problems of the World," directed by Jerry Rodriguez. While the two of us sat in the warmth of the crew's van, Simmons spoke excitedly about his brother's rap group: "Ya gotta do a story on them ... they're gonna be large!" he screamed. Those words still echo in my head. I never wrote a word about this up-and-coming crew. And, to say the least—they exploded.

In 1983/84, crews like the Fearless Four, Furious Five and Soul Sonic Force were on the cutting edge of this new Black Noize, but they still dressed like costumed funkateers Earth, Wind & Fire or Parliament/Funkadelic—that urban Indian or leather spacemen shit that was considered *coool!* Run-D.M.C. was having none of that, preferring to dress like regular fellas, brothers in the street. In his book, Bill Adler reported that Run-D.M.C. once had a slight confrontation with the Fearless Four in a New Jersey club while they were playing the same bill. The Fearless Four tried to dis Run-D.M.C.'s street attire, not thinking it was proper stage wear. Jay looked at the crew and said, "Yeah, that's right! That's the way we are. No leather suits and no homo boots." Within a year, the Fearless Four had faded from the rap scene. And Run-D.M.C. proved, in both voice and image, that they were "tougher than leather."

Run-D.M.C.'s image, aggressively marketed by their label, is what made them so instantly special. Like Madonna's belly button or Michael Jackson's glove, the crew's black hats and unlaced Adidas sneaks were things consumers grabbed on to quickly. With their iconic look reflecting an outlaw spirit that white, middle-class kids already reveled in via reggae and heavy metal, their sound naturally followed suit.

But, drawing on the distinguishably different rap traditions of engagement with social issues (from early Sugar Hill releases) and of gritty, roughhouse energy (from twi-night jams in neighborhood parks), *Run-D.M.C.* wasn't all ill shit; it created a new style in two ways. Though their debut twelve-inch, "It's Like That," carried a message a la Grandmaster Flash and the Furious Five, it did so over a spare machine beat sliced through every few bars with sharp synthesizer hits; none of those live *band* arrangements and *none of those brutal visions of urban realism either.* Supervised by Larry Smith and Russell Simmons but directed by Run and D., the song expanded its scope to include the sorry dilemmas of the world-at-large as well as the ghetto. Instead of them each rapping every other verse—that's the old way—the Run and D. intertwined their forceful voices, finishing each other's lines in thrilling exchanges that went about tackling a topic that might have seemed heavy-handed; not deploring the problems it presented, "It's Like That" achieved added power (thus, authenticity) through subtlety as well as spareness; it was still kinda smooth and adulterated, though.

The B-side, "Sucker MCs," was more cut-to-the-bone, the track being just a beat co-producer Larry Smith programmed to be a knockoff of the one on Orange Krush's "Action" (Russell Simmons's first production in 1982, which introduced raw vocalist Alyson Williams to the pop world). Part autobiography, part B-boy fantasy, "Sucker MCs" was the beginning of the modern "dis" record, its tart, serrated words directed at Bronx crews such as the Treacherous Three, the Fearless Four and the Furious Five. It went a little som'n like, "We're live as can be, not singing the blues/Not five, not four, not three, just two."

Run-D.M.C. contained another cut, "Hard Times," that sounded like "It's Like That." Over a track of hypnotic breathing and a throbbing bass that vibrated with images of slaves working in the field of some down-South plantation, the pair's warbles have weaved an inspirational message for the worked-up, done-in masses: "Hard times in life/Hard times in death/I'm gonna keep on fighting till my very last breath." Fortunately, there was, in addition, something that evolved from "Sucker MCs" in "Hollis Crew." The former tune became known as "Krush Groove 1," and the latter, naturally, was called "Krush Groove 2." In the language of hip hop, a krush groove is a monster jam, a big-footed, dubbed-down stampede. As its opening salvo, "Sucker DJs who did not learn/If you don't this time we shall return," indicates, this second jam is a variation on a lyrical as well as musical theme. And if this rap attack wasn't enough, Run and D. talked more shit about those old-school Bronx "freaks" wrapped in feathers and cowboys outfits in "Rock Box," a few of its most memorable lines also giving some justification for their own "down" street look: "Calvin Klein's no friend of mine/Don't want nobody's name on my behind/Lee on my leg, sneakers on my feet/D. by my side and Jay with the beat."

Even though "Rock Box" harnessed melodic axe riffs by Eddie Martinez, they devastated only those bourgeois Blacks whose usual tastes run toward the pseudo-jazz jack of saxophonists George Howard or Kenny G. As Russell Simmons says, "Rock Box had a pussy guitar; it was rock for niggers!" While it won fans throughout MTV Land, "Sucker DJs" was a more exciting rock 'n' roll record simply because it was meaner and set a new pop order. Even more raw was "Jam Master Jay," a percolating, homemade beat layered with the brother harassing the hell out of perfectly good records and being *most* abrasive. "That's the kind of shit that white kids were looking for in a rap band!"

While Run-D.M.C. continued fusing rock with rap on *King of Rock,* they were still pussyfooting around, their guitar flash still coming off less comforting than agitating, more radiant than explosive. Like on "Rock Box" before, Eddie Martinez's axe on this album doesn't blaze a trail across dusty pastures, his effects box acting like accelerator pads; his fuel gauge for any aggression here is running on E.

Things start off with fleeting images from "Rock Box" trying to disguise themselves in a dub called "Rock the House." Slamming (or should we say rolling) directly into this retread is the title track, whose rockish swirls were bolstered by another no-holds-barred rap attack on the status quo: "It's not a trick or treat/And it's not an April Fool/It's Run-D.M.C.—never ever old school."

Still, this track's music supported nothing progressive or fresh. And when the band included another unforgivably generic imposter to the title of angry rock 'n' roll anthem in "Can You Rock It Like This," it was becoming clear that the kings of rap were this close to only sitting on the throne occupied by jaded, tired farts opting for security over ingenuity. Then they laid out "Roots, Rap, Reggae," whose attempt to bridge continents falls short of the span by a mile. Though featured vocalist Yellowman drops some amusing lines in Jamaican patois ("Five plus five equal to ten/Everywhere I go I got a lot o' girlfriend/Music is sweet, music is nice/Yellow have about 24 wife"), the ugly albino's charm loses its zing against this lumbering, plain track. Run-D.M.C. were prophetic enough to ride the cusp of the ragamuffin wave years before it hit the States, becoming the dominant style in the concrete jungle during '89/'90; why, though, did Run-D.M.C. leave its zing back in the islands?

Thankfully there's the nonchalant aggression of Jam Master Jay's turntable cutting in "Jam Master Jammin'" and "Darryl and Joe (Krush Groove 3)" and the sharp boom of "You're Blind," which features guitars (played by Rick Rubin and Larry Smith) that actually scorch the aural tarmac that's its beat. Clearing the air of a street hustler's smoke ("Livin' your life just to perpetrate") and replacing it with a purple haze that suggests seeking knowledge (or, as Run puts it, wearing "some glasses like D.M.C."), the track has the power to raise the Black nation as it moves a crowd. Now, this is the way to rock a house.

Fall 1986: After carefully sipping from a steaming cup of herbal tea and staring out the window at the chocolate, Afrocentric *Essence* gal strolling under the beaming sunlight on St. Mark's Place, Vernon Reid turns his attention toward me, saying, "Sorry. What was that last question?" Realizing that most musicians are far more intense (i.e., strange) than other mere mortals, I hide my frustration from his sad eyes and move the tape recorder slightly across the table. "I wanted to know what artists recorded your favorite albums this year."

And in his whispery voice Reid mumbles, "What artists?" His mind drifts for a moment, lost in the stars or a cloud of Ernie Isley solos; on his gentle-landing back to earth, he glances at the portable Sony. "Well ... three of my three favorite artists this year are the Bad Brains, Anita Baker and Run-D.M.C. Yeah, I think *Raising Hell* is a masterpiece."

After recruiting former dope-boys Aerosmith to gasp and strum on their remake of the rock classic "Walk This Way" (Run-D.M.C.'s attempt to crash the walls between rock and rap, as the video demonstrated), these bogus gangsters/kings of rap were able to transcend into millions of living rooms/bedrooms/kitchens via the magical airwaves of MTV in heavy rotation. Yet, to merely state that this track was overrated in the earholes of the masses would be an understatement. Though I have nothing against the sound of the '70s (memories of roaring through Baltimore wit my home [white] boy J.T. as we blared *Toys in the Attic* while puffin' on Tiajuana Red back in the day when "Walk This Way" was my favorite jam), this song could have worked if the change had been radical enough. Yet one gets the impression that the main reason this song was re-recorded in the first place had more to do with producer Rick Rubin's fantasies of working with his once-upon-a-time idols than anything else; the only reason Russell Simmons didn't disagree had something to

do with the dollar signs blinding his sight. But then again ...
who knows?

"The turntables might wobble, but they don't fall down,"
Run says on "Peter Piper" (which uses the carnival-style break
from the Bob James–composed "Mardi Gras"), the most hip-hop
track on the first side. Although this track is not (another) one
of the faves, the song that follows, "It's Tricky" has an ill,
nervous beat that strolls nearer to the edge of rock culture than
"Walk This Way" could ever think of.

The distance of five years (this record was released in
1986) has nothing to do with my contempt of Run-D.M.C. or
rock culture, it has to do with the awkward way that the (rock)
music was introduced. In my mind, a group like Public Enemy
(although *Village Voice* critic Greg Tate voted them one of the
best *jazz* groups of 1990) would become more influential in
swaying Black youth toward the new rock aesthetic than any
Rick Rubin track on this album.

"Kings from Queens, from Queens come Kings/We're raising hell like a class when the lunch-bell rings," the crew raps on
the album's title track. Although this is another guitar-soaked
song, the axe-wail is not as obnoxious as in "Walk This Way,"
because it works more in the structure of hip hop without being
an overbearing pain in the ass.

Overall, *Raising Hell* ain't all that, forget about all that
hype. The best (purist) tracks on the disc are "Son of Byford"
(which, unfortunately, is about forty seconds long), "Dumb Girl"
(look, Ma, no guitars!), with its minimalist beats and sonic echo,
and "You Be Illin' " ('cause it got that goofy ending, "Talkin'
'bout my mom's, talk' 'bout my mom's").

Perhaps it was Vernon Reid's electric-guitar paradise dreams
that made him vote *Raising Hell* one of the best albums of
1986, but then again, maybe his mind was drifting in the clouds.

After two years of Run-D.M.C. overexposure—hearing their
collective voices of positivity creeping from the radio and TV

PSAs urging urban youth to just say no to drugs or to stay in school; seeing them chillin' with bulky professional wrestlers or posing in giant subway ads for national sports chain Athlete's Foot; watching their videos enough times that they were haunting my dreams (leaving me bored and tired come morning), and gettin' into a scary argument with a bunch of knuckleheads clad in black T-shirts and untied Adidas while chillin' at the *Raising Hell* tour at Nassau Coliseum, the hoods sayin', "Ya don't know who you fuckin' wit!" while the self-proclaimed Kings from Queens were strutting onstage, bouncing back and forth, holding their dicks and shouting the lyrics to "Hard Times"; after all this, when the UPS dude delivered the green Profile envelope containing Run-D.M.C.'s latest piece of black vinyl, *Tougher Than Leather,* I was less than thrilled. After spending many nights grooving at the Knitting Factory, getting rocked and jazzed by the sonic screech of Jean-Paul Bourelly, the blare of Steve Coleman's sax or the soulful wail of Cassandra Wilson, my aesthetic had shifted to a new contemporary vanguard—one that was more downtown boho than crossover chic. After listening to the record once (with one deaf ear), I merely flipped it onto my growing pile of dusty discs and forgot about it. One friend asked my (*humhh!*) learned opinion on *Tougher Than Leather* and my answer was simply, "Fuck that shit ... it's wack."

That was 1988. Three years have passed since I heard the now-age Kings of Rock (the sound you hear is Elvis turnin' in his grave) and, damn, I made a mistake.

With the exception of the Rick Rubin–produced "Mary, Mary" (a lame rockist track that stumbles with feet of concrete) and "Ragtime" (a vain attempt to place Scott Joplin in a B-boy context while the boyz parodize Doug E. Fresh and Slick Rick), Run-D.M.C. created an album that rocked harder than the aging-hippie rhythms of "Walk This Way." In contemplating a theory in which to define this work, I am reminded of the concept of *Negritude,* which was developed by two philosophers, Sedar Senghor, and Aime Cesaire, between 1934 and 1948. Of the several broad meanings, as explained by Janheinz Jahn in *Neo-African Literature,* two of them bring *Tougher Than Leather* to mind: (1) It was more often the style, feeling, and vision of a poetical work that mattered than its content. And (2) it was rhythm sprung from deep emotion and feeling states, and from humor. In other words, never have I felt that these brothers were great poets (can't touch Chuck D. or Doug E. Fresh on the printed page), but the way they say what they say within the context of their style can blow any sucker MC from the stage of the Apollo. As for their rhythms—check out the futurist soundscape of "They Call Us Run-D.M.C." and "Beats to the Rhyme" to hear how advanced their sound could be once they were left alone in the studio (this was the first album that didn't have the interference of Larry Smith or Rick Rubin); these two cuts sound like they were tracked at a NASA space-station hovering over Mars.

During the late '80s, a crew of Black musicians, writers, artists and critics got together in New York to form a group called the Black Rock Coalition. Although this organization would be instrumental in "discovering" powerful bands like Living Colour, 24-7 Spyz, Eye & I and PBR Streetgang, the reason for its existence could be found in its manifesto: "Rock 'n' roll is Black music and we are its heirs." From Little Richard to Chuck Berry, Jimi Hendrix to Funkadelic, this aural history may not be played on local "classic rock" stations, but hey—them's da facts. On their amazing title track, "Tougher Than Leather," Run-D.M.C. snatch the roots back from those dusty MTV pinheads, stir in some funky wah-wah (something about that sound creates a musical Hoo-Doo that moves even the *deadest* bodies) and abrasive lyrics, constructing their best rock song since Rick Rubin and Larry Smith's fingers bled on the "Rock Box" solo.

Perhaps a lot of folks had grown bored with Run-D.M.C. by the time *Tougher Than Leather* was released, since this album didn't exactly burn down the house in the sales department. After groovin' to Big Daddy Kane or MC Lyte, buying the latest Run-D.M.C. album might have seemed like a step in the wrong direction. But this is perhaps the most underrated hip-hop album—of 1988 or any year. (P.S. But don't go thinkin' ya should rent their movie of the same name, 'cause that's BULL-SHIT G!)

No longer the B-boys to watch, hip-hop hippies De La Soul and Ruthless gangstas N.W.A. among the many crews now outflanking them, rap's first dick grabbers walked their separate ways for two years before coming back together for *Back From Hell* in 1990. Run virtually disappeared from sight, becoming a blissed-out born-again Rasta and preferring to chill at home with his wife and two kids; D.M.C. became a fixture on the party circuit, where, after downing a couple of forties of Olde English 800, he would test his new rhymes out on friends and acquaintances till the break of dawn; and Jam Master Jay started the Rush Associated JMJ label, working with the Afros, while Run and D. launched JDK Records, whose first artist, Smooth Ice, froze below expectations.

Figuring that since they could resurrect aging arena-scale rockers Aerosmith, who went on to win a 1990 MTV award, these deposed kings of new rock 'n' roll resurfaced with "Pause" in 1989, intent on erasing the hell critics and fans had given them over their last few projects. With its recombinant technofunk hybrid of soul and rap, this jittery anti-drug/we're-all-in-the-same-gang jam of inspired sloganeering (originally the B-side to their spastic *Ghostbusters 2* theme song) delivered a rush to hip-hop and dance aficionados alike, taking them on a trip along melodic curves hooked up by the group in collaboration with Queens keyboardist Stanley Brown. Notable not just for its shuffling hard-jack production, this track represents the first time Jam Master Jay has rapped on a record. Sporting a headful of new-age braids in the song's video, he demonstrates a new dance called the Pause before introducing Brown, who is wielding the same over-the-shoulder synth favored by Teddy Riley. The sly smile that Brown maintains on his baby face while going for his in a get-busy solo seemed to be sending a bold and large message to the new-jack mack: "Yo! We got our own thing!"

In another blues-informed tumble that occurs deep into *Back From Hell*, Guy lead voice Aaron Hall is featured in a loopy, rousing chorus that supports the assertive, get-busy emotion of the song's verses. This track had the muscle to pound dancers and postmod freaks into submission. Question is, Did Run-D.M.C. have the stuff to make the hardcore/hardheaded brothers on the corner, reveling in the group's fall from grace while slurping from brown paper bags, grab their dicks?

The first three tracks on *Back From Hell* briskly sweep any such skepticism into the wind. After taking a quick fifty-second bite out of their own "Sucker MCs" for "Sucker DJs," they stomp into a chaotic track, titled "The Avenue," that details how junkies, drug dealers and stick-up kids are "fucking up" the streets of Hollis; the same blocks that once represented Black middle-class respectability (an escape from the ghettos of Brooklyn or the Bronx) are now creating bronzed victims of violence and addiction. As Run says toward the end of the track, "Nobody give a damn, that's how they're livin' on the Ave." The irony of second-generation suburbia youth destroying what their families worked hard to build can be heard in their voices. The soundscape is rather chilling, as one can hear sirens, bullets, and the cries of victims in this nightmare of confusion. This track is obviously influenced by the brutal street journals of Ice Cube or N.W.A., yet Run-D.M.C. doesn't in any way celebrate ("I got a feeling the illing will never pay") this lifestyle of destruction.

After they've portrayed their neighborhood as an urban Sodom and Gomorrah, one supposes that the logical follow-up question would be "What's It All About?" While appropriating its main rhythmic thrust from the popular Manchester group the Stone Roses, this track doesn't pretend to answer the inquiries of noir America, but instead it lifts the podium to a universal level. After comments on the blight of the homeless, the decay of buildings, and damaged spirits of our youth, Run-D.M.C. talk about the fall of the Berlin Wall and the freeing of Mandela. In other words, no matter how slowly other parts of the world are trying to get their shit together, America seems to be drowning in a sea of her own rhetoric. Or to quote a Funkadelic record from the '70s, "America eats her young." At times Run & Co. sound like a trio of preachers or teachers ("If you don't like what me and my crew are doing ... then fuck you!" D.M.C. screams), but their words are valid and their beats are seriously slammin'. If the crew came "back from hell" to face a mirror image of another inferno, then they must be slightly disappointed.

After reporting on the sorrow of the world, the brothers pile into their rides and roar over to the popular Q Club: couples sway to the dancehall stylee/dub track of "Bob Your Head;" fellas hold warm Guinnesses in sweaty palms, and *rub* the tight-dressed hotties in a way that suggests Erica Jong's concept of "the zipless fuck." With its mixture of dancehall and hip hop, the track doesn't sound like it was imported from the islands (the fellas rappin' in Jafakein accents), but it still rocks.

These tracks certainly don't equal the power or the fury of propulsive assertions like "I'm Not Going Out Like That" or "Hit It Run," but these tunes, along with the pumping "Not Just Another Groove" (which sounds more Uptown than Rush) and the too short ragamuffin pit bull "P Upon a Tree," are sufficiently ragged to tear shit up like the old days, when things were heavenly for Run-D.M.C. It would be a mistake for the crew to believe that they are still the Kings of Rap—their crown was snatched around the time *Tougher Than Leather* was released—but, yeah, they're still in there!

SALT-N-PEPA

HOT, COOL & VICIOUS (NEXT PLATEAU), 1986

A SALT WITH A DEADLY PEPA, 1988

BLACKS' MAGIC, 1990

Between bites of her tofu sandwich at Dojo's, my friend Francine reminisces about her pre-teen years in the depressing city of Poe (Baltimore): of the marble house on North Avenue where every Saturday night there was a roaring party, the sounds of Motown and the din of drunken voices drifting through the dusty vents, floating into the dainty bedroom she shared with her three sisters. "Daddy useta play all them Motown songs," she says, her eyes dancing with memories. "Ya know, Marvin Gaye and Junior Walker and Smokey Robinson? When he played 'Ooh Baby Baby,' we knew that the lamp with the red bulb had been plugged in and everybody was dancing close. Hell, the entire house reeked of cheap perfume and spilled beer, sweaty bodies and whispered secrets."

"Yeah, kinda reminds me of the first adult jam I ever went to," I say, gulping down a Bloody Mary. "Me and my brother was in Pittsburgh and my Aunt Rickie and Uncle Ed took us to this wild party 'cause they couldn't find a babysitter. And my cousin Dee was 'round the side of the house kisisn' this dude who had just come from the Army on leave. Jesus, I swear they played 'Let's Get It On' about a million times that night! I don't tell this to many folks, but I cried the day Marvin Gaye was killed!"

"Me too," Francine says, sighing. "But ya wanna know when me and my sisters really got crazy? When Daddy useta play them girl groups: Martha and the Vandellas' 'Dancing in the Streets,' something by the Ronettes or the Supremes. Talk about niggers goin' bugged! Hell, we would be jumpin' on our beds and screaming at the top of our lungs. But no one ever heard us 'cause they was into their own thang. We was sisters and in our young minds all those girl groups were sisters, too."

"The party's over, it's time to call it a day/You burst my pretty balloon . . ."

And on Sunday mornings, while most of Black Baltimore was snoring off a drunken Saturday night or calling on Jesus to "wash away their sins," Francine and her sisters were thumping down the squeaky basement stairs, tripping over discarded beer bottles or sleeping bodies, sneaking into the rear of the room where the hi-fi rested on a rickety old table. Sorting through a pile of scratched seven-inch discs smeared with fingerprints, li'l sis Wanda would find her favorite record ("Anyone see da plastic thang that go in da middle?"), "Baby Love." Still dressed in their flowered pajamas, the girls flicked on the dimming red light and instantly their basement was transformed into the stage of the Apollo. While they pantomimed in front of the mirrored wall, the record played and the audience (in their minds) cheered; their flowered pajamas became sequined gowns as these three supreme young girls danced elegantly for their adoring fans.

Twenty years later, Francine says, "Being a member of a girl group was always our fantasy."

Smiling, I say, "Yeah, that's cool. But you know what I always wondered? Why do girl groups always come in threes— like the holy trinity of pop, I suppose?"

From the Marvelettes' "Please Mr. Postman" to the Crystals' "He's a Rebel," Vanity 6's "Nasty Girls" to Exposé's "Point of No Return," the detailed history of girl groups in modern pop can be traced back to the late '50s when groups like the Shirelles could be heard drifting from car radios, wailing broken-hearted mini-dramas or romantic anthems of love. And yet the paradox of girl groups throughout the canon of pop is the fact that the words and music are mostly fueled through the creativity of male songwriters and producers. These aural Pygmalions (Phil Spector, George Morton, Berry Gordy, Prince, etc.) are often given more credit than the voices heard on record.

If one were to judge Salt-n-Pepa solely from their sultry teen-mag pinups or their sexy music videos, one might suspect that these three Queens natives (Sandy Denton, Cheryl James, and DJ Dee Dee Roper) are hip-hop sirens created by their producer, Hurby "Luv Bug" Azor—just another product from Hurby's noisy machine factory. Yet nothing could be further from the truth. . . .

Granted Hurby did discover Salt-n-Pepa while they worked the telephones in Sears' sales department (if this were a film, it would now dissolve to the corny scene where the innocent young

Salt-n-Pepa, Black-magic women. © Ernest Paniccioli, 1990.

actresses are discovered in the drugstore by a Hollywood agent); the only catch to this scenario is the fact that Hurby was also slaving *his* days away at Sears while attending the Center for Media Arts. He got together with Sandy and Cheryl when he was assigned a class project that involved making a record. As the Showstoppers, Salt-n-Pepa's first production was an answer record to Doug E. Fresh's popular hip-hop tracks "La-di-da-di" and "The Show." It was extremely raw and amateurish, yet it did manage to open doors for the team. After playing "Showstopper" for Juice Crew producer Marley Marl, who managed to get this crew hooked up with a single deal from Pop Art Records, the wheels of steel started rollin'.

Although there have been other girl groups in the canon of "South Bronx dada" (early '80s Sugar Hill group Sequence released a handful of singles and two albums) Salt-n-Pepa was less of a musical hallucination, more of a hip-hop influence to a legion of young B-gals "hiding in the light," searching for something to call their own. And yet, in their four-year history, Salt-n-Pepa has been labeled everything from hip-hop womanists to crossover opportunists to the new power of soul. It's interesting to note that all three terms apply to Salt-n-Pepa, because with each of their three albums, they approached their musical canvas from diverse angles; each of these discs have progressed the once-silent voice of women into the rock-hard world of hip hop.

To best document the soundscapes that Salt-n-Pepa travel, each album should be placed under a heading which best describes their missions as they venture through the superhighways of Black pop.

1. Looking for the Perfect Beat. "The most progressive forms of this music are too hard-edged for women," hip-hop kingpin Russell Simmons chauvinistically told journalist Nelson George in 1985. One year later, Salt-n-Pepa dropped their debut album, *Hot, Cool & Vicious,* onto an unsuspecting audience to much critical acclaim and with a huge hit in the orgasmic sex song "Push It." As a blueprint for all future hip-hop divas, this album is evidence that Salt-n-Pepa was more than a cute novelty act. Although the group never pretended to be feminist in the Gloria Steinem *defi*nition of the word, Salt-n-Pepa's voices blared from speakers, declaring their independence to both B-boys and flye-girl crews. Talk about complete arrogance, Salt-n-Pepa just say what they wanna and do what they say: in the eyes of their male fans (looking at their image first, thinking of their lyrics last), nothing they could say would be insulting. Call 'em a "Tramp" ("You know that kind, wit nothing but sex on the mind") and the art of double standards are reinforced; as the male voice in the mix says, "Yeah, I'll be a tramp . . ." Although this song attempts to put urban slickie boys in their proper context as it explains their gigolo methods to the "sisters" of America, as Salt-n-Pepa told a scribe from *Spin* magazine, "Men are not insulted by that track, they take it as a compliment."

Working both sides of the hip-hop fence, Salt-n-Pepa displayed their vamp fangs in the (sub)urban moonlight of the bouncy track "I'll Take Your Man." With the so-called shortage of Black men in the urban communities of America (I'm reminded of a Woody Allen joke: "If there's four women to every man, then someone must have eight"), da sisters failed to recognize the humor in this track. Over fierce, funky beats that sound like a wild party on New Year's Eve, Salt-n-Pepa throw Tyson jabs ("Ho don't ya know, can't ya understand/If ya miss wit me . . . I'll take your man"). This track had neighborhood Gucci gals suckin' their teeth and calling this new "juice crew" a buncha bitches—if Shaharazad Ali's *The Blackman's Guide to Understanding Blackwomen* was ever made into a film, this would be the soundtrack. Yet on their remake of the Pointer Sisters' "Chick on the Side," these gals try to redeem themselves. As the title explains, even if they did take your man, it's a shot in the dark that he'll be faithful to them; like my homegirl

D. says, "What goes around, comes around, and payback be a mutherfucker!"

Two tracks that celebrate the passion of the music more than the sexual desire are "Beauty and the Beat" and "My Mike Sounds Nice." The latter details the art of "rockin' and shockin' ... and kickin' ass" in the studio, while the former is less hard, more seductive. With *Hot, Cool & Vicious,* Salt-n-Pepa became the first girl group to be taken seriously in the hip-hop arena. They might have made the music more sensual, but more than that, they made a wide enough crack in the holy walls of rap to allow other women to slip through. One should not forget the brilliance of Hurby, but without these "queens from Queens," his sound would have been lost in the stars.

2. Crossover Dreams. 1988 was the year these hip-hop divas crashed the aural/visual race bar of the MTV zombie generation. Like the Supremes twenty years ago—under the hawk eyes of Berry Gordy, Diana & Co. bum-rushed the gates of Las Vegas ballrooms in flowing sequined gowns—Salt-n-Pepa was no longer a "ghetto" act segregated to the back streets of Red Alert or Mister Magic's weekly New York radio shows. "You can't play me boy/I'm no game," Salt-n-Pepa rap over the addictive beats Hurby laid down on the album's title track, which is bomb-squad chaotic, guitar-heavy and drum-happy; but there was little need for the sisters to worry, since they were playing *themselves* on much of this album. Not to say that *A Salt With a Deadly Pepa* is all-the-way wack, but terrible records seem to lurk in the mind like cancer: they can be lethal, but if they don't kill ya, they're not something you'll forget easily.

In the same way that no one will ever remember the Beatles covers that Diana Ross and her Detroit posse wailed beneath the white lights of Caesar's Palace, Salt-n-Pepa's re-make of the four mop tops' "Twist and Shout" will not go down in the B-boy hall of fame as the best hip-hop record ever. But the question is, Who shall we blame, Salt-n-Pepa or Hurby? It's understandable that their "supa def dope produsa" would have delusions of crossover swimming through his mind (picture this scenario: Luv Bug is sittin' in da studio and says, "You bit—er ... I mean girls, you're gonna be the first rappers to do the National Anthem at the World Series!"), but as future sisters like Janet Jackson and Miche'le would later prove, there's no need to go skinny-dippin' in polluted waters to be accepted by the masses. Worshipping at the altar of '60s rock culture (Hurby even adds an electric guitar solo in an attempt to prove that he is fab-culture literate) was not only depressing, but rather foolish. In the age of new technology, if the past is to be *lifted* and placed within a postmod concept, then the process should be handled gently—the listener should not be reminded that the process of appropriation is taking place. Salt-n-Pepa's version of "Twist and Shout" is not only a bad cut, it's bad art.

On "Shake Your Thang," their collaboration with Washington, D.C., funk (go-go) band E.U., Salt-n-Pepa prove that the promise shown on their first album had not faded, and that they were also walking with their ears tuned to the sounds of the underground. Although go-go was once hailed as the hip-hop nation's second cuz—the next big beat to drop a bomb on mainstream America—this thumpin' bass and drum-heavy artform never fulfilled its promise as The Next Big Thing.

Contributing to the mythology of hip-hop culture, the story of Salt-n-Pepa's first meeting with these post-funketeers is quite interesting: One night, after E.U. opened for these rapping soul sisters in some hotter-than-July Washington, D.C., venue, Spinderella's turntables crashed and the air lurking in the dive was dead. Having left their instruments onstage, E.U. volunteered to aid Salt-n-Pepa in halting the unpleasant roar of the audience. With their "snot-nose funk" and Salt-n-Pepa's sweet-as-chocolate voices, the savage beasts were soon calmed. Months after the fact, Hurby remembered the expression of bliss this collaboration induced on the faces of the sepia-toned crowd.

Although the sound of D.C. funk was still chiefly the soundtrack of music critics' dreams, director Spike Lee achieved a feat many record companies could not; by employing E.U. to record the Marcus Miller–penned "Da Butt" (for his film *School Daze*), Spike helped the godsons of soul extend themselves into the radio-tuned earholes of other chocolate cities besides D.C.

With their ode to the art of dirty dancing (and with booming booties like theirs in skintight jeans, the heat was risin'), Salt-n-Pepa lifted the grooves from the Isley Brothers' classic "It's Your Thang" and layered it with the innovations of New York and Washington funk. "Shake Your Thang" was not the first time that go-go had crawled into bed with hip hop (Kurtis Blow's "I'm Chillin'," recorded with Trouble Funk, still haunts my memory), but this track would prove to be the most successful relationship of Blax-on-Blax dance music. "Oh, I like hip hop mixed wit the go-go baby/It's my thang and I shake it crazy," Salt says. Somewhere behind the bounce of bass and congas, the sound of fierce finger-snapping echoes in the studio.

Any daydreams that *A Salt With a Deadly Pepa* would metamorphosize into a funk fest are soon shattered by the wailing electric guitars that open yet another cover, "I Gotcha." I've always felt that when any artist(s) produce a cover jam, their track should be better than the original production. And after Salt-n-Pepa's version of "I Gotcha," I'm sure that Joe Tex is flippin' in his grave. 'Nuff said.

"Salt-n-Pepa with mics, Spinderella with cuts/Let's get paid," Salt raps on "Solo Power (Let's Get Paid)." Although most critics aren't on the business side of "da biz," it might be idealistic to think there are other ways to make money, without selling one's soul. "Push It," the smash from their first album, went Top Forty without losing any of the group's street appeal, but *A Salt With a Dead Pepa* damn near killed any vibe that was left.

3. *Back in Black.* "It's the '90s, the year for change/Can

you prove it?/I made this beat ... and I produced it!" Salt smoothly says on the album's title track, *Blacks' Magic*. The first change one notices is translated through the album's cover art: Instead of the cutesy girl poses one expects from Salt-n-Pepa, we are treated to a haunting airbrushed painting by Charles Lilly. *Blacks' Magic*'s graphic design shows our three heroines depicted sitting in the semidarkness of a library after midnight, their eyes fixed on the text within the *Blacks' Magic* book which Pepa holds firmly in her hands. As the trio stares fascinated by this glowing Hoo-Doo Manifesto of Black popular music, the creative spirits of Billie Holiday, Jimi Hendrix, Louis Armstrong, and Minnie Ripperton hover overhead, casting spells of inspiration.

On "Expression," the album's first single, one can witness Salt-n-Pepa's second change by listening to guest vocalist Jacci McGhee (Keith Sweat's background singer) wail away on the song's chorus like an African muse. After hearing her smooth voice ("Express yourself, you gotta be you and only you baby/ Express yourself and let me be me") floating through the mix, one's thoughts aren't that she emerged from the shiny doors of a Baptist church; yet it signifies that Salt-n-Pepa have awakened from their crossover dreams into a theater of soul. Although Brit critic Simon Reynolds tries to brutally assault the body of Soul in his essay "All Souled Out" ("Soul? My arse—the Queen is dead and her name was Aretha Franklin!"), *Blacks' Magic* proves that the sonic architects within the hip-hop nation have designed a new body for her: Call it *cybersoul*.

"We've always been push it, shake, twist it out—you know, that type of group," Salt told journalist Lisa Kennedy in the pages of *Mother Jones* magazine. "Well, we're older now and have a lot more responsibilities ... we're in a different frame of mind now." With "Negro Wit' an Ego," these sisters in rhyme have made the conscious decision to lay down their party outfits and feed the audience some brain food. One might view this song as Salt-n-Pepa's attempt to jump on the Public Enemy/ Afrocentric bandwagon, but in the words of noted feminist Kool Moe Dee, "Knowledge is king," and on "Negro Wit' an Ego," these women are dropping science. Starting in the middle of this aural protest, Salt-n-Pepa sing, "Put some faith in your race" over Hurby's loopy beats, before summing up their mission by rapping, "I'm Black and I'm proud to be an African-American soul sister/Using my mind as a weapon, a lethal injection ..." Angela Davis couldn't have said it better.

From the shaking of bodies to the body politic, Salt-n-Pepa have recorded two soulful (images of Simon Reynolds's ears bleeding cloud my mind) tracks that discuss the reality of sex. Without being overly romantic or dreamily passionate, both "Do You Want Me" and "Let's Talk About Sex" are funky, uncompromising companion pieces that express a woman's need to control her body. In other words, if you wanna, cool (just know what you're doin'); and if you don't wanna, don't do it. When Salt says, "Be my friend not just my lover/Share your thoughts with me/Love my mind not just my body, baby," one might think she's being old-fashioned, until you scope the statistics of teenage mothers in our country. Without being preachy, Salt-n-Pepa are just "tellin' it like it is." Note that the chorus of "Do You Want Me" is sung by men. "Ain't got no time for silly games," they say when the women resist their language of lust, reducing their machoisms to a pile of shattered-ego dust.

It's interesting that both of these tracks feature more singing than rapping, giving me the idea that Salt-n-Pepa might come back next time with no rap at all. That would be a loss, but to paraphrase Rakim, whatever they do, I know it'll have soul.

THE 7A3

COOLIN' IN CALI (GEFFEN), 1988

One steamy July night in 1988, I was hangin' out at Manhattan's Calliope Studios, on a mission to interview Stetsasonic's li'l-man Daddy-O. Sitting in a swivel chair, sipping cold coffee, I watched as Daddy-O jumped up from a mixing board, screaming, "Damn, sometimes I wish I was a Latin Rascal [those editor/producers of jerky dance tracks] 'cause they got the dope beats!" He wasn't talking to anyone—in fact, he was gazing out the window, not even noticing me in the studio.

Across the room, lounging on the black leather sofa, was a fella who was later introduced as Bretty B. (from the Cali hip-hop crew 7A3). Although Ice-T was on the scene, most New Yorkers hadn't any idea that rap music had much impact on West Coast culture. This was before M.C. Hammer or N.W.A., Ice Cube or Tone-Löc.

The track that Daddy-O was producing was a lackluster piece titled "½ Bouldin, the Other ½ Ince." It was yet another bigger and deffer tune that aspired toward an old-school sound (real old—sounds like it was recorded in a cave), utilizing springy acoustic drums and an interesting guitar sample that floats over the mix like a Stratocaster jet dropping bombs on corpses in an aural jungle. Unfortunately, though, the guitar sound is buried so deeply in the mix, one is left with the feeling of electric-axe wet dreams, yet still unfulfilled. Granted, this was one of Daddy-O's first production gigs outside of his regular stint with Stet (check out his groove thangs with Queen Latifah, the Black Flames, and Timmy Gatling for a more mature, sexier sound), but this track is just quickie filler.

The main problem with the 7A3's debut album, *Coolin' in Cali*, is that it suffers from producer(s) overload, a disease common to new kids on the avenue who lack an artistic agenda or aesthetic vision. By spreading six producers (including Philly gangster Schoolly D., party-boy Cash Money, another Stet-man, DBC, and da underrated Joe "The Butcher" Nicolo) over twelve tracks, this disc screams of aural schizophrenia. Just listen to "Groovin'," a track that seems to pay homage to the deconstructed grooves of Tackhead producer Adrian Sherwood: a brutal attack of found sounds and live instrumentation (layered with a heavy-funk bottom) that conjures up haunting images of ghosts dancing in one's nightmares. And though this "collision of mess and precision" has a chaotic appeal, *the shit ain't no hip hop.*

With 7A3's paint-by-numbers approach to hip hop (dig the Fresh Prince-ish tune "A Man's Gotta Do What a Man's Gotta Do"), what pisses me off the most is the knowledge that these fellas must have had *some* ambitions when they began this project, 'cause two of the tracks are damn-near brilliant, diamonds buried beneath a heap of trash. "Like Sinatra, do it my way," Bretty B. screams on the title track, "Coolin' in Cali," an ode to B-boy highlife on the Left Coast. Constructed by sonic architects Hank Shocklee, Keith Shocklee and Eric Sadler, the sheer savagery of the grooves induces a high that can only be matched by either drugs or religion. Although 7A3 tries to play the role of neo-soulboys on their other eleven tracks by using *real live musicians* (searching for authenticity?), Shocklee & Company prove that the humanist touch ain't what makes a great hip-hop record. By sampling Sly Stone's "Thank You (Falettinme Be Mice Elf Sgin)" Kool & the Gang's "Hollywood Swinging" and other big-beats, more beauty can be heard leaking from computers than from a thousand Hammond organs. All hail the Fairlight bandits. . . .

If "Coolin' in Cali" is 7A3's chronicle of chillin' in the L.A. sunshine, then "That's How We're Livin' " is its noir companion in leisure crime, an anthem of nighttime decadence that slams like a souped-up limo roaring down Sunset Boulevard: "Saw the homeboys from the days of delirium/'89 Benz's, guess who's steerin' 'em/Hop into the ride, cold coolin' with the crew/They puffin' on the cheeba and guzzling the brew," Bretty says over beige soul-stirrer Boz Scaggs's "Low Down" groove. Produced by Philly Joe Nicolo, this track reeks of raw urban funk that reminds me of Muhammad Ali in his prime: Black, bold and sweaty as hell. Damn shame 7A3 wasn't living this bad throughout the remainder of *Coolin' in Cali*; guess that souped limo caught a flat.

SAM SEVER

SEE MS. MELODIE AND 3RD BASS

SHABBA RANKS

AS RAW AS EVER (EPIC), 1991

The bass riffs rippling through the streets of Gotham the last year or more have frequently belonged to ragamuffin trax, those hybrid reggae jammies pumped up by the same machines in rap's arsenal. With its synthesized punch, nagging bass lines and chatting-style lyrics, dancehall is the gangster music of Jamaica that's swiftly running up on hip hop in its hometown. And the performer waging the most savage attack over this concrete playground is flyeboy–sex symbol Shabba Ranks. Before signing with Epic Records in 1991, this _draped_ twenty-two-year-old recorded several hits ("Roots & Culture," "Wicked In Bed," "X-Rated") for Jamaican independents. Now he's looking beyond his dubwise core of fans.

Shabba's major-label debut makes two blind thrusts for mainstream U.S. acceptance. These are "The Jam," a yawsy boast/toast produced by and featuring KRS-One, and "Housecall," an awkward pairing with Kingston-soul crooner Maxi Priest.

It's when Shabba and his regular session producers are left alone that things really take off. Riding knotty beats spiked with dub elements, the performer runs his deep voice (complete with deep patois) into whatever gets in his way—a speeding "Trailer Load of Girls," a chopping "Flesh Axe," for example. He offers contradictions—sexist boasts one moment, moral upliftment the next. Like he drops "Flesh axe—the land of de woman body fe chop . . . /Flesh axe—keep on choppin' de land de woman got" then asks, "Where Do Slackness Come From?" But in ramajam dancehall dives, no one really cares about the answer.

SHINEHEAD

ROUGH & RUGGED (AFRICAN LOVE), 1987

UNITY (ELEKTRA), 1989

THE REAL ROCK, 1990

L ike the sonic boom of hip hop, the island riddims known as reggae began as rebellious music against the politics and repressive nature of the ruling class—the soundtrack of urban blues for the worked-up, done-in masses. Both styles developed traditions of social criticism, comedy and boasting, but while reggae had been gliding along smoothly, circling around ghetto heaven in America, rap—full of brash intensity—had been bopping forward on another Ave. That's surprising since the musical roots of B-boy culture lie in the distinctive Jamaican sound-system scene of the late '60/early '70s (U Roy, Big Youth, Ranking Trevor). Its power and crispness migrated from Kingston to the West Bronx in 1967 via a DJ name Kool Herc.

Although Herc was blowing away other neighborhood disco setups by 1973, he still wasn't moving crowds. North American Black audiences just didn't rock to rock steady, so Herc began giving up the funk. Crowds began responding, but to keep things fresh, he also talked over his B beats (what he called back-to-back breaks). Rap started coming into its own, employing found sounds from jazz to soul to rock 'n' roll.

Back in Jamaica, DJs were filling floors with similarly inspired cut-and-mix melanges. Using technology imported from the U.K. and the U.S., they began experimenting, creating textures that resembled those in rap. They started forging a path toward the hip-hop nation in America. Eventually, the worlds of reggae and rap collided, creating a milky club cocktail of Rastaman vibrations and flye-boy intonations.

While this fusion quickly gained many followers, including the Fat Boys and Run-D.M.C., the man leading the movement since 1985 has been Shinehead. Born Edmund Carl Aitken in London and raised in Jamaica and the Bronx, Shinehead cut his first LP on the independent African Love label (owned by his manager and main producer, Claude Evans). With an ambitious blend of hip-hop boasting, ragamuffin toasting and love-man crooning, it gelled together under an invisible bead of grace and power, and throughout there were hints of the performer's personality, which lurks on the edge of lunacy (in one interview he responded to questions using the impersonated voicings of John Wayne, Robin Leach and a thespian).

The standout track on *Rough & Rugged* was "Who the Cap Fits," a serious attack on evil, power-hungry snakes, with a serious bounce. After languishing in New York's underground for months, the tune got picked up by urban-contempo radio outlets WRKS-FM and WBLS-FM and became reggae–hip hop's first monster cut. Based on a Bob Marley and the Wailers classic, it had an aim that was straight and on-target: "Control of the soul is your ultimate goal/And you couldn't care less who's left in the cold/Principals/Morals/Scruples/Love/Yeah, I know/These are things you ain't *ever* heard of . . ."

"Who the Cap Fits" (re-mixed with a new funk break and dreamy synth strings) and four other tunes from *Rough & Rugged* moved on to Shinehead's major-label debut, *Unity.* Of these, "Hello Y'all" honored his love for reggae music, and "Know How Fe Chat" demonstrated how limber his tongue is. But on to the LP's new stuff:

Hooked up with a brisk groove that's based on the Beatles' "Come Together," its title track, produced by Davey D. and Run-D.M.C.'s Jam Master Jay, screams for an end to rap's reputation for outsized egos and knucklehead violence. "When are you gonna stop this negative crap?" asks the performer. The songs ends on a hopeful note, with him singing "We Shall Overcome." This may be so, but when?

From an idealist stance, the next cut whisks us back into reality, through the restless underbelly of New York City's snaking subway system. A playful ride—called "Chain Gang Rap"—it's the album's hardest assault on hip hop. It conjures up glimpses of characters ranging from pickpockets to Guardian Angels, sweaty bums to booming flye girls. There's even a bullshit artist shooting his spiel for handouts.

After this wobbling trip atop numerous snare rolls and a fantastic, cascading bass, Shinehead returns to the smoothness (and breakneck lyrical pace) of dancehall/lovers' rock via "Ragamuffin" and a remake of Nat King Cole's "Golden Touch." The former illustrates how fertile Shinehead's tastes are, and how stirring his falsetto is. It, moreover, spells out what Shinehead has.

With his latest effort, *The Real Rock*, the performer continues borrowing melodies from the classics, but here he lifts melodies instead of singing them, recontextualizing Sly and the Family Stone's "Family Affair," Jimmy Castor and the Castor Bunch's "Potential" and Frank Sinatra's "Love and Marriage" (better known to new-jacks as the theme to shock TV' "Married With Children"). The catchiest tunes, however, are complete originals. The title track, where Shinehead raps about God ("Running around with the notion that you can't be stopped/But your'e gonna have to answer to the real rock"), is at once ferocious and hypnotic. "Dance Down the Road," distinguished by singing, a Jamaican rap and an American one, is a jamboree of cheerfulness. And "Till I Kissed You" is a sweeping jaunt through the tunnel of love. After blazing a musical trail, commenting on some of the blemishes encountered along the way, and teaching a few lessons in morality, Shinehead's still exploring. That he isn't feeble yet is a testament to the heft of his talent. Not the real rock, but a pretty sturdy structure nonetheless.

HANK SHOCKLEE/ BOMBSQUAD

SEE ICE CUBE, L.L. COOL J, PUBLIC ENEMY, 7A3, AND SLICK RICK

SLICK RICK

THE GREAT ADVENTURES OF SLICK RICK
(DEF JAM/COLUMBIA), 1988

I n walk two young tenders, statuesque and stylish. I'm lounging on the A train, Duke Ellington playing on the radio in my brain, gliding toward 125th on the uptown Black-folks express. In a corner sits a tattered soul swigging on a bottle of Wild Irish Rose, across the aisle, three Harlem slickie boys are scoping the cuties, but only for a moment. The one honeychile who caught *my* eye is wearing bamboo earrings and cut-up jeans, a tight spandex bodysuit revealing tits that would make a vain man cry. Cracking cherry-flavored Bubble Yum, honey turns to her girlfriend and says, "You know that dude Wise who lives on a Hundred Forty-seventh? Yo, he was trying to gas my head yesterday with all this yag." She laughs. The second girl, whose rust-colored extensions hang down her back, flashes a smile. "He kinda nice," she says. "You should give him some play." Ms. Spandex laughs, her voice soaring over the steady din of the roaring subway. And she says, "Yeah, he nice and all, but he ain't got no gold. Any nigga that wanna step to me *gotta* have some gold—a few chains, a coupla rings, or something." Her girlfriend nods her head in skeptical agreement.

And so I'm reminded of the first time I saw Slick Rick: Two years after his million-seller ("La-Di-Da-Di/The Show," with Doug E. Fresh) had slipped quietly from the *Billboard* charts, rail-thin Ricky was hanging large with his crew at New York's trendy China Club. Sitting in the semidarkness gulping champagne and Heinekens, Slick Rick possessed a sinister persona that sent ice water racing through my veins. Like a hip-hop Captain Hook, Ricky wore a pirate patch over his left eye (he was blinded in that eye as an infant by flying glass) and a tilted leather cap. From my seat at the bar, I could hear Ricky talking in his smooth Black-Brit accent, gold teeth with diamond studs gleaming in the shadows; his skinny fingers were covered with gold nuggets and there were enough truck jewels dangling from his neck to choke a bull.

On his debut album, *The Great Adventures of Slick Rick,* with a few sidebars to warn young 'uns about the dangers of crime, our man of the moment mostly has boning on his mind, along with teaching the art of ghetto coolness and sending positive messages of the Lord's light "still shining on you" ("Hey Young World"). But ask Trick Daddy Ricky about his secret to a lasting, mature relationship and he'll reply, "Treat Her Like a Prostitute."

Often I'm surprised at the childish dirty talk of my peers, of the misogynist locker-room "humor" that slips into men's conversations when women are not around. Be they book-smart or street-savvy, the lingo remains the same—from "the bitches" to "the ho's," many fellas relate to women on distant levels when they are not within the boundaries of our wild and loose tongues. This isn't an attempt to say "sorry" for Slick Rick's "Treat Her Like a Prostitute" ('cause like G-Mann says, "Women don't like no sorry men"), just a way to explain the essence of the track. Anyone who grew up in Black America, hung with the

Slick Rick. Photo by Alcindor, courtesy of
Def Jam/Rush Artist Management/
Columbia Records. © 1989 CBS Records Inc.

---

youngbloods on basketball courts, or chilled on the stoops of
tenements should understand that the tone of Slick Rick's voice
is not to be taken seriously—close your eyes and you can see
his golden smirk. Hell, this ain't social crit or even street lit,
more like an extended smut joke told after a few forties have
been downed and the bodega is closed.

"Here's an oldie but goodie!" Rick screams at the beginning of "Treat Her Like a Prostitute," and one isn't exactly sure
if he is referring to the track or to himself, 'cause this flye boy
been around for a while. While you're listening between the
lines, I'll tell ya a tale: Once upon a time there were a coupla
neighborhood pals who got together and decided to form a rap

crew. There was the human beatbox Doug E. Fresh, the dapper Brit Slick Rick, and the drivers of the wheels of steel, Chill Will and Barry B. After kicking around concepts and song ideas, this group of teen prodigies (now dubbed the Get Fresh Crew) released their 1985 dual masterpieces, "The Show" (arranged by the future of the funk, Teddy Riley) and "La-Di-Da-Di." Standing in an uptown subway station or walking through midtown, one could hear young men slinging Doug E. Fresh or Slick Rick lyrics like electric lassos. Although this popular hip-hop quartet toured the world and clocked dollars, all was not well in their Black Paradise.

Anyone who has ever dropped their jaw in awe at the Black noize of hip hop is well aware of the egoism that radiates from the cult of personality: ebony arms of steel reaching from the grooves, grabbing ya collar and screaming in ya face. In real life the art of egoism is a tiring game—one that both Doug and Ricky soon realized. While Doug wanted to soar "all the way to heaven," Rick chose to walk on the wild side. "Treat Her Like a Prostitute" was recorded while the Slick one was still down with the Get Fresh Crew, but he soon departed due to that old show-biz standby, "artistic differences." Somehow tapes of "Treat Her" got out and became a smash in the hip-hop underground; bootlegs blared from hundreds of sonic street boxes.

"Gather 'round party-goers—that's if you're still livin'/And get on down to the olde Slick rhythm," Slick Ricky Walters boasts on "The Ruler's Back." He's like a hip-hop holy trinity displaying three Ricky's in one body: lyricist, producer and actor. Whereas many rappers speak in the same tone of voice (or become part of a vocal team that explores their diversity, i.e., Digital Underground), Ricky is an aural dramatist—like in the days of early radio shows—who invades the soul of his characters, speaking in their voices, with a vocal repertoire that includes little children, jealous boyfriends, and coke-head nymphos ("The Moment I Feared"), or a young, dumb, fulla cum (as well as "crabs with spears and Indian drums/Singing hey-yah, hey-yah, hey-yah-hey!") "Indian Girl."

Although he is teamed with the Shocklee posse on six of the album's twelve tracks, Slick Rick proves himself more than handy in the studio on the solo-constructed track "Children's Story." Told as a gritty bedtime story of a misled young boy who becomes a neighborhood stickup artist, gets beat up by the police, encounters strange characters and has a mad chase in a stolen car before getting blasted, the drama of "Children's Story" is built not only in Ricky's voice, but in its minimal textures (i.e., a brutal yet seductive piano that lurks throughout).

After listening to Slicky Ricky's madcap outlaw and sexual adventures, it's somewhat startling to hear Rick let down his B-boy defenses and show his vulnerable side on a track. "Teenage Love" is more Rick Walters than Slick Rick, more melodic realism than hyped character study, beginning with Rick's boyish voice saying (begging) "Don't hurt me again" before launching into his short stay at Heartbreak Motel. In the amusing companion video to this track, one sees Big Daddy Kane sweet-loving Slick Rick's gal on the train. Hey—shit happens!

Although *The Great Adventures of Slick Rick* did well on a street level, selling 1.5 million copies, most mainstream critics chose to ignore or dismiss it. The "Dean of Music Crit," Robert Christgau, called Slick Rick a "girly-voiced rapper" and a woman hater. Please. . . .

Who knows if there'll ever be a follow-up to this album. Slick has since been involved in his own "Children's Story" and might have to spend a few years in jail before returning to the studio. But for now *The Great Adventures* is part of the recorded canon that made Def Jam one of the most important labels in hip-hop history.

SPECIAL ED

nviting listeners to his stomping ground—also home to
Chubb Rock, UTFO, and Full Force—Special Ed, on his
debut LP, rhymed: "I recommend you get off your soft
tush/Come down/Come around/To the 'bush." He was referring
to East Flatbush, a middle-income residential district in Brooklyn, consisting mostly of one- and two-family houses. Until the
late '60s, it was an Italian-American and Jewish enclave, but
today it is overwhelmingly African-American. One can ascertain
this—even if the streets are empty—by observing the hue of the
models on the Newport and Hennesy billboards. Likewise, one
could also guess that many East Flatbush residents have West
Indian roots. Walking along main stretches like Flatbush or
Utica avenues, one notices that stores carry tropical delights
such as salt codfish cakes and roti and curry. And in the
summertime, folks cool out to reggae and calypso along with hip
hop.

The success of *Youngest in Charge*—it sold more than
500,000 units—took Ed far beyond the confines of the 'bush, to
stages all across the country and around the world. But he's still
a resident of the place where his brilliant debut was conceived.
Its wit was especially surprising since much of it was written
while the rapper was only fifteen years old. And tellingly enough,
the line "I'm young/But my tongue speaks maturity" (from his
first single, "I Got It Made") was a statement that was firmly
proved by most of the LP, produced and arranged by "Hitman"

239

Howie Tee, who lives (and records) across the street from two of Ed's cousins.

Though he sounded a bit congested, Ed's raps on *Youngest in Charge* cascaded smoothly from his mouth. While many other hip-hop fledglings were marching down the sociopolitical trail newly forged by Public Enemy and the Jungle Brothers, Ed was continuing down rap's braggadocious dirt track, that winding stretch dotted with rotting human debris: countless skeletons belonging to MC underlings slayed in battle, long lines of deposed monarchs left with no more loyal subjects to rule over. This was no place for lower-level lyricists or sonic architects with no rhythmic clout. The Hitman hardly ever fired blanks, and Ed showed heavy mettle in this eco-jungle of words.

Instead of boasting about expensive cars or fine hotties, Special Ed claimed to own entire islands in the West Indies and to be able to afford solid-gold bones for his pooch. His frisky, fun style was a power trope, and he was always putting sucker MCs in their place. In "Taxin'," he affirmed, "I'm Special Ed and you ain't." In "Think About It," he asserted, "My rap is like a trap that you fall into/I'm Special Ed—now who the hell are you?" Dismissed.

From the effortlessly gliding "I Got It Made" to the madly shifting "Club Scene," the countrified "Hoedown" to the city-slick "Fly M.C.," *Youngest in Charge,* aside from being witty, was a tantalizing cocktail of catchy breaks that Special Ed's voice served chilled.

Still cool and confident, Ed stayed the course on his second release, *Legal.* Between the two albums, he turned eighteen, his voice matured and he became a certified sex symbol thanks to his smoth, sharp features and naturally curly hair. But unlike Big Daddy Kane or L.L. Cool J, he didn't play up to the females, surrounding himself with trite loverboy raps like "To Be a Man" or "I Need Love." On top of more irresist-ible bass-and-drum combinations—he co-produced four cuts

Special Ed. Photo by Michael Lavine,
courtesy of Profile Records.

himself—he created a whole new batch of playful ego boosters.
This time, though, he managed to weave a few social concerns
into his aural tapestries.

Expressing his feelings about public school's lack of a
proper Afro-American curriculum, he declares from "Come On,
Let's Move It": "I am the one who seeks special education/
'Cause I can't learn from the system in my nation/Or should I
say residence/Run by dead presidents?" Later, in "See It Ya," a
guest toaster named Koolie Man chants some "culture lyrics"
about the Afrocentric meanings of the colors red, green and
gold.

But the best cut on *Legal* is the thick, cushiony, totally
escapist "The Mission." By meshing James Bond's cinematic

theme music with Billy Squire's pounding "Big Beat," producer Tee fashioned a raw but sophisticated track. Fittingly, the rapper does more with it than just brag. With a hook ("We're on a mission!") sampled from Salt-n-Pepa's "I desire," he scripted an aural spy flick, complete with violence, love interests and yucks.

Opening scene: Ed is putting the make on a cutie named Suzanne. The phone rings. At first he tries to ignore it, still petting his PYT. Then, disgustedly, he stops what he's doing and walks over to the annoyance. When he picks up the receiver, a voice on the other end informs him that there's a package waiting for him in his mailbox. As he retrieves it, he notices it's a tape. Anxiously, he sticks it into his player. Someone has stolen one of his dope beats! Amidst protests from his companion, he urgently proceeds to "do what I gotta."

Scene two: Aboard an Air Force jet, he makes his way toward Japan, where he steps to his nemesis with "intent to kill." Stabbing the sucker doesn't work. Neither does shooting him. Ed throws up his hands and proceeds to fight him "Flatbush style." Triumph. Though down on his ass, it's a pretty safe bet this particular fella won't be taking Ed up on his visitation inducement from the 'hood. More likely he'll be moving to that hip-hop wasteland east of nowhere.

3RD BASS

THE CACTUS ALBUM **(DEF JAM), 1989**

THE CACTUS REVISITED, **1990**

DERELICTS OF DIALECT, **1991**

BEIGE BOYS IN THE CHOCOLATE FACTORY (A FILM TREATMENT)

ESTABLISHING SHOT of the Harlem-based campus of Columbia University, a beautiful marble-limned and tree-lined campus.

ENTER Pete Nice, white (home)boy English major with an attitude. He's in college after years of hanging in the Brooklyn yards with his B-boy friends, absorbing the positives and negatives of Black culture while playing hoops till dusk (his father, Ray, is one of the best-known high-school coaches in New York), hangin' on the ave in Queens, slowly going *def* as hip hop rocked the funky boulevards, maxing in his bedroom reading LeRoi Jones's *The Dutchman* or pondering the meaning of a Langston Hughes poem. On this night, Pete is sitting in the offices of WKCR, Columbia's radio station, spinning discs from the latest "Top of the Hip-Hop" charts, surrounded by his homeboys Hawk and Dog and Clark Kent, who are clad in jeans and Public Enemy T-shirts, slick leather bombers and gold chains. Everyone in the room gives a "shout-out" to someone special "from around the way." The next day when Pete goes to the station to pick up some records, he finds a memo to the effect that his show is over. Canceled. *Finis.* These halls of progressive learning just can't cope with the new artform that cultural theorist Greil Marcus once dubbed "South Bronx

Dadaism"; can't cope with the young Blacks ("They're not even students!") who are the innovators of this groove hanging out on the campus after dark. . . .

VOICE OVER by Chilly C. from Hammel Houses in Brooklyn: "Yeah, we useda call him Serch 'cause he was always hanging with the brothers. Ya don't find too many white boys chillin' with Blacks, 'cause most of them are scared or they're afraid of what their moms might say. *(On screen we see the tall, slightly husky Serch being chased through Far Rockaway's Redfern housing project by three Black teenagers carrying sticks. Serch's glasses fall to the ground, shatter. Watching Serch run blind, the Black teenagers stop and begin laughing.)* Yo, even when they was trying to fly that head, Serch would still come back to the 'hood. It wasn't like Serch was trying to be Black, he was just being himself. He was accepted, ya see. And being accepted in the 'hood meant a lot to him."

VOICE-OVER by Dante Ross, producer: "I remember the first night those two, Pete and Serch, met outside the Latin Quarter and the first thang they did was battle. Pete was dropping shit like, "In the garden of rap you're just a dickweed." Serch had already put out "Hey Boy/Go White Boy" on Idlers Records; that was when he was workin' with Tony D. *(On screen we see midtown Manhattan at night, neon gleaming on the wet sidewalks. There is a group of young Black and Latin teenagers dressed in late '80s B-boy gear, waiting to enter the small doorway of the Latin Quarter. The line stretches around the corner, and the sounds of chatter and laughter can be heard. Jeeps parked across the street are blaring the savage "South Bronx" by Boogie Down Productions. Five-O drives slowly past the youths, silently staring.)* Pete had been working in the studio with my homeboy Sam Sever. Me and Sam kinda grew up together. Anyway, Sam knew Serch, too, so he introduced

3rd Bass, beige-boys in the chocolate factory: Pete Nice and MC Serch. © Alice Arnold, 1990.

———

'em. Before that night them boys couldn't stand each other. 'Bout a year later they was in the studio working under the name Three the Hard Way."

FADE TO BLACK.

Whiteboy angst in the hour of chaos: All boom-boom static and karate kicks, 3rd Bass storms into the ears of the listener like hip hop's answer to '70s junkie/poet Jim Carroll—hard-voiced and brutal beats, walking on the wild side with an uptown swagger. Not the parody of hip-hop culture that the Beastie Boys had become; not sporting gold Volkswagen hood medallions or grabbin' their dicks on MTV. The first track on *The Cactus Album* (da one after the Little Rascals music, which serves as introduction), "Sons of 3rd Bass" beats down any questions one might have on this dapper duo being anything like the Beastly Brats. Attacking with a blissed tone, words shatter into walls of sound as Prime Minster Pete Nice and MC Serch ("Three boys

buggin' to the a.m./You step to the Serch and I slay 'em")
unleash a string of insults that be flying heads. Forget about
those Led Zeppelin samples and get with the program. Hell, the
Beasties never even played the Apollo.

Joining ranks with the production team of Hank Shocklee
and his Brotherhood of Badness, 3rd Bass cut their first single,
the bouncy "Steppin' to the A.M.," a track that could serve as
the perfect soundtrack to *Death Rollerskating 2000*—Spike Lee's
venture into the art of science-fiction filmmaking. Serch once
told me that the group wanted to pass this track along to Eric B.
& Rakim, but when Rush's Lyor Cohen offered it to Rakim, the
R. smashed the phone down. Although this track doesn't pack
da punch of Eric B. & Rakim's "Follow the Leader" or "Eric B.
Is President," Shocklee and crew had constructed the perfect
sparing partner for 3rd Bass to be introduced to the hip-hop
arena; "Steppin' to the A.M." comes out fighting and refuses to
stagger.

Droppin' science one minute, fetching for laughs the next—if
the members of 3rd Bass were silent film stars, both of 'em
would be Charlie Chaplin. In much the same way that the
world's most famous tramp shifted from the comic to the serious in the blink of an eye, Pete and Serch change musical
landscapes often, joking around in the four-color wonderland of
Pee Wee's Playhouse before transporting to a bleak world of
gray skies. After flippin' stoopid on the Professor Prince
Paul–produced romp "The Gas Face," the album's second single, 3rd Bass offers the eerie funk of "Monte Hall," the album's
masterwork. As produced by the third beige boy in the chocolate
factory, Sam Sever (who collaborated with our heros on the
majority of *The Cactus Album*) this track is surreal space jazz,
mod poetry layered by haunting bass lines and hypnotic drums.
When a voice intones, "This place is everything," one has the
feeling of being in a hip-hop Twilight Zone.

Having worked with Big Audio Dynamite and Just-Ice,

Mantronix and Run-D.M.C., Sam Sever is a cyberfunky machineman creating virtuoso performances in the studio. He is well-versed in the art of sonic manipulation, throwing in dialogue from the Little Rascals, Abbott and Costello skits, John F. Kennedy speeches, old radio commericals, and a carload of funk that attacks the senses, holding the listener within its sonic web. With the release of *The Cactus Album* in 1989, Sam Sever joined the pantheon that includes Marley Marl, Hank Shocklee, Doctor Dre of N.W.A. and Hurby "Luv Bug" Azor—stylish innovators of sound. To paraphrase author David Henderson, these producers are huge monsters of rhythmic energy threatening to take over music.

The other standout track is the autobiographical "Products of the Environment," which traces the lives of Pete Nice and MC Serch. Over soulful Stax horns, brutal scratches and hypnotic drums, Serch throws his rhymes into the dizzy mix: "Redfern Houses, where no MC would ever go/Is where I did my very first show/ ... And on that stage is where I first learned/Stick out your chest or be a kid and get burned." The narrative reminds one of *Down These Mean Streets* translated into hip-hop speak.

Following the lead of Bobby Brown and Chaka Khan, 3rd Bass became the first hip-hop crew to release a re-mix album, *The Cactus Revisted.* Offering new arrangements and (in some cases) new lyrics, this album merely gives an alternative vision of the group's sound. A year after their first album, it would have been preferable if the energy had been used to create new material. Not to say the re-mixes don't work on an aesthetic level—Marley Marl's noisy dub arrangement of "Brooklyn-Queens" is brillant—it's just that, as Mickey Spillane once said, "In this business you've got to progress, you've got to keep ahead or else you just stay behind, being imitated."

The one new track is "3 Strikes 5,000," produced by Dante the Scrub (see the De La Soul album jacket) and his production crew, the Stimulated Dummies. The beat sounds a little slow, but it can still move booty; it's Pete and Serch who don't quite work. Compared to the way their smooth-as-polished-glass voices attack other tracks, "3 Strikes 5,000" sounds like someone just woke them at three in da morning—kinda tired.

Hip hop as an artform is not really in need of any great white hopes, but if beige boys wanna raid the chocolate factory, they should be careful not to burn it down after they're fat. Since Vanilla Ice has already poured gasoline all over the factory and the Beastie Boys have been barred from entering ever again, 3rd Bass could do well to be an upstanding example of their race.

When 3rd Bass dropped their *real* second album, *Derelicts of Dialect*, they were no longer the novelty whiteboys on the block—or the most popular ones. Vanilla Ice had dashed to the top of pop, causing MC Serch to tell *Rolling Stone*: "I opened the door for this kid. I apologize for that. If I thought something so miserable would have come of it, I would've stayed home and worked at Wendy's."

These weren't 3rd Bass's last words concerning "Vanilla Wafer" (or, for that matter, any other rapper who appeals to crossover tastes). In "Pop Goes the Weasel," as Peter Gabriel's "Sledgehammer" supports them, they throw words like poison-tipped arrows at performers "who can't be artistic" on the mic'.

They can, and on the rest of *Derelicts of Dialect* 3rd Bass's appeal lies in their intelligence and humor, traits found in their literary wordplay, use of obscure samples and even the names of their songs. If James Joyce was still kickin' today he'd be jealous of titles like "The Merchant of Grooves" and "A Portrait of the Artist as a Hood," or he'd be down wit' 3rd Bass. Their extensive use of jazz on *Derelicts of Dialect* might have surprised some fans who were used to them being funky. But, to paraphrase George Clinton, Who says a hip-hop crew can't be jazzy, and who says jazzy hip hop can't be funky?

.

TONE-LÖC

LÖC-ED AFTER DARK (DELICIOUS VINYL), 1988

As irony would have it, me and my homeboy Paul P. were in California the first time I heard Tone-Löc's "Wild Thing." We had just left a club called the Red Onion, where the women dress in Day-Glo miniskirts, tight jeans and biker shorts that reveal *much* smooth, brown flesh. They were quite friendly, but the fellas, playing Daddy Cool, leaning against the wall dripping jerri-curl juice and attitude, made me want to laugh; they gave the hotties *no* rap!

"Yo, Paul," I said after an hour or so of being dazed and amazed. "Let's blow this scene." Back in the ride, I flicked on the radio and started cruising through the urban jungle of Compton. Ain't nothing like that movie *Colors*—didn't see any drive-by shootings, just palm trees swaying in the night breeze. And from the kickin' Alpine speakers, a laid-back, husky voice commanded, "Let's do it." The music moved at the pace of a slow train before an electric guitar swung into the mix. At first this track took me for a loop—who the hell *is* this? As the jam faded out, the radio jock screamed, "That was Tone-Löc with his new song, 'Wild Thing.'" Who? This had to be some Cali new-jack, 'cause I had never heard of him on the New York hip-hop scene.

"Hey, wanna know why Lost Angeles hip hop is so wack?" I said jokingly to Paul. "Because they got palm trees in the ghetto!" We both laughed as our rented Benz glided down a darkened street. But, ultimately, Tone-Löc had the last laugh—all the way to the bank. "Wild Thing" became the biggest-selling commercial single in the history of the Hot 100—second only to U.S.A. for Africa's "We Are the World." Much of its success had to do with its video, which was a parody of/homage to Robert Palmer's "Addicted to Love" clip (oh yes, another irony: cuz Robert has made a career of rippin' off R&B tracks, reducing their soul factor and gettin' paid-in-full; for once *he* got Memorexed).

The sound of "Wild Thing" (co-written by Marvin Young, a.k.a. Young MC) is the sound of lightning striking, thunder rolling—Big Tony Löc coming. Shooting some new spunk at a familiar guitar riff (from Van Halen's "Jamie's Cryin' ") while riding the rhythm of a hard, pumping beat, he tells us how he spells relief after a forty-hour grind. "When the weekend comes I go get live with the honeys," he says in a muddy Mississippi drawl. This former computer operator, introduced to rap only a few years ago by a friend, tuned Middle America into a Black ghetto slang for shagging, rolling in the hay, making mad, passionate love. Wrapping (or is it rapping?) the phrase in smiling, color-blind textures—even the calculating (cheap, attention-grabbing) video was shot in stark variations of gray—gave a generation raised in the age of sexual anxiety a reason to cheer, not fear, the act most postpubescent folks dream of constantly.

Whether it's crusing down the avenue or stalking the mall, chilling with the crew or flying solo, Tone is a man always on a temporary-love mission. He's one of the horned-up masses until he encounters a skeezer pleezer who's willing to take just fifty dollars to make him holler (despite what chill brother Mic once said: "All fifty dollars will get ya these days is a kiss on the cheek!")

But, yo, if that's all ya got, Tone has the solution: a fantastic hyper-aphrodisiac called "Funky Cold Medina." As this track (constructed using much of the same rap-meets-rock-meets-sex elements as "Wild Thing") begins, Löc is cold-chillin' in da spot, proving very easy to resist. "Like Mick Jagger says, 'I can't get no satisfaction,'" he complains. Glancing across the room, he noticed a "no-name chump" getting all the play. After strolling over to Mr. Softee-cum-Mr. Goodbar, he inquires, "Why you so flye?"

"Funky Cold Medina!"

Back discussing more familiar drugs, Löc clears his throat, all smoke and brew, and proceeds to fill us in on the shit that sparks his creative process. In an early interview, he said: "I get a great big ol' quart of Olde English. I light up a joint, play a beat over and over again. And as it comes into me, I write." "Cheeba Cheeba" ("reefer" said twice in ghetto parlance) has a slow, gangster-bop beat that displays frisky bits of wah-wah guitar and Fender Rhodes piano. It's a track that helps affirm the identity of the mean Los Angeles streets that turned Anthony Terrell Smith out. From a middle-class kid whose biggest passion was soccer, he became a street urchin who eventually gravitated toward gangland. It was there that he adopted his handle—Löc is short for *loco,* which is Spanish for *crazy* or *wild.* Today his favorite hobbies are collecting soft friends and guns.

In "Löc'ed After Dark," the rapper conjures up wintry images from back in the days: of carrying a .357 like an American Express card (never leaving home without it), of "tearing up towns," of casting tombstones on a stretch called The Shaw. This grisly place gets its own tune in "Löc'in on the Shaw." A moody and cinematic instrumental, this cut displays no viciousness—but it's felt. The ghostly voice of some character from a blaxploitation soundtrack glides across the soundscape asking, "What's up, bro?" in a tone that suggests a thuggish beatdown—Flatbush style, as Special Ed would say.

Back in New York: Like me, many brothers and sisters initially slammed Tone-Löc for not being a *true* hip-hop artist. By that they meant he wasn't Black enough. They were responding to him based solely on the hit singles they were bombarded with all summer long. But the tracks used for "Löc'in on the Shaw" and "Löc'd After Dark" are as street as anything by Rakim or Big Daddy Kane. And "Wild Thing" and "Funky Cold Medina" are Black simply because Tone-Löc (one of rap's most compellingly interesting voices) is rapping on them. His husky drawl could not have been delivered by, in the words of Norman Mailer, "a white Negro." And as Afrika Bambaataa once said, "Hip-hop music is colorless. It's what goes on top that makes it Black or white."

TOO SHORT

LIFE IS ... TOO SHORT (DANGEROUS MUSIC/ RCA), 1988

SHORT DOG'S IN THE HOUSE, 1990

THE BALLAD OF OUTLAW JONES

Nineteen sixty-four. Chill winds blow through the deserted streets of a planet called Harlem. Broken glass and shattered bottles reflect the moonlight that seeps through cracks in the midnight fog. Nighthawks swoop over battered trashcans and broken dreams, their fragile wings scraping the tarred roofs of leaning tenements; down on the avenue, a choir of tomcats scat a blues hymn as they search for food. Inside the womb of Well's Bar: sepia-toned glamour boys order shots of Jack Daniel's and Schaeffer chasers, flashing wads of cash as the smooth voice of Mary Wells croons "My Guy," whispered desires blaring from mono speakers, Black hips swaying to the beat. The smell of passion and spilled beer taints the air like a decadent incense. Uptown funk and Kangol caps tilted to the side. A drunken roar from the rear, "Coolsville, Daddy. Coolsville."

Well's Bar is an oasis to the hustlers of Harlem, a gathering place whose red bulbs (highlighting the erotic black-light posters taped to the wall) attract them like ebony moths. The jukejoint overflows with bad attitudes, flared pants and loud voices. Two-thirty A.M. (tick-tock, tock-tick), reads the clock on the wall; time moves swiftly, yet no one seems to notice. Taped to the smudged mirror above the bar is a faded photo taken last New Year's Eve—all slickie boy grins and shots of poison.

And so enters Scarface Jones: spit-polished Stacy Adams and nasty vibes, processed hair and a crimson-colored suit. Five years past, one of the aging whores in his stable (breasts the size of overstuffed pillows, legs as thick as tree trucks), Maggie Dream, sliced his cheek with a razor blade. The reasons are blurry, but a hundred neighborhood folks witnessed Maggie catch a bullet in her heavy bosom, wobble on gold spiked heels and fall in the middle of 125th Street and Eighth Avenue; one old cat claims the Devil himself came to pick her up.

"Yo, Scarface!" a voice from the crowd screams. "Old lady got ya babysittin' or somethin'?" In his thick, bronze-toned arms, wrapped in a red silk blanket, wearing white booties and a sky-blue cap, is Scarface's son, Craig Jones, a.k.a. Outlaw—precious as rain, yella as dawn. Daddy Jones smiles, light reflecting off his polished gold caps. On the night the baby was born, Scarface was in Well's passing out cigars and buying drinks for the crowd. From the bowels of the bar, a drunken woman staggered to Scarface's chair and asked in a slurred voice, "Is he gonna be an outlaw like his daddy?" A hush crushed the din, everyone staring at Scarface. His eyebrows twitched and he began to laugh. "Damn right!" he yelled. "Gonna follow in Big Daddy's footprints." From then on, folks called the baby Outlaw; the name just kinda stuck.

Nineteen eighty-eight. Another summer. Healers, wheelers, and cocaine dealers, Outlaw Jones has seen them all—speeding down 125th in slick Benzes, modeling their fresh cuts in the lighted mirror at Shalamar's Barber Shop, sipping champagne with the chocolate honeys in the Showman or Palm Cafe or the Fox Hole (" 'Cause that's where all the foxes went," his mother once said). As he stares from the window down to 123rd and Seventh Avenue, the block that Sugar Ray Robinson once owned, he thinks of the father he never knew and muses about the fast dollars a smart hustler like himself could make off the suckerass vics on the ave. Like Outlaw's favorite rapper of the moment Too

Short would say, "Everybody's got that same old dream/To have big money and fancy thangs." Outlaw marvels at the way Too Short's monotone voice seems to glide over the bass-heavy rhythms, cold stompin' the bass line that Eric B. & Rakim made famous on "Microphone Fiend." Something about Too Short's voice sounds like ice water flows through his veins, like he'll shoot ya now, ask questions later. "Ya can close ya ears and run your mouth/And one day ya soon find out life is . . . too short." If that ain't cold, Outlaw thinks, then I don't know what is.

There are some Cali boys who will tell ya that Too Short is the real voice of Oaktown, that M.C. Hammer is just a screamer who can dance. Boyz is da hood say, "While Hammer was a goddamn batboy, Too Short was in his crib making tapes with

Too Short. Photo courtesy of Jive/RCA.

255

his homeboy Freddy-B, sellin' 'em on the street and clocking dollars." Whereas Hammer be yellin' about not puttin' your hands on whatever (can't touch ... what?), Too Short creates anthems that salute his homeboys. On his debut album, *Life Is ... Too Short,* our man Todd Shaw has a melodic track called "Oakland," which features silk-voiced girlies singing while Too Short, reaching into his bag of simple rhymes, says, "Straight from the west/Oakland is the best/Baby, it's so fresh/Just call it the big bad O ..." Surprisingly, with its new-jack ballad keyboards and drum machines, this track has the sound of B-boy Quiet Storm. Hell, homies gotta get lovin', too.

But don't go away thinkin' that da boy is soft, because like every gangsta rapper's literary companions, Iceberg Slim and Donald Goimes, Too Short would be the first to brag that he put the *M in Mackin because everyone else was only ackin.* Listen to the semi-misogynist theme of "Pimp the Ho," where Too Short (sounding as though he's spitting fire in the mic') drops lines like "But the cute young tender in the tight red dress/She has a soft booty and a real big chest/She said I love ya, said it again/At the motel freaked her and her friends/Like Too Short rappin', everybody knows/Like the Mack said, homie, pimp the ho." One of more surprising elements of this track is how Too Short uses the word *ho* as a metaphor for rival rappers and then again for the mixing board in his studio. "It's like twenty-four ho's/Better known as tracks," he says.

But for all his gangsta pose, Too Short has a sense of humor about his tough talk. Before Ice Cube even thought about recording "It's a Man's World" with Yo-Yo slam-dunking his sexist remarks into the nearest trash bin, Too Short recorded "Don't Fight the Feelin'," where lady rappers Entice and Barbie (from the Danger Zone posse) reduce his badassness to dust; the three of them go dis for dis like a hip-hop duel (or duet). Too Short opens the track by asking, "Do ya like to fuck?" Anybody else would've gotten slapped, but Too Short just continues on his trail to the booty (like a smutty Transformer, his dick is also used as a compass). Over electro-beats that sound like hardcore Mantronix, mainman Todd swims deep into the gutters of Oaktown to fish out rhymes like "I won't ask and I sure won't beg/Reach right over and rub your leg/I let my hand slide between your miniskirt/Slip my finger in your panties, straight go to work." Bum-rushing the mix, Entice and Barbie counter with, "Do they call you short because of your height or your width?/Dis me boy, I'll hang your balls from a cliff." All right, so this isn't the type of discourse that feminist critic Michelle Wallace might throw at propmaster Greg Tate, yet the feeling is the same. Like the ghost of Roland Barthes told me in a recent daydream, "Fuck semiology, let's get funky."

In a track that could apply to New York or Detroit, Baltimore or Philly, Too Short composed a funky, laid-back soundtrack of urban America, "City of Dope." He documents a day in the life of a drug dealer: of "fat ropes and shattered hopes," flye cars and begging women, of lost friends and dead enemies. It's a scene many of us view everyday, a scene that refuses to disappear. Music critic Stanley Crouch once said, "You cannot make a powerful Afro-American culture if you're going to base it on what hustlers and pimps think about the world." But what Crouch refuses to understand (as he floats on his bourgeois cloud nine) is that what hustlers and pimps think, folks in the ghetto see everyday. And pretending that these problems don't exist does not mean they will fade away.

Nineteen ninety. Yet another summer. Two years have passed since Outlaw Jones was rockin' the scratched disc of Too Short's first album on his mom's tattered stereo. Two years have passed since he had to sport out-of-style kicks or return his sad-eyed mom's empty forty-ounce bottles of Olde English to the smelly bodega just to reap a couple nickels. "Your daddy had a good heart," his moms once said, her voice strained. "He just didn't leave us no money when he went off to Jordon." But Outlaw knows the truth 'bout his daddy; the graying hustlers who hang on the block have told him the complete story, which his mother is either ashamed or afraid of, including how a jealous slickie boy gunned Scarface down in the lobby of the Theresa Hotel. "Scarface was a bad muthafucker who pimped fallen angels and spit in God's eye," Ralph Cherry said. Ralph was this old queen who had trimmed and shampooed every Harlem diva from Billie Holiday to Dinah Washington to silver-haired gospel singers; Outlaw useta see him lounging in front of his shop when he breezed past on his way home from the pool parlour. But that was then: These days there is no time for games. These days the art of the deal is all that matters—dealing guns, dealing drugs, dealing any damn thang that produces fast money.

Glancing at the diamond-studded gold Rolex on his thin wrist, Outlaw strolls to the corner of Seventh Avenue, where Crackhead Don ("The walking dead," he thinks to himself, the stench of urine filling his nostrils) is washing and waxing his ride. "Here ya go," Outlaw says, a ten spot in his palm. "Go get yourself a megablast." Crackhead Don laughs and then bolts into the night. "If that muthafucker ain't thin dizzy, then I don't know who is," he mumbles, getting in the glittering gold Jag.

Snaking through heavy traffic, Outlaw reaches into the tape-cluttered glove compartment, randomly takes out Too Short's second album, *Short Dog's in the House.* Popped into the Awai deck, blaring from the Alpine speakers, Cali-boy Too Short becomes Harlem's funky soundtrack as Outlaw cruises past burned-out brownstones, walking dead gathered 'round a garbage-can bonfire, 'round the way girls (bamboo earrings, Fendi bags) posing in front of Korean delis, clad in colorful maxi-leather coats, puffing on their Newports. Like the fusion-soul group War once sang, "The world is a ghetto." Seems to Outlaw that the whole world has come to Harlem to get in on his deals.

*   *   *

Before Black pop's conservative wave swept through the valley of funk, hanging on to the coattails of Luther Vandross and Anita Baker, the ghetto sounds of the '70s were a realistic translation of the street—Any Ghetto USA, from Marvin Gaye's "Mercy, Mercy Me" to Curtis Mayfield's "Freddy's Dead," these grooves feature snapshots, four-minute documentaries of urban blues combined with platform dancing shoes. Following the ideas of jazz purist Branford Marsalis, "Hip hop might not be the *new jazz,* as Harry Allen says, but it damn sure is the *new R&B.*" And like the rhythmic blues of the Me Decade (in the Chocolate Cities of Black America, it was more like the Us Decade), hip hop became the chief communicator of the '80s Ebony Nation—ain't talkin' 'bout no magazine either. By borrowing the beats of past decades, rap artists have discovered a fresh medium to relate ideas from aged agendas.

Taking the hook, line and title of Donny Hathaway's '70s classic "The Ghetto," Too Short made the best song on his second album, also its first single. Just as Hathaway's tune became a theme of urban sorrow, Too Short revises this language of despair to conform to a '90s viewpoint. Or perhaps *conform* is too soft a word when one realizes that the landscape of Hathaway's pain has become bleaker in the last twenty years. Too Short's 1990 version of "The Ghetto" is laid-back funky despair of "dope fiends down with a pipe in their mouth," and of the government's misguided war on drugs. "Instead of adding to the task force, send some help," Too Short says. After painting a portrait of addicted friends and nine-months-pregnant blood sisters suckin' that glass dick, Too Short escorts us to the other side of the canvas, where the dealers gather to show off their new clothes and exchange tales of their sexual conquests. In his gruff, monotone voice, none of these details sound romantic. There's a thin line between junkies and dealers—both are addicted to their lifestyles (either lowlife or highlife) and both are trapped within the crumpling walls of the ghetto. Most dealers live fast lives, make fast cash and spend it fast; and most folks know that the street life of a hustler is limited.

Too Short works with various producers on *Short Dog's in the House*, and his musical maturity is evident, but the text of his raps merely retraces the steps that he stomped on *Life Is ... Too Short* two years before. If he isn't fucking your girl "In the Oaktown," then he's calling her a bitch in porn fantasies ("Punk Bitch"). Too Short seems to equate each sexual encounter with a ride on the terror train, a one-way ticket to motel hell. It's possible that these tales could be slightly amusing if Too Short were a better storyteller, but his limited vocabulary works against him. On "Ain't Nothin' But a Word to Me," Too Short joins hands with Ice Cube to give their reasons for using the B-word so often. Produced by Lench Mobster Sir Jinx, this track is boom-boom Jeep funky, but the rhymes are nothing more than sexist garbage that could cause leading feminists like Queen Latifah and Monie Love to jump them both in some dark alley and feed their balls to the *other* dogs. And Too Short also places himself in an awkward position by trying to go blow for blow with Ice Cube—it's like sending Pee Wee Herman into the ring with Mike Tyson. Perhaps the spectacle will amuse for a moment, but everyone knows it won't be a fair fight. In this case, Too Short is knocked out ugly.

Clicking off the tape deck, Outlaw parks his car on Riverside Drive and 147th Street. If he were to leave the Jag in front of the coke house over on Broadway, five-o would surely run a check on the plates. As he emerges from the Jag, smoothing the wrinkles out of his black linen suit, Outlaw hears booted footsteps running behind him. Before he can reach for the shiny .350 Mag stashed under the Jag's leather seats, five shots are fired and Outlaw is swimming in a sea of blood. Dizzy, the world has spun off its axis and a parade of voices fills his mind—humming, rapping, pleading. And then silence.

A TRIBE
CALLED
QUEST

PEOPLE'S INSTINCTIVE TRAVELS AND THE PATHS OF RHYTHM (JIVE/RCA), 1990

1. Speaking on the subject of hip hop as a revolutionary artform, jazz modernist Max Roach said, "Innovation is in our blood. We [African-Americans] are not people who can sit back and say what happened a hundred years ago was great, because what was happening a hundred years ago was shit: slavery. Black people have to keep moving." And yet the hip-hop nation circa 1990 appeared to be in brake mode. With the exception of groups like Public Enemy, who can always be counted on to release a flye single, and new-jack bohos like Digital Underground, the so-called cutting edge had become just another ragged road to tread; when major record companies began signing almost anyone who owned a turntable and a microphone, it was easier finding a needle in a haystack than an innovator in a record rack.

2. "So you write about hip hop," the drunk blonde said, slurring her words over the din of Living Colour's "Cult of Personality," blaring from a tattered jukebox. While axe-monster Vernon Reid's wailing chords battled demons, Ms. Thang ordered another rum and coke, then she turned toward me saying, "Not to be insulting or anything, but don't you think rap is just a fad? I mean, it's not even real music." *Real music?* I thought. I laughed out loud at the foolishness of her question. My mind drifted for a moment, then I recalled what Afrika Bambaataa told me a few years past: "As long as Black folks can talk, there will always be rapping."

A Tribe Called Quest, introducing da hip-hop nation to da be-bop past. Photo courtesy of Jive/RCA.

---

3.   The first time the hip-hop nation heard funki-dread rapper Q-Tip, he was coming from Calliope Studios, collaborating with his homeboys De La Soul on "Me, Myself and I." While he was lounging on the noir sofa after midnight, producer Prince Paul yelled, "Yo, Q-Tip! Why don't you drop a coupla words on this track?" After struttin' over to the microphone, he relaxed for a second and said, "Black is Black." His contribution was simple indeed, yet with these three words Q-Tip had etched his voice into the minds of them folks looking for new-style hip-hop saviors. Along with his soulmates the Jungle Brothers and De La Soul, Q-Tip defined a new breed of rapper in the hip-hop kingdom: the av-garde Afrocentric bohemians. Had these fellas been around twenty years ago, they would've probably been clad in COLTRANE LIVES T-shirts and African beads and baggy jeans; they would have been trapped in the Black art-

world ghetto reciting blackadelia poetry in dank, downtown lofts with LeRoi Jones and Larry Neal, while a free-jazz trio squawked anarchic blasts of noise. Yet by embracing modern means of communication and mass production, yesterday's boho chic have become today's pop stars.

4.   And last night I dreamt of Armageddon: me and Q-Tip cruising through the debris of urban ghettos in a battered Caddie, under skies of blood, radio blaring "the beat, the rhyme, the noise" of A Tribe Called Quest's debut album, *People's Instinctive Travels and the Paths of Rhythm,* perhaps the first hip-hop album that consciously merges the elitism of jazz with the pop structure of hip hop. Driving past an abandoned building, I saw a long-haired dude dressed in black-on-black emerge from the shadows. "Fuck you!" he bellowed, throwing rocks at our car. Jamming his foot on the gas pedal, Q-Tip raced away with a sonic blast. "Who the hell was that?" my shaky voice inquired. "That was Lou Reed," Q-Tip answered. "He been doin' that bugged shit ever since I sampled 'Walk on the Wild Side' on my track 'Can I Kick It.'" Outside the thin walls of my nightmare, I heard a car crash. And I awoke to . . .

5.   The soft cries of a baby drifting through a jazz dream opens *People's Instinctive Travels* with a sense of optimism. This voice of innocence was the signal that one will not be entering a nightmare world of brutality where the language of criminality is spoken by the majority. What *Melody Maker* critic Simon Reynolds once dubbed as "oceanic rock" (". . . an attempt to rediscover lost innocence and peace. It's hypnotic, or narcotic, a fall back into the blissful continuum of unconsciousness") best describes the world that da Tribe found while chasing break-beats down a rabbit hole. Following their bliss like a sepia-colored Alice, these fellas discovered a wonderland of sound where post-bop trumpet players blow "in a silent way" while hip-hop DJs scratch in various collages of aural chaos. But as Q-Tip softly says during the closing moments of "I Left My

Wallet in El Segundo" (the album's second single), "We can go, but we gonna come back home."

6. Coming back home (back to reality?) the Brothers Quest—which also includes Jarobi, DJ Ali Muhammad Shaheed and Phife—strip down the layers of excess dominating the genre, experimenting with the form to maintain its excitement. Witness the sitar that slowly slides into the mix of the brilliant "Bonita Applebum," hip hop's brightest moment of romanticism; marvel at Q-Tip's laid-back voice and surreal poetics ("Rhythm is the key as we open up the door," he says on "Rhythm [Devoted to the Art of Moving Butts]"). These cats are smooth and I don't mean slippery.

Not to say that *People's Instinctive Travels* is devoid of big beats—listen to the hardness of "Description of a Fool"—but the majority of the album's cuts show the B-boy generation that jazz can be used as a soundtrack of desire and pain, reason or rebellion. I'm not sure if this sound was what Harry Allen had floating through his mind when he boasted that "hip hop is the new jazz," but this album is bound to change our perceptions of the status quo.

ULTRA-
MAGNETIC
MCS

CRITICAL BEATDOWN **(UPTOWN/NEXT PLATEAU),**
1988

Though writer Frank Owen dubbed it "a sort of poverty theme park, a carefully preserved spectacle of deprivation designed to strike fear in the hearts of decent, law-abiding citizens across the world," the Bronx—whose images of decay (drugs, inadequate schools, random violence, etc.) became world-famous via flicks like *Fort Apache, The Bronx* and *Enemy Territory*—still managed to create the most potent, dominant form of popular musical expression in the '80s, hip hop. You'd think nothing beneficial could grow and prosper in such desolate, malnourished soil, but as Owen explained, "Hip hop is not so much a product of the Bronx environment as a triumph over it."

Springing out of the self-destructive structure of street gangs, linking itself to the more peaceful graffiti art movement that "bombed" miles of subway cars, then settling down with beats and rhymes, hip-hop culture was a way for poor Blacks left out of the American dream of upward mobility and material validation to say, "Look, I'm somebody, too!"

In rap's early days, crews using one microphone, two turntables and mega-watt amps would plug into street lamps in parks, kids riding through on bikes nodding to the boom, B-boys' hanging off posts chilling to the rarefied air from pumping speaker cones. When the atmosphere was cool, rappers tied up their throngs with upbeat, self-aggrandizing lassos ("When I was born my momma gave birth to the baddest MC on the goddamn earth").

When the music made the transfer to records, immediately its brutal quality began being removed by bands (cf. the Sugar Hill house band, now known as Tackhead). Moreover, many of the Bronx pioneers (Kool Herc, Coca La Rock) were unable to capitalize on mainstream interest in their invention due to bad business deals and other problems. Queens and Brooklyn began asserting themselves, then came entries from the outer limits of Los Angeles and Philadelphia. Madison Avenue jumped on the bandwagon, too, and slowly but surely the graininess of those original rap performances was squeezed out of the genre.

Lamenting this situation, Kool Keith, lead speaker of new-generation Bronx crew Ultramagnetic MCs, said in 1988, "Rap is cluttered with happiness now and it hurts to see that style getting over—like DJ Jazzy Jeff and the Fresh Prince. I thank God for groups like Eric B. and Rakim and Kool G. Rap and Polo. Rap is about hardcore attitude and competition."

The stirring hip-hop tradition of tough breaks and self-centered, venomous rapping—you can almost feel the hot breath of MCs Ced-Gee and Kool Keith—continues on *Critical Beatdown*. The album was an unusual release for Uptown, a label known for fostering rap crews "smoothed out on the R&B tip," as Bell Biv Devoe would say—Heavy D. & the Boyz, Father MC, and *GQ*-styled new-jack crooners like Al B. Sure! and Guy. Perhaps that's why this LP was largely ignored when it was released: with their Gucci track suits, high-top Adidas sneaks and Kangol caps tilted to the side, Ultramagnetic MCs simply didn't fit into Uptown's shop of new-age chic. But it shouldn't have been ignored. Though it's sometimes lyrically hollow, *Critical Beatdown* is engaging in many ways. It's a little rough around the edges, with homegrown charm and other-worldly dialect. In his opening remarks, Kool Keith dismisses those who don't appreciate his greatness as roaches, germs and MC Ducks. While not *remarkably* witty, these, one must admit, are amusing new ways of referring to rival rappers.

Practically all of *Critical Beatdown* is constructed with loops from the *Ultimate Breaks and Beats* compilation discs. But Ultramagnetic MCs—the name, they say, stands for "the highest form of attraction"—doesn't just bite, chew up, then spit out familiar funky rhythms. They add drum rolls and play sampled overdubs on different notes along a keyboard; they employ turntable cuts and scratches to create excitement along linear groove lines. Loaded with putdowns direct enough to make challengers squirm, the song "Kool Keith Housing Things" zips along at a revved-up speed, a metallic guitar snaking its way through pounding, jittery drums from beginning to end. When the rapper declares, "Quickly, I'ma rip your brain off/ Throw it down so the blood could drain off," a James Brown grunt underscores his intensity. When the tune settles into its hook, DJ Moe Love name-drops ("Kool Keith/Koo/Kool Keith") over a mournful minor-key riff, waving Keith Thornton's handle in everyone's face with more than a slight suggestion of danger.

This LP is full of such insinuations and depictions of harm, killer jokes with a deadly edge. They're giving other hard-style rappers a tough time competing, and Ultramagnetic MCs can't see why anyone would even bother. As Kool Keith once said, "A lot of people are jealous of us. We look good, we sound good ... It's a shame. Everybody else should just give up!"

VANILLA ICE

TO THE EXTREME (SBK), 1990

Poor Vanilla Ice. Though he became real big real fast, selling well in excess of seven million units out the box, a whole lot of homefolks couldn't help wondering what to make of his debut LP, *To the Extreme.* In these enlightened times scrutiny and distrust of any white hip-hop artist is to be expected. It was the ethnic mimicry in the way Ice speaks that rubbed Nava P. the wrong way. Maxi, meanwhile, couldn't get with Ice's frequent though ignorant use of street slang (peep the line "I wore a jimmy [penis] that I slapped on" in "Ice Cold"). And Chas became irritated by Ice's hard posing (represented on the record jacket by a half-closed left eye, and in the grooves with awkward PG imitations of two other Ices—Cube and T.). While white appropriation of hip hop is no longer a novelty, Vanila Ice comes off to aficionados of the music as an especially calculating and barefaced counterfeit.

His poser attitude grates even more because it's successful. With radio stations that purport not to play rap kicking "Ice Ice Baby" (the album's initial smash) into their rotations, a lot of brothers and sisters saw yet another example of how intricately racism is woven into the fine fabric of American society. Ice is rap's great white hope—more homogenous than either the Beastie Boys or 3rd Bass. He didn't go through the channels, gaining street acceptance before crossing over, and like Paul Whiteman and Elvis before him, he's riding the coattails of a Black art form all the way to pop culture heaven. ("Ice Ice Baby" became rap's first number one pop single, and when *To the Extreme* bumped MC Hammer's *Please Hammer Don't Hurt 'Em* from the top spot on *Billboard*'s Top LPs chart, it was the first time two rappers headed up that list in succession. Ice even won an American Music Awards prize for *best* new rap artist!)

From his lofty perch Vanilla Ice is frequently bathed in frenzied adulation and lust from white 'ronis who sport tacky examples of suburban shopping mall chic. It's a different story back on the Afrocentric pastures below, though. Here Vanilla Ice is reviled and viewed as a threat to the hardcore regiments in hip hop's army. His rise has certainly clouded the vision of the many A&R reps in the banking business, but it also altered the thinking of more than a few take-no-prisoners B-boy capitalists, including Kool G. Rap & Polo and the Bomb Squad (which includes Public Enemy's Chuck D.), who have either produced or are about to produce white hip-hop acts. Packaging their ideas in whiteface seems to be a means of survival to these relatively uncelebrated artists, who are frustrated by no airplay and a slack touring climate.

But even as he was rhyming "I'm a throne overtaker/Not an MC faker" from arenas where he was the opening act for that other plastic poet, MC Hammer, Ice's claim was being challenged. In a November 18th story in the *Dallas Morning News*, reporter Ken Parish Perkins uncovered "numerous contradictions" in Ice's record company bio as well as some of his interviews. Apparently, to gain legitimacy in Black circles, the rapper had said he was "from the ghetto" (where he was once supposedly stabbed in a gang fight), when actually, he grew up "a middle-class kid from Dallas," according to the *Village Voice*. He was also purported to have attended the same Miami high school as Luther Campbell of 2 Live Crew (as if such an association would add credibility to his case), but there was no proof of this either.

His were lies without conscience, and they showed utter disrespect for Black culture. They didn't end with him falsifying his background either. The Black fraternity Alpha Phi Alpha had been shouting "Ice Ice Baby" for years, and Vanilla Ice was quoted as saying he had never heard it before. Yet his chant sounds suspisciously similar to the Alphas'!

The truth about Vanilla Ice's music is that it's paint-by-numbers hip hop, devoid of flair, wit and startling drama. He's neither a gifted poet nor flipmaster, and his rhymes—mostly all of them are about girls and himself—frequently border on sheer idiocy. Besides the jimmy reference in "Ice Cold," he reveals that "the freaks are jockin' [him] like Crazy Glue," and that's he's "smooth like slime." Now, that's braggadocio!?

Beyond the numerous wackisms throughout *To the Extreme,* the sample hook in "Ice Ice Baby" *is,* one must admit, grabby. It's the only fitting element in an otherwise throwaway ramble that features Ice perping as a gangster driving a 5.0 (Jeep). As he's cruising down a highway later, police officers on an investigation passed him up and, instead, "confronted all the dope fiends." In "Ice Ice Baby" not only does Vanilla Ice reveal that he's a sucker, he shows that in America one is above suspicion if one is white.

Having plundered David Bowie and Queen's "Under Pressure," Vanilla Ice anxiously climaxes one of the verses in "Ice Ice Baby" with "check out the hook!" With its cascading bass notes it's the last thing on the album really worth noticing, because the songs aren't compelling at all. Granted, there are a few cool break beat implosions, but they aren't showcased flatteringly. Two other appropriations—the Jackson's "Dancing Machine" in "Dancin'" and Scotty's "Stop That Train" in an homage named after the original—aren't layered with wit either. "I think I'll let the hook try to explain," he suggests at one point. One assumes that the reason one doesn't hear any excuses is that these tracks are too ashamed that they've been forever soiled by the trash heap of musical history; iced by Ice!

THE WEE
PAPA GIRL
RAPPERS

THE BEAT, THE RHYME, THE NOISE (JIVE), 1989

BE AWARE, 1990

Hardly a peep has been heard from the hefty musical canon of Great Britain that cannot be linked to the history of African-American pop. The '70s punk movement is, perhaps, the only anomaly, an English style that can't be traced directly to any Stateside form of Black music. But on a global scale and in theory, punk and the Bronx-born product called hip hop are somewhat related. Punk was a do-it-yaself artform, one that required little or no formal musical training to execute. Moreover, as much as punk was a revolt against the politics of the land, it was also a revolt against the bubble-gum music that the elders of pop like the Rolling Stones or Elton John were creating for the plastic ears of the BBC and the world at large. Punk was an uprising of teenage rebel culture, and its players did not give a fuck about anything or anyone—save the fellas banging in their bands or the tarts buying them brews.

At the same time that punk was becoming the movement of the moment in London, hip hop was becoming the new subculture of the young, Black New York underground (and who knows where else, since tapes were sold, the sound transported to different cities throughout America). Punk and hip hop were created on the same principle: that youth could be a moveable force in a culture with limited means. And like punk, one of hip hop's early disadvantages was the sexual politics practiced within

The Wee Papa Girl Rappers, Brit gals on a mission.
Photo courtesy Jive/RCA.

the movement. Although there were women who stood on the sidelines and pumped the DJ or hung with the graffiti bombers in the darkened train yards, their roles as active participants in *creating* this new street culture were limited. In punk's later (dying) years, female groups like the Slits or the Raincoats tried to define a female aesthetic that would be accepted by women *first* and the male rockers second; unfortunately, the punk movement died before the female voice could be clearly heard on vinyl or above the static of the airwaves.

In the beginning, producers of British hip hop unreeled strained machinations that revealed nothing of the artist's world view or lifestyle. And when they weren't adopting a distinctly U.S. ghettospeak, they were employing the tricks of American track layers with mixed results. For instance: Stetsasonic's Daddy-O. Studio craft was barely art when he produced tracks on the wack *Born This Way*, contributing to the crumbling of the Cookie Crew; nor was Professor Griff's work with the She Rockers any great masterpiece. And yet Teddy Riley, whose slippery fusion of rough street collages and techo-smooth beat wizardry was making inroads into R&B, revived the short but fading careers of rap duo the Wee Papa Girls.

This duo, which consists of kindred vocalists TY Tym and Total S., got robbed of cash and much of their desire to be MCs when they recorded a cut that appeared on the compilation disc *Street Sounds* called "He's Mine." While touring the U.K. behind this fluky regional semi-hit, they got a lift when a Jive Records talent scout spotted these sisters (not only in the skin, but in the blood) whose collective handle has its source in the same place they did—their father. As TY Tym once related, their pops (who was born in St. Lucia and speaks French patois) used to walk around their Acton, England, home bleary-eyed, chanting, *"Oui, Papa, Oui, Papa,"* French for "Yes, Father." Taking the pronunciation but not the spelling of this expression they heard echoing down their hallway gave the Wee Papa Girls their name.

So after hooking up with Jive and, subsequently, Riley (who was signed to the label's publishing arm, Zomba), these rhyming rhythm sisters tracked the tellingly titled "Faith." With a song whose intro took an ironic bite from James Brown's "It's a Man's, Man's, Man's World," these two teenaged sweet girls entered the predominantly male rap arena, where basking in the spotlight were brooding, self-aggrandizing materialists sporting dookie gold chains and Troop suits. Even if the roar of women had not been heard in the Brit punk arena, the Wee Papa Girls would be *damned* if their voices would be silenced in the hip-hop nation.

Though the Wee Papas' "Faith" repeats the title of George Michael's gray-boy soul smash, the two records are markedly different in mood. While Michael transmitted a careful whisper to the Top Forty's audience of aging, white baby-boomers, the

Wee Papas' tune, a revolutionary hype-beat hybrid of Euro-dance, '70s funk and '80 hip hop, was the sound of a new generation raised in the global digital marketplace, where styles and colors are regularly up for grabs. Jittery, effervescent, but never over the top, the attitude in "Faith" is: Don't be persuaded against putting your dreams into action. While TY Tym and Total S. never balked at going for theirs—they often used to sneak out at night to explore London's club life—the pair still have a few reservations to reveal: "I remember the time I would try to rhyme/Said to myself I've got to find the words/'Cause this vocab ain't it/All these words I know they don't fit."

Riley's other contribution to *The Beat, the Rhyme, the Noise* declared "You've Got the Beat." This screeching, propulsive jam throws playful irreverence at rival rap crews over cool, dense samples. Appropriating some new Harlem rhyme for their Brit noise, Total S. declares: "Ain't no future in frontin'/Some rap groups they think they're runnin' things." Working with Riley made them part of the new avant-garde, thus their self-assuredness.

As Riley's swingbeat was gaining momentum in America, the soundtrack of hip house was becoming popular (on a limited scale), too, Chicago houseboy Chip E. rockin' the turntables in the Windy City, New York posses like the Jungle Brothers collaborating with Brooklyn acid (house music) king Todd Terry on the monster track "I'll House You." Although Chip E. might have been the first to experiment with the hybrid of B-boy/dance-queen culture, it was the Jungle Brothers who made this style accepted in the hip-hop nation.

So you're saying to yourself, "What does the rise of hip-house culture have to do with these two Brit chicks?" *Check it:* The acid soundtrack of Thatcher's Grooveland, the chaotic beat that kept on movin' da bodies and souls of those strobe-light angels floating toward post-disco heaven, was influenced by the psychedelic fugues of a man called Todd. With hypnotic sound (repetitive, haunting notes that offered dangerous visions of both house and hip hop, ghettos of mainstream culture), Todd Terry's "acid" noise guided dance music to a Twilight Zone of both drugs and movement. On "To the Trip," one of the standout tracks on their debut disc, the Wee Papa Girls say in their voices of pure ecstasy, "I will take you higher and you can take me higher/To the trip." Although not a direct reference to the 1960s LSD film directed by Jack Nicholson (*The Trip*, released on American International Films), both of these pop artifacts operate as products of enlightenment. Even though "To the Trip" masquerades as a love song, an ode to some unnamed dude lurking in the background ("I hope that you come and take me, yeah [take me to the trip]/I hope you love only me, yeah ... *take me to the trip*"), the true origin of this track lies within the drug culture of Brit rave parties. As produced by Detroit necromancer Kevin Saunderson (guiding light behind the Motor City band Inner City, as well as one of the originators of Techno-Sound), the Wee Papas were attempting to introduce the sound of the future to the universal spectrum of dance music.

Another track that speeds past the usual hip-hop dance-floor mix is "Heat It Up," produced by Andy Cox and David Steele of the Fine Young Cannibals under the name "Two Men and a Drum Machine." Using the cold, industrial sound of Brit house (which has none of the elegance of New York Garage/ Chicago warehouse music), this track rides the aural cut-and-paste collages made popular by Coldcut and M/A/R/R/S. In this soundscape the vocals function as background chatter for the noise of computers gone haywire. "It's like that, yeah," the girls say as the bleeps and beeps and cosmic rhythms wail in the foreground. This is the science fiction of *Logan's Run* transferred to house culture. Although Cox and Steele are inventive in the studio, their music is quite a distance from the hip hop one expects. This is the music of dreams, heard while still awake.

Given a peek into their West Indian roots on "Wee Rule" and "Bustin' Loose," one hears the Wee Papa Girls' affection for reggae. The first nods its head in the dancehall, while the second attempts to combine Public Enemy static with the Wee Papas' smooth interpretation of island sounds. Without thinking twice, "Wee Rule" is the better of the two: The girls' voices are energetic, while the music is rough and ready, holding back no punches. To paraphrase the Wee Sisters, say "This rules the dancehall" three times.

Without the beatwise ammunition of producers Riley, Saunderson, Cox and Steele, the Wee Papas' *Be Aware* isn't as commanding as its predecessor. The crew filled their follow-up disc with producers (Coldcut, Dancin' Danny D.) who had provided bits of ecstasy-driven disco before, but their ingratiations here lack the buzz of their past hits. Even Carl Bourelly, who juiced up Bell Biv Devoe's "Do Me," seems to have shot his wad, "Best of My Love" (with a lengthy sample of the Emotions' song) and "Westside" revealing very few of the upbeat and down elements that made BBD's song so nasty and notorious.

"A group of MCs"—with insinuating synth blips, blurs and buzzes—comes close to being the album's most deadly weapon, but the Robert Clivilles/David Cole–directed "The Bump" is a higher-caliber bullet. With a chorus of anxious party people whipping up its milky, piano-driven house beat (dotted by gentle percussion and get-busy keyboard squirts) with "Here we go/Here we go/Here we go"s and "Ow"s alongside an African-sounding chant delivered by children, this song has what it takes to galvanize any dance floor. So when TY Tym and Total S. aim "Move your butt and then shake your thighs" at your body, don't try to dodge their directive; let the rhythm hit ya.

WHODINI

WHODINI (JIVE/ARISTA), 1983

ESCAPE, 1984

BACK IN BLACK, 1986

OPEN SESAME, 1987

GREATEST HITS (JIVE/RCA), 1990

I t's been said that whenever the rallying cry "Brooklyn's in the house" was heard in sold-out jams, that was the cue to grab one's fat pocketbook or thick gold ropes before someone else got them. Posses from this New York borough, dubbed *Crooklyn* by the rest of the Apple corps, injected fear into the hearts of party people everywhere, and their antisocial behavior became notorious for its frightening enthusiasm and viciousness.

With their silk-suit-and-button-up-shirt look, their polished tracks and mellow-voiced tone, Whodini was a beautifully kept building in the middle of Brooklyn's ghetto heaven, personable characters floating gently through a turbulent sea of hardcore attitude and crush-groove madness. Most of their records were tracked outside of Gotham in foreign locales such as London and Cologne, Germany (Cologne? Hmmm, guess that explains Whodini's sweet-smelling veneer!).

The trio joined the ranks of hip-hop hopefuls in the early '80s when keyboard wiz Thomas Dolby—the boy knew how to make his synth toys purr and talk smooth early on—brought an electro track into Jive's Zomba publishing arm. Its prexy suggested getting someone to rap over it. The label ended up with not one but two vocalists in Jalil Huthchins and Ecstasy. As Whodini, they added text to Dolby's texture, spinning a tale about rare-breed personality-jock Mister Magic, then host of the

"Rap Attack" on WHBI-NY (the show subsequently got picked up by WBLS), which gave hip hop a much-needed broadcast showcase.

Galloping to a rigid Simmons-drummed (as opposed to funky-drummed) blap beat accented by a wash of synth strings and sequencer squiggles, and underscored by the constant low roar from a seething mass of ravers, "Magic's Wand" explains what a rap attack is ("DJs jamming in the street/MCs rapping to a beat") before defining the genesis of rap through Magic: "The moment he went on the air/It was plain to see a new phase was here."

After this dance-electric track hit, avoiding the urban wasteland of New York but landing atop new-music summits throughout Europe, Whodini wandered into "The Haunted House of Rock," sort of an updated version of Bobby Boris and the Crypt Kicker Five's '60s novelty smash "The Monster Mash." At the beginning of Whodini's walk on the horrific side, we hear footsteps marching through a creeky door, lightning cutting into a cold gray sky. Drums start to pound and percolate as a bass fog rises revealing a bright Japanese-sounding melody that in its current context seems more eerie than joyous. But there's definitely a party goin' on, bug-eyed, gravely voiced Wolfman Jack rockin' da wheels of steel between breaks by the grateful dead, an MC bustin' tunes from the black lagoon.

After jettin' out of this London dive *fast*, Jalil and Ecstasy hustled over to Germany to get with industrial-noise architect Connie Planck for more tracks for their first LP, Planck hooked the pair up with a "Nasty Lady" and a "Rap Machine." The former is a gurgling techno bang that gets up on the downstroke for a rapacious woman; the latter gets the clap for being too damn wack.

Aside from being the LP that paired them with their longtime producer, bassist/drummer Larry Smith, *Escape* is the Whodini album everyone remembers most. Containing the rap classics "Friends," "Freaks Come Out at Night" and "Big Mouth," it earned Whodini its first gold record award and turned Jalil and Ecstasy into ambassadors who opened up the airwaves as well as the ears of non-rap fans who are more receptive to melodic sheen than minimalist bombast. If Whodini were completely rejected by members of the rap fraternity out of the box, this time around they were at a happier medium. Smith didn't compose perfect pop tracks for Whodini, pasting their voices on in some postmodern collage experiment. And though sweetened and smoothed-out, his grooves maintained some degree of funky swagger and hardcore appeal. No aural visions of black films or flashbacks to jams at the local P.A.L. center will be conjured up, but Whodini had brought a B-boy attitude to those *Escape* sessions.

"I'm gonna give you what we got/And baby that's plenty/ 'Cause never have so few rocked so many," boasts Jalil in "Five Minutes of Funk." And for a while—before the rap attacks of L.L. Cool J's *Radio* or Run-D.M.C.'s *Raising Hell-Escape* (which eventually earned an RIAA platinum certification) was the highest-selling hip-hop LP ever; so the rhyme was more than just empty braggadocio.

Without any vocal, the scraps of squirmy melody and soft-machine bounce from "Five Minutes" comes back to haunt on the track "Featuring Grandmaster Dee," which one suspected would contain some emotional cutting from the crew's DJ, Dee. But this blue-eyed brother was probably just standing on the sidelines, keeping time—or something—while an engineer lowered the faders on the tune's vocal channel and made a straight pass. One wonders why this instrumental was included in the package; maybe paucity of imagination or, perhaps, it's an accommodation for bonus-beat hunters. Whatever, this track has served Ralph McDaniels and Lionel Martin (co-creators of the popular New York music vid show Video Music Box) quite well over the years. It's played on thousands of TV sets daily, over the program's opening montage of pop stylists, and during its closing credits.

Not as pervasive but even more durable is "Friends," from the same album, a booming hip-hop ballad concoction with a deeply cynical outlook. "Friends/How many of us have them?" it asks. "Friends/Ones we can depend on." It has an apprehensive tone rooted in greed and deceit. "Big Mouth," another booming track, warns all rumormakers with "We made the beat big enough to rock the house/But we also made it big enough to fit in your mouth!" Which doesn't mean that Whodini don't have everlasting tongues as well. Elsewhere they say: "I am the man of a thousand rhymes/Couldn't say them all in a week's time."

"There" turned out to be the mostly ho-hum *Back in Black*, which had nothing to do with the ballsy rock of AC/DC (whose classic 1980 album also bore this title). By the time Whodini's third LP was released, seventeen-year-old newcomer L.L. Cool J was the B-boy to watch. As produced by former NYU film student and punk-band axe-grinder Rick Rubin, junebug's *Radio* and the feel of a rock album even though it employed no fuzzy lead guitars. Then Run-D.M.C. stepped up to the mic' with Aerosmith's Steven Tyler and Steve Perry keeping the pulse. Compared to these, *Back in Black* was another trilling R&B-rooted release that swayed when it should've rocked. One track, "Fugitive," harnesses an extended and layered heavy-metal guitar solo onto a tense drum pattern, but the juxtapositions don't result in a jagged wall of sound; the track's textures, more forced than forceful, aren't crackling, thrashy or doomful, and like Journey's hip gyps (bland but hooky pop tunes that purport to be arena-scale pump-your-fist power rock), elements of teen-age anger and rebellion are here reduced to a cocktail of adult lethargy.

After chilling on the lam for a few days in "Fugitive," Jalil and Ecstasy take a long stretch and emerge hungry for some soft cookies to go with their chocolate milk. "He's the rapper

J/I'm the rapper Ecs/We're known for playing tag-team sex," they declare. For guys who dedicate their albums to their wives and first loves, this is a surprising revelation. More expected is the pro-monogamy cut, "One Love," which melds a swirling, richly contoured mid-tempo groove with loverboy wisdom, content and praise: "I was known for having the upper hand/I was known as a stone-cold ladies' man/If it wasn't for you I'd be that way still/But lately there's a change in Jalil."

For "Funky Beat," the crew steps down in Funkytown—not the center of the city, covered in litter and grime, but its somewhat gentrified suburb. In this song, which asserts that their DJ also raps, braggadocio and sheer energy slip into high gear. This is the most exciting moment on *Back in Black*. Instead of cushy arrangements, sexual as well as musical, there's B-boy badness being elevated to a higher degree.

Another lumbering cut with rock 'n' roll axes leads off *Open Sesame*, whose cover features the trio lounging on a flying carpet, hovering over some pyramids and palm trees, and wearing satin suits and Cole-Haan loafers. "Rock You Again (And Again & Again)" explores being p-whipped, while "I'm Def (Jump Back and Kiss Myself)" discards any outside object of affection in favor of narcissism. Though Larry Smith again directs on this album "I'm Def" and one other cut, "Be Yourself," makes room for some collaboration with Roy Cormier and a team known as Sinister.

Sometimes referred to as the first female rapper, Millie Jackson spices things up on "Be Yourself," which sports the first-ever break-beat loop heard on a Whodini disk. With thin, cheesy synth horns accompanying a tired-ass TR-808-driven beat, this corny sermon is wack as hell, but hearing hoarse-voiced Jackson scream, "You know how much money I could've made being someone else?/Diana Ross wouldn't been the boss—I woulda been!" makes me want to snatch the title Queen of Royal Badness away from Latifah and give it to Mildred.

From there, Whodini wax brisk and groovy and boring about the pitfalls of materialism ("Cash Money"), about love as a drug ("Hooked on You") and about being knocked out by hotties posing on the corner ("You Take My Breath Away"). All these spotlight Whodini's refusal to evolve along with the artform of rap and it's fickle audience. As a result, this attraction, once the biggest thing on Planet Rap, filling halls like Madison Square Garden with supporters, soon became obsolete and, despite high ambitions, *over*. Releasing a backward-focused compilation is a move that many once-lofty acts now on the bread-and-butter circuit make while plotting their brilliant comebacks. All of Whodini's magic (including many of their bad tricks) are regurgitated on *Greatest Hits*. Full Force produced a new "bonus track" titled "Any Way I Gotta Swing It," which Juice Crew member Kool G. Rap co-wrote. Even though Full Force are also from Brooklyn and the song was originally on the *Nightmare on Elm Street 4* movie soundtrack, it still speaks easy and couldn't hardly put fear into *anybody's* heart.

WRECKS-N-EFFECT

WRECKS-N-EFFECT (ATLANTIC), 1988

WRECKS-N-EFFECT (MOTOWN), 1989

From bebop to hip hop, the Beatles to the Sex Pistols, each new generation of pop stars has influenced the fashions of the times. In '50s England, the first "rock fashions" were defined by the Teddy boys, an urban subculture that critic George Melly described as "the dark van of pop culture." Inspired by the radical chic of American screen idols like James Dean and Marlon Brando, the Teds were working-class styleographers of (white) pop, noisily awaiting a movement. Unlike style-conscious American rebels (clad in leather jackets and tattered jeans), the Teds wore "uniforms" that were modified Edwardian fashion: long jackets with velvet collars, tight trousers, bootlace ties and suede loafers.

Hyperspace to new-jack city, where the eroticisms and chaos of inner-city America (crack dreams and B-boy swagger; street aesthetics and new technologies) have been absorbed into a network of noise pioneered by producer Teddy Riley. What began as a hybrid of old-world soul and new-school hip hop on tracks by Bobby Brown, Keith Sweat, Al B. Sure! and his own band Guy, swing beat or new-jack swing (a term coined by writer Barry Michael Cooper) became the dominant sound on Black radio during the late '80s/early '90s.

"Regular dance beats are straight—'*boom-da, boom-da,*'" said independent producer/Heavy D. & the Boyz member Eddie F. in 1989. "Most all your rap songs up until now used straight beats. But now you got the swing beat. It goes '*boom-pa da, boom-pa da.*' It makes you move because it sounds more real."

And at twenty-two, Teddy Riley became the king of swing beat, his most important contributions to the language of Afro-pop arriving through collaborations with the hip-hop nation: Heavy D. & the Boyz's "We Got Our Own Thang," Redhead Kingpin & The FBI's "Do the Right Thing," Kool Moe Dee's "I Go to Work."

These crews can be dubbed new-age Teddy boys. Besides forging a new sound for radio-wise urban dance music, they created a manifesto for a new B-boy attitude. With tailored, oversized suit jackets, pleated, baggy trousers or leather skips (no sneakers), they're one part buppie chic, one part gangsta slick. Like the '50s Teds, these current tastemakers are inspired by outlaw film images, only in this case the movies are *The Mack* and *Superfly*. Still, the new-age Teddy Boys have taken the thug out of hip hop, replacing it with glamour.

Paying homage to this movement from their second album while bombing the air with, perhaps, the most inspired street-corner soundtrack of summer '89 was Wrecks-N-Effect. On "New Jack Swing," producer Riley (who is only credited as a control-room mixer) transports the listener through a hyperactive musical mine field with exploding street parties, blipping sirens, jagged turntable cuts, P-Funk samples and hip-hop ego. This Harlem unit, whose name is uptown parlance for "making things happen," gets credit for this brash, frisky tune even though Riley raps on much of it. After a flippy intro where sixteen-year-old group member/lead voice Aquil Davidson tries to impress a jingling, irresistible around-the-way hottie, Riley starts showing off: "I made the new-jack swing/Yes, T.R. is my name/Makin' you dance to my thing." Reeling off a list of the luminaries he's collarborated with. Riley next brings it all home, briefing members of Black Metropolis on the revolution he's spearheading, an inspired mantra of cyberfunk innovation.

While "New Jack Swing" is badder than a souped-up Batmobile, it doesn't leave everything else on this second Wrecks-

N-Effect record in the dust. With pounding, floating grooves constructed on samples from such funky sources as Mtume, Strafe and James Brown, a number of the cuts on this record, while not the future, should have been the boom radiating through the air via black radio or kitted-up rides.

Textures here flow from laid-back chuggers to bristling bop, cushiony blues pop to minimalist Black noise. The crew, which also featured Brandon "B Doggs" Mitchell (who died after being hit by a stream of high-caliber steel) and Markell Riley (Teddy's younger DJing brother) changes gears many times, Aquil playing a B-boy Superman/Clark Kent. One minute he's forcefully spinning egoist fantasies about his skill on the mic' or his ability to get any party started right ("Wipe Your Sweat" and "Leave the Mike Smokin' "), then, changing into a mild-mannered gent the next, he's crafting provocative poems of seduction or edgy landscapes of urban survival ("Juicy" or "V-Man"). He moves through his corridor of poses without missing a beat, spreading his words evenly on every cut like crunchy peanut butter or, better yet, raspberry jam. The somewhat boyish tone of his voice only makes his topping easier to swallow.

Aside from the fact that it contains half as many tracks as their second LP and that its title's the same (are these guys lazy, forgetful or what?), the first thing one notices about Wrecks-N-Effect's debut album is that it showcases a different lead rapper. Twenty-one when the tunes were tracked, Keith KC, who has since left the group, was older than the rest of the fellas in the band. Bringing with him the experience of performing in a little-known collective called The Masterdon Committee ("Funkbox 2" and the Duke Botee–produced "Get Off My Tip" on Profile), he boasts on the record's leadoff single, "I'm a rap veteran/ And I'm better than/Anybody that you would be considerin'." His tongue is quicker than his wit, but he keeps the cut moving, whipping up the track's busy go-go froth, speeded up on the new-jack/hip hop tip.

Going back to Chocolate City (Washington, D.C.) funk for inspiration, Wrecks weaves the voice of that scene's reigning grandpa (Chuck Brown) throughout "I Need Money," a bristling showcase that begins with Aquil addressing a low-income, high-post wannabe poser. Then the vocalist imagines the exploits of a nice earner: "What if I had all the money in the world?/That's just a thought/I'd be sipping up Moet."

Unfortunately, the crew's big thrust for fat pockets (flye video and all) got shamelessly shunted when traditional jazz guitarist turned soul crooner George Benson bum-rushed the show. Both artists covered the Staple Sisters' languid "Let's Do It Again" (the title theme from the '70s film starring Bill Cosby), but in the strangely isolated world of Black radio, where rap is still ghettoized and/or ignored completely (despite its proven strength in the marketplace), the better, more irresistable remake of this classic jam lost out to bourgeois aesthetics and finishing-school politics.

"Wrecks-N-Effect," the album's title track, is repeated on this album—there's an instrumental, too. It proves to be the worst cut. You needn't listen beyond a few seconds for evidence that this tune is clumsy and left-footed. Clearly, Teddy Riley was still perfecting his language of studio poetics on these tracks, as was Wrecks-N-Effect. As is evident by the multicolored sweat suits that the group wears on the album cover, this album is more old-school than new-jack, more retro than techno.

X CLAN

From African tribes to hip-hop crews, James Brown to Bobby Brown, Black folks have always moved to the streams of bubbly, pounding sounds created by drums. Young brothers and sisters from the rhythm nation know this, but for years they've missed (or dismissed) other motivational voices in their heritage: the raging rebels such as Nat Turner; the velvet-toned speakers such as Adam Clayton Powell Jr.

This state of affairs started to change in 1987, when Public Enemy bum-rushed the cold-getting-dumb show (headlined at the time by B-boy parodists the Beastie Boys), armed with beats for the feet, food for the mind. Since then, throngs of other consciousness rappers have emerged speaking truth to power. One of the latest additions to this culturally aware posse is X Clan, a New York City quartet that includes manager/leader Professor X—the Overseer, Grand Verbalizer Brother J., Rhythm Provider Sugar Shaft and Architect Paradise.

In any other hip-hop crew, J., Sugar Shaft and Paradise would be rapper, DJ and producer. But, according to their press handout, X Clan isn't just any other hip-hop crew. These self-proclaimed "revolutionists for justice" call their music vainglori-ous ("the coming of the gods"). They declare they're not in the entertainment business but the awareness business. And they assert they're not rappers but messengers of truth who hung with Biblical figures like Mohammed and Issac.

Beyond the bullshit, X Clan is a brilliant, exciting amalgam whose debut LP, *To the East, Blackwards,* is informed by the theories of authors Martin Bernal and Cheikh Anta Diop, who believe that the roots of civilization as we know it are Black, and that math, the sciences, philosophy and the arts began in Egypt, not Greece.

X Clan communicates these convictions in their songs—"verbal milk," if you will—intent on making Blacks aware of their ancestors and the contributions they made to the world. In "Heed the Word of the Brother," Aristotle, Plato and Socrates are forcefully told to "step off." Dismissed.

Brother J., who raps with the patience and passion of a teacher, then proceeds to clear the way to Blackness using a combination of knowledge, mysticism and sardonic humor. All three of these elements are evident in the leadoff jam on *To the East*, "Funkin' Lesson": "Born in a cosmos/Where no time and space exist/Mortals label me as illogical, mythological/They couldn't comprehend when I brought the word/A street called verb, a Black steel nerve/Teaching those actors and actresses/Who write a couple of lines about what Black is—really?/Then they makin' me a sin/When a brother just speaks what's within/I guess I'm Blacker than a shadow in the darkest alley/That they're always scared to go in—boo!"

Elsewhere, J. takes us back in time for a walk along the banks of the Nile, where we're introduced to Osiris, Isis, Solomon, Jesus and others. We're lifted up, jetted through outer space, then dropped back into the cruel realties of racist modern America—of institutional enslavement, of cold-blooded murder by the hands of "the other man."

Fed up with this vicious, oppressive status quo—the last straw being the slaying of Yusef Hawkins by an Italian-American mob in Bensonhurst, Brooklyn—thousands of African-Americans took to New York City's streets in 1989 in a day-of-outrage protest that stopped traffic on the Brooklyn Bridge for nearly two hours. As part of Blackwatch, a Brooklyn-based activist organization, X Clan took part in this declaration, proving they're more than just

X-Clan, back to da muthaland via Flatbush Avenue.
© Alice Arnold, 1990.

talk. They recount their involvement in "A Day of Outrage, Operation Snatchback."

While the tune's Billy Squire big-beat backing fits its narrative ("I'll walk with the lions/Stalk with the elephant"), it's nowhere near as frisky as the George Clinton funk rhythms used on the rest of the LP. But it still kicks.

Another recurring element on *To the East* is Professor X's booming voice, which interrupts with the authority of a higher being. His words of wisdom are usually preceded by "Vainglorious" and end with "sisseeee!" (which has become slang for ignorant sucker). Crossroads, a word embodied in X Clan's name as well as its leader's, is one more thread. Basically, the crossroads is where you're at. Now what?

The fact that Professor X is part of the new Black movement in rap should come as no surprise. As a youngster, he played baseball with Malcolm X, and his father is the renowned activist Sonny Carson. Professor X, whose real name is Lumumba, has also managed King Sun and Just Ice, and promoted shows at hip-hop hangout the Latin Quarter. He started conceptualizing Blackwatch and X Clan in 1987.

The group's big break came when video director/video jock Ralph McDaniels allowed them to appear between videos on New York's top-rated "Video Music Box." They just spoke a few sentences, but their striking look—rings in their ears and noses; lots of leather, bamboo and stone around their necks; wooden canes in their hands—fascinated people all over the tri-state region of New York, New Jersey and Connecticut, including Island Records, which signed X Clan. Thanks to the label, the crew's rhythmic transmissions from all points in the Black experience started rippling through the rarefied air throughout African-America, charging its inhabitants (in Jeeps, study rooms and clubs) with an understanding of their rich heritage. This was fuel to move forward and continue the struggle—and an invitation to dance to the drummer's beat.

YO-YO

lthough she stomped into the '90s modeling bedroom-baby eyes, no-joke Button Flys and long, fake hair flung above thick thighs, phat sista Yo-Yo ain't no stunt posing for bitch-killa misogynists gathered 'round smoking loose joints or gulping cans of Olde Gold while talkin' shit amidst strains of "Jingling Baby," This nineteen-year-old flava is a long way from being a homeboy-skeezer pleezer, G!

In the race for womanist respectability in rap land, Yo-Yo took the baton from such artists as Queen Latifah and Ms. Melodie and ran with it, but not before adding a deadly edge along the sexist trail. She's the guileless flirt in "You Can't Play with My Yo-Yo," the second single from *Make Way for the Motherlode*, whose retort to a 'ack-daddy threatens to run his blood cold: "See the booty—yeah it's kinda soft and/If you touch it you're living in a coffin." Moreover, she's the streetwise USC (that's University of South Central) grad who's brave enough to face off against Ice Cube (da man whose first album uses the word "bitch" more times than any other disc by a nigga) in "What Can I Do?" She dissed him with a touch more ladies first on "It's a Man's World," from *AmeriKKKa's Most Wanted*, and maybe won. Here Cube gets the best lines (dudes will laugh, their disgusted honeys'll shake their heads) *and* the last word. This time there's no competition.

That's not surprising though. Along with Sir Jinx, Cube functions as producer of *Make Way for the Motherlode*. The pair bathe their Lench Mob homegirl in a tub filled with zingy funk and slinky "pimp" beats. After layering alongside the Bomb Squad on *AmeriKKKa's Most Wanted,* Cube and Jinx have become smooth mixdown operators in their own right. Yo-Yo spreads countryfied hardcore drawl over the fellas' sonic water, leaving behind a film consisting of humor and wit, if not uncompromising direction.

Yo-Yo views herself as a hip-hop activist and feminist-assassin; that's why she started the Intelligent Black Woman's Coalition, or IBWC. It's "an organization devoted to increasing the self-esteem of *all* women," according to a press handout. But during "You Can't Play with My Yo-Yo," the rapper brags about the 8-Ball and Cisco liquor she gulps, and she ruthlessly schemes on a sister's man, even threatening to "smoke her" if the you-or-me issue is confronted. Further contradicting her agenda of feminine solidarity and upliftment Yo-Yo puts down a rival MC with the line "You're wetter than a hot ho in the snow."

Because of this, a homey now swears the IBWC is the creation of some brilliant marketing pimp. But when Yo-Yo stands in front of packed high school auditoriums, chatting gender-specific with sullen teen-dreamers uncertain of their futures on this male planet, she is, nonetheless, an inspiration who enourages independent thinking, a homegirl who implores fellow sisters to go do it for themselves.

YOUNG MC

STONE COLD RHYMIN' (DELICIOUS VINYL), 1989

Fueled by the fact that its performer penned Tone-Löc's "Wild Thing" (the single that waged the biggest pop assault since "We Are the World"), and driven by raps packaged in buoyant, loopy beats, Young MC's *Stone Cold Rhymin'* became one of hip hop's most successful LPs during 1989, selling over two million units. With a mellow voice that rolled along like a well-oiled machine—it packed sixteen to thirty lines into a verse rather than the standard eight to twelve—Young related tales of adolescent angst and playful braggadocio. Like the output from DJ Jazzy Jeff & the Fresh Prince, his tunes were safe and pleasant, examples of gentrified hip hop. But while Prince and Jeff ground the traditional B-boy rebel image to a nub, turning out shiny and sharp pop, Young retained a few denticulations, working some truly dope beats into his music mix (which was programmed and performed by producers Matt Dike and Michael Ross, the Dust Brothers and Quincy D., a.k.a. Quincy Jones Jr.). From Washington go-go to Euro jive, from smooth Chi-town soul to nasty Ohio funk, all of Young's escapism got captured inside frisky, bad-ass samples.

But in interviews the twenty-three-year-old rhymer always made a point of stressing his good-guy, collegiate standing. Speaking to one journalist, he said: "I really never focused on rap as a career. My first priority was always my education."

Preferring a book over a jam, Young (whose real name is Marvin Young) was, not surprisingly, more homebody than

Young MC, making rap safe for the masses.
© Tina Paul, 1990.

———

homeboy growing up. Born in London to Jamaican parents and raised in Hollis, New York (home to Run-D.M.C. and L.L. Cool J), he started writing lyrics about fairy tales before reaching adolescence. At the age of ten he was turned on to hardcore rap by a neighborhood buddy, and from listening to pioneering MCs Melle Mel and the Sugar Hill Gang as well as Jamaican toasters Yellowman and Peter Metro, he developed his distinctive roll-of-the-tongue style. Following stints in a few local crews during high school, he made his exit from rap when he entered the University of Southern California to study economics. Through a mutual friend, he was introduced to Matt Dike and Michael Ross, former Los Angeles club DJs who had just started the independent label Delicious Vinyl. After auditioning for the pair over the telephone, Young was signed in December 1987. The following year he debuted with the swaggering "I Let 'Em Know." Though not the bulging smash the label had hoped for, it received good critical notices in the United States and England.

Then Young got his big break, co-writing "Wild Thing" as well as its follow-up hit, "Funky Cold Medina." Up to this point his career was an extracurricular activity. After graduating and releasing *Stone Cold Rhymin'*, he focused all of his energies on somersaulting up the charts.

Using vocal yelps similar to those in Rob Base & DJ EZ Rock's "It Takes Two," along with a teasing chicken-scratch guitar sample and a drum sound as tight as his dream baby's tush—in 1989 Young dated *Penthouse* Pet Amy Lynn—"Bust a Move" became the performer's breakthrough single. With some vividly detailed advice to bashful Romeos ("Don't hang yourself with a celibate rope"), it shook like Jell-O in a swaying breeze, while a perilous/funny high-school adventure, "Principal's Office," moved languorously, snaking through the modern music universe like the little engine that could.

With the exception of "Just Say No" (which gives a too familiar, too simplistic solution to the complex drug problem), the rest of *Stone Cold Rhymin'* is pure ego-boosting/putdowns delivered with speed (and clarity). In "Pick Up the Pace," Young takes a jab at his slow-tongued comp, then he jets through (we're talking Concorde here!) the fifty-three-second "Fastest Rhyme" a capella.

But quickness isn't Young's only gift. Like he advises during "I Come Off," his braggadocio is "not run of the mill." In one song he boasts, "If every rapper were Hawaiian I'd be Don Ho." In another, speaking to those old-school suckers who dissed him early on, he proclaims, "You're an 8-track tape and I'm a compact disc." In other words, he's on top and they're over now.

From his lofty position (whose rewards include a Grammy, as well as commercial endorsements from Sprite and Taco Bell), Young shot down early perceptions that he's just into cheerful (though inspired) fluff. Having participated in the Stop the Violence movement, rallying against Black-on-Black crime, he wrote and recorded two politically charged cuts for Sly & Robbie's KRS-One–produced *Silent Assassin* (Island). The brusque "Under Arrest" explores the feelings of lost dignity that compelled N.W.A. to explode "Fuck Tha Police!" "Living A Lie," sleek and languid, hands urban rebels a gloomy forecast: "People doing bad today/Somewhere down the line there'll be a price to pay."

These cuts are glimpses into Young MC's future. In a *Rolling Stone* interview he said, "It's all well and good that people can identify with school or shy men meeting women, but there are other things that need to be addressed as well."

Boombox on Coney Island, old school hip hop. © Tina Paul, 1981.

THE
ESSENTIAL
TWENTY-FIVE

For anyone new to the field, here are our recommendations of twenty-five essential records that can form the core of any hip-hop collection. In alphabetical order by artist:

Beastie Boys • *Paul's Boutique*
Big Daddy Kane • *Long Live the Kane*
Biz Markie • *Goin' Off*
Boogie Down Productions • *Criminal Minded*
Neneh Cherry • *Raw Like Sushi*
De La Soul • *3 Feet High & Rising*
Digital Underground • *Sex Packets*
The D.O.C. • *No One Can Do It Better*
EPMD • *Strictly Business*
Eric B. & Rakim • *Paid in Full*
Ice Cube • *AmeriKKKa's Most Wanted*
Ice-T • *Freedom of Speech*
Jungle Brothers • *Straight Out the Jungle*
L.L. Cool J • *Momma Said Knock You Out*
Marley Marl • *In Control, Volume One*
N.W.A. • *Straight Outta Compton*
Poor Righteous Teachers • *Holy Intellect*
PM Dawn • *Of the Heart, Of the Soul, and Of the Cross: The Utopian Experience*
Public Enemy • *Yo! Bum Rush the Show*
Public Enemy • *It Takes a Nation of Millions to Hold Us Back*
Run-D.M.C. • *Run-D.M.C.*
Salt-n-Pepa • *Blacks' Magic*
Slick Rick • *The Great Adventures of Slick Rick*
3rd Bass • *The Cactus Album*
A Tribe Called Quest • *People's Instinctive Travels and the Paths of Rhythm*

ACKNOWLEDGMENTS

And so Havelock and Michael would like to send a shout out: Janine McAdams, Greg Tate, Nelson George, Faith Childs (our agent), Michael Pietsch (our editor at Harmony for lotsa patience!), Bill Adler, John Goodman, Mitchell Smith (the glue), Havelock's Mom (for tolerating our confusion and noize), Tracy Miller, Leyla Turkaan, Ursula Smith, Robert Perlman, Scott Paulson-Bryant, Grace Heck, Laura Hynes, Monica Lynch, Charlotte Hunter, Jon Schecter, Bönz Malone, Peter Wetherbee, Tonia Shakespeare (Will's illegitimate great-granddaughter and Havelock's galley girl), Alice Arnold, Judy Womack, Beth Jacobson, Dante Ross, Tony Johnson, Russell Simmons, Fab 5 Freddy, Marie Moore, Awesome Two, Ralph McDaniels, Lionel Martin, Barry Michael Cooper, Ben Mapp, Michelle Vernon-Chestly, Frank and Chene Owen, Jackie Rheinhart, Armond White, Nava (The Underweight Lover) Parker, Ann Carli, Chris Reade, Darryl Clark, Duane Oliver Taylor, Kelly Haley, Shelby Meade, Sara (from Virgin), Victoria Clark, Lisa Cortes, Lyor Cohen, Tina Wynn, Rush, Priscilla Chatman, Dave Gossett, Elisa Keyes, Gerrie Summers, Jerry Rodriguez, Sylvia Rodriguez, Jimena Martinez, Deena "Baby" Rhodes, Leonard Abrahms, Kate Ferguson, Kim Greene, Vincent Jackson, Vincent (Jamaica Boy) Notice, Dan Charnas, Lala Cope, Krystal Kelly, Marisa Fox, Carlos Gonzales, Cynthia Badie-Rivers, Hazel, Shelly and da twins, Randy, Cedric Booker, Corwin and Calvin (for giving us gills and driving us crazy), Gary Porter, Linda Duffany, Howie Weinberg & the entire Masterdisk gang, Dee Dee Sharp, Kev-Nice, Greg Grant, Fancy Footwork, The BTX, DJ Odyssey, Full Force, Ira McLaughlin, the Horsemen, Gerald Woods, Jackie and Darryl Lawson, Francessa Spero, Bob Payne, Marley Marl, T-Money, Hank Shocklee, Super DJ Clark Kent, Red Alert, Ernie Paniciolli, Tracy Morris (for transcribing), Kevin Gibbs, Harmony, KRS-One, D-Nice, Camille Nicholson, Francine Brown, Jean-Paul and Carl Bourelley, Simo Doe, Lauren Zelisko, Kangol, Mixmaster Ice, Doctor Ice, Sharon Washington, Van Silk, Cathy Camaccho, James Jaz-Graham, Paul Price, Bernita Ewing, Lisa (Big Sister) Miranda, Jeff Wright, the entire hip-hop nation (for inspiration).